TO REMEMBER THE TRAIL
Drawing by Jose Cisneros

Covered Wagon Women

Diaries and Letters from the Western Trails 1853–1854

Volume 6

Edited and compiled by
KENNETH L. HOLMES

Introduction to the Bison Books Edition
by Linda Peavy and Ursula Smith

University of Nebraska Press
Lincoln and London

© 1986 by Kenneth L. Holmes. Reprinted by arrangement with the Arthur H. Clark Company.

Introduction to the Bison Books Edition © 1998 by the University of Nebraska Press

Manufactured in the United States of America

⊗ The paper in this book meets the minimum requirements of American National Standard for Information Sciences—Permanence of Paper for Printed Library Materials, ANSI Z39.48-1984.

First Bison Books printing: 1998

Most recent printing indicated by the last digit below:

10   9   8   7   6   5   4   3   2   1

Library of Congress Cataloging-in-Publication Data
The Library of Congress has cataloged Vol. 1 as:
Covered wagon women: diaries & letters from the western trails, 1840–1849 / edited and compiled by Kenneth L. Holmes; introduction to the Bison Books edition by Anne M. Butler.
p.   cm.
Originally published: Glendale, Calif: A. H. Clark Co., 1983.
"Reprinted from volume one . . . of the original eleven-volume edition"—
T.p. verso.
"Volume 1."
Includes index.
ISBN 0-8032-7277-4 (pa: alk. paper)
1. Women pioneers—West (U.S.)—Biography.   2. West (U.S.)—History.   3. West (U.S.)—Biography.   4. Overland journeys to the Pacific.   5. Frontier and pioneer life—West (U.S.)   I. Holmes, Kenneth L.
F591.C79   1996
978—dc20   95-21200   CIP

Volume 2 introduction by Lilian Schlissel.
ISBN 0-8032-7274-X (pa: alk. paper)
Volume 3 introduction by Susan Armitage.
ISBN 0-8032-7287-1 (pa: alk. paper)
Volume 4 introduction by Glenda Riley.
ISBN 0-8032-7291-X (pa: alk. paper)
Volume 5 introduction by Ruth B. Moynihan.
ISBN 0-8032-7294-4 (pa: alk. paper)
Volume 6 introduction by Linda Peavy and Ursula Smith.
ISBN 0-8032-7295-2 (pa: alk. paper)

Reprinted from volume six (1986) of the original eleven-volume edition titled *Covered Wagon Women: Diaries and Letters from the Western trails, 1840–1890*, published by The Arthur H. Clark Company, Glendale, California. The pagination has not been changed and no material has been omitted in this Bison Books edition.

Introduction to the Bison Books Edition

Linda Peavy and Ursula Smith

Late in 1980, as Kenneth Holmes worked on his proposal for *Covered Wagon Women*, he noted in a letter to his prospective publisher, Robert Clark, that he thought "this could well be another classic set of books," though he still had "some sorting out of ideas to do."[1]

Those lines have proven to be prophetic. The eleven-volume series of women's diaries and letters brought out by the Arthur H. Clark Company over the next thirteen years was indeed "a classic set of books"— but one that has required "some sorting out of ideas" by readers as well as by the editor.

The sorting out continues with this reprint edition of *Covered Wagon Women*. But the musings of the reader today are informed by the work of the many scholars who, during the fifteen years since the first volume appeared, have given us a basis for looking at the frontier experience—especially the woman's experience—in previously unthought-of ways.

Indeed, it is tempting to assume that the letters and diaries of the ten women represented here will yield definitive answers to some of the major questions raised by recent scholarship. Did migrant women look to the West with fear or with anticipation? What effect did the move have on family dynamics? Were men and women affected differently by the journeys? Did pioneer women gain cultural and economic freedom in the West? What of racial interaction? Was it different for the westering female than for the westering male? And did pioneer women themselves perpetuate the "cultural and habitual" sexism and racism of the nineteenth century?[2]

However, one would be hard put to find sufficient commonality of experience on which to base the answers to such questions. Consider the highly diverse backgrounds of the women included here. The three Butler sisters, natives of Kentucky, were born frontierswomen whose family history bespoke the restless American. Boston-born Amelia Knight, the wife of a physician, was pregnant with her eighth child when she crossed the plains. Celinda Hines was an unmarried schoolteacher traveling in the company of her parents and her extended family. Sarah Perkins, an Indiana farmwoman with minimal education, had lost several children before she joined her husband on the journey west. Carefree Rachel Taylor turned fifteen during her journey. Forty-five-year-old Hannah King, an upper-class Englishwoman, a Mormon convert, and a published novelist and poet, traveled toward Zion with her husband and four of her children. New York native Mary Burrell celebrated her nineteenth birthday during a crossing made in the company of her family and her fiancé. Elizabeth Myrick, a Wisconsin farmwife who had given birth to her first child while her husband sought gold in the West, now joined him in a move to the fertile farmlands of northern California.

Despite such diversity, there are some interesting parallels to be found in the experiences of this panoply of pioneers. For example, to a woman, these diarists are acutely aware of their environment. Even Sally Perkins, whose entries are typically as sparse as the high prairies she crossed, recorded the scenery: "roling preraris" caught her eye on April 25, 1853, and on August 31, her journey almost complete, she wrote of "heavy hills and very stoney." Amelia Knight noted on May 26, 1853, that she "went up on a high bluff, and had a splendid view of platte and her beautiful timbered Islands." Celinda Hines was often swept by what she observed: "All day the scenery was most enchanting intirely surpassing in loveliness & originality any thing I had ever beheld" (June 17, 1853). Equally prone to effusive descriptions was Hannah King, who noted on the edge of the Rockies that "it seems something marvellous & mysterious that our Cavalcade should pass along breaking the Eternal Silence of these wild places" (August 28, 1853).

The reader is struck not only by each woman's eye for detail but also by the varied responses of different women to the same natural phenomena. On July 8, 1853, Amelia Knight visited "Steamboat Springs, a great curiosity . . . [that] spouts up about a foot and a half, out of a hole in the solid rock." Seventeen days later, Celinda Hines devoted over three hundred words to the wonders of "far famed Soda Springs" and "Steam-boat spring . . . so called from the noise of its ebullitions." In contrast, after an August 16, 1853, visit to "the celebrated Soda and Steamboat Springs" area, Rachel Taylor declared that she "did not feel paid for [her] trouble" in going there. Yet nearly one year later, on July 16, 1854, Elizabeth Myrick was intrigued by Steamboat Springs: "it boils furiously all the time."

The reader is struck as well by the abrupt mood swings evident in the daily records of some of the women. On June 26, 1854, Mary Burrell, an exuberant and observant nineteen-year-old, wrote of seeing "12 different kinds of flowers within 1/2 a mile." Yet delight turned quickly to despair. "Mother is taken sick," she fretted in that same passage. "Oh Dear me! what if we all get sick!" Two days later, with her mother "on the recovery," her spirits rebounded and she wrote of "Many new flowers & very fragrant." On September 15, 1853, on the brink of her long-anticipated entry into Salt Lake City, Hannah King was so beset with worries over her son-in-law's obvious intention to wed two more of her daughters that she wrote of "beautiful Bluffs—beautiful Kanyons" and of "sorrows & troubles & tears! &c &c . . . mixed up with the beauties of nature."

With such shifts in circumstance and mood, one would expect diarists on the overland trail to write of their loneliness for those back home. Yet passages of this sort are far more common among the letter writers than the diarists represented in this volume. Six months after settling in Polk County, Oregon, Margaret Butler Smith wrote to relatives in Monmouth, Illinois, "[I] grieve so much about you all and my native land." And three years after completing her journey west, Elizabeth Butler Hutchinson asked a niece back in Illinois to "go to that little hickory grove on the west of the old home and pick two of the nicest oak leave you can find and send them in your next letter also two hickory ones . . . [and] continue to send until you send every kind of leaf that grows in the old granate State" (August 3, 1856).

Nothing quite so wrenching appears in the entries of the diarists in this volume, perhaps because, as Glenda Riley has noted in *A Place to Grow*, women caught up in the ceaseless activities of the trail had little time for such reflections. In addition to (1) performing day-to-day chores under the added duress of the trail environment, (2) meeting the physical demands of moving themselves, their families, and their goods across the continent, and (3) acquiring and honing the skills essential for their survival in their new homes on the frontier, women on their way west were also proccupied with (4) making the psychological move from looking back on what they'd left behind to looking forward to their new lives in the West.[3]

The diaries in this volume are replete with passages concerning activities that fall into one or another of Riley's four categories of on-the-trail activities. But how are we to categorize the very activity through which we've gained most of what we know about everyday life on the trail—the act of journal keeping itself? Scribbling in their little books approached a passion with these women. Day after day, no matter her circumstance, each of these travelers gave in to the urge to record that day's highlights. One can only wonder at the dedication that prompted a dispirited and pregnant Amelia Knight to take up her diary not once, but twice, on April 14, 1853:

> Quite cold   little one crying with cold feet, sixteen wagons all getting ready to cross the creek, hurry and bustle and get breakfast over, feed the cattle, and tumble things into the wagons . . . and away we go the sun just rising
> Evening we have traveled 24 miles to day, and are about to camp in a large prairie without wood, cold and chilly east wind, the men have pitched the tent, and are hunting something to make a fire, to get supper, I have the sick headache and must leave the boys to get it themselves.

For five months and one week—from the beginning of her trek on the banks of the Des Moines to its end on the banks of the Columbia—the day before her eighth child was born—Knight wrote in her journal every single day but one.

Equally faithful was Sally Perkins, the barely literate farmwife whose 142 terse notations ("May 8   15 miles   verry good times" and "August 12. laid by" constitute complete entries) cover all but two days of her journey west. Less faithful if more expansive than Perkins, Hannah King took pains to explain her periodic lapses, noting on August 28, 1853, that "much has transpired & I have intended every day to write—but something has always prevented me." Mary Burrell, who never missed a day's entry over the length of her four-month trip, seemed, on July 3, 1854, to be more puzzled than pleased by her dogged dedication to keeping a journal: "Myself sitting on the edge of the wagon box until it hurts me and what am I doing? Writing this nonsense—"

If Burrell herself could not explain her compulsion to write "this nonsense," to what are we to attribute the scrupulous fidelity of these women to their journals? Was it their awareness of being part of a historic movement? Were their jottings a way of marking—and hastening—the interminable days? Did keeping a diary during a journey that a woman might or might not survive provide a means of leaving a legacy?

Whatever the reasons they were kept, these journals give us invaluable knowledge about the worries that beset these women as they traveled west. The greatest fear of most of the diarists in this volume was the possibility of losing a loved one through illness or accident. The graves that dotted the prairie—and that were duly and frequently noted by some of the diarists—were ample reminders of the suddenness with which tragedy could strike.

When Celinda Hines's father was drowned during a river crossing, she described the accident in considerable detail, then provided a stark reminder of how life went on despite such loss. "With hearts overflowing with sorrow we were under the necessity of pursuing our journey immediately as there was no grass for the cattle where we were," she wrote that very evening, concluding her entry with two telling words: "Wolves howled" (August 26, 1853).

The women whose writings make up this particular volume show, on the whole, a fascination with, rather than a fear of, the indigenous peoples of the West. "Saw the first indians to day," Amelia Knight noted on April 29, 1853, some two and a half weeks after her departure from Vernon, Iowa. "Lucy [age 8] and almira [age 5] afraid and run into the wagon to hide." Three days later, Knight observed, "Indians came to our camp . . . begging money and something to eat   children are getting used to them."

Appearing equally easy in the company of Native Americans, Rachel Taylor reported on July 7, 1853, that she and her friend Mary had "visited some more Indians Wigwams, where there were some squaws. They shewed us some of their ornamental work, and seemed very friendly." Nearly a year later, Mary Burrell, who shared Taylor's fascination with native customs and who was far more careful than most diarists of the period to identify Indians according to tribal affiliation, noted on June 4, 1854, that her train had met with a large party of Sioux. There were "402 Indians, or more," she wrote, certain of the number since she had "counted them besides ponies & dogs, & plenty of children about 2 to a man & 3 ponies to a person & 5 dogs half wolf."

Burrell, like Elizabeth Myrick, who also crossed the plains in 1854, wrote more frequently than had the diarists of 1853 of hostile encounters between whites and Indians, the inevitable result of increased migration and continued disregard for Native American rights. "Met an army of indian fighters going to fight the Pawnee," Myrick wrote on May 19, 1854. "They were dressed in full indian uniforms with their guns bows an arrows an lances an bayonets & shields."

Conflicts of another sort are evident in some of these diaries. "Husband is scolding, and hurriing all hands (and the cook)," Amelia Knight wrote on April 16, 1853, barely a week into her journey across the plains. But later tensions eased, and she noted, "husband brought me a large bunch of flowers, which he said was growing close to the snow" (June 21, 1853). Hannah King avoided telling her husband her worries because she "wish[ed] to make his path as smooth as [possible]" (June 24,

1853). Yet her efforts were often in vain. "Mr King was in a grumbling spirit which marred [the day] as he often does," she noted on July 13. A day later, overwhelmed by "harshness," she admitted, "Oh! how I wept! for I felt how changed were all things around me — & . . . how changed were those who were so lately *all* to me!"

Hannah King was not the only woman dismayed by the changes that took place during the journey west. Operating in uncharted territory of more than one kind, these women were sometimes disconcerted by the speed with which familiar habits were altered to fit new and difficult circumstances. Looking back on her own overland emigration some six months earlier, Elizabeth Butler Hutchinson wrote to relatives back home in Illinois, that "this great journey with its numerous inconveniences, and dangers; take man, and beast, through a material change. yea and even women—it seems to arouse, and set to work all the selfish and beastly passions, a natural consequence, when all restrictions are taken from over them" (April 1854).

Not all restrictions were, in fact, lifted. For instance, even as Hannah King was assigned the traditionally masculine task of driving a team, she was also admonished to wear her bonnet, lest her complexion be "spoilt." Driving, a task "few women would have cared to have done," shook King's nerves "into a muddle," and by mid-July she had handed over the reins to her thirteen-year-old son, choosing to walk, if need be, rather than continue to drive as she "had been *made* to do" (May 30, June 24, July 15, 1853).

Did King's refusal to continue to drive mean that she was unable or unwilling to take on new and unfamiliar roles? Or was her public defiance of her husband's orders an indication of a newfound ability to stand up for her rights? Would she have ever driven a carriage *or* openly defied her husband's wishes had she remained in England rather than sailing the Atlantic and joining a wagon train bound for Salt Lake City?

That destination was uppermost in Hannah King's mind at every phase of her journey. "We are now only 300 and a few miles from the Valley Marvellous! wonderful!" she wrote on August 28, 1853, then added, "I rejoice & yet I dread I hardly Know why Either." A century and a half later, neither do we. And yet we sense through King's mercurial musings a bit of what it must have been like to embark on a journey that severed a woman's ties with one world and bound her so inextricably to another.

In a sense, we are the latter-day confidants of Hannah King and the other "covered wagon women." Though our limited acquaintance means we cannot hope to really know and understand them, we realize that, individually and collectively, these frontierswomen belie the nineteenth-century stereotype of woman as weak, emotionally insecure, and capable of functioning only within the confines of the home.

And we have learned enough through a close reading of the diaries and letters in this volume to appreciate the simple yet profound truth of Mary Burrell's final journal entry, written September 1, 1854, soon after her arrival in Sonoma County, California: "Here we stopped . . . — thus ending a journey which for care, fatigue, tediousness, perplexities and dangers of various kinds can not be excelled."

NOTES

1. Kenneth Holmes to Robert Clark, December 24, 1980, in *Covered Wagon Women: Diaries and Letters from the Western Trails*, vol. 11 (Spokane WA: Arthur H. Clark, 1993), p. 9.

2. Anne M. Butler, introduction to *Covered Wagon Women: Diaries and Letters from the Western Trails, 1840–1849*, vol. 1 (Lincoln: University of Nebraska Press, 1995), p. 1.

3. Glenda Riley, *A Place to Grow: Women in the American West* (Arlington Heights IL: Harlan Davidson, 1992), p. 82.

Contents

Illustrations

Introduction to Volume VI

It appears we are destined for years to mingle in one common herd
with the sap heads of every country and clime.

The above words were written by Elizabeth (Butler)
Hutchinson in a letter to a relative in Monmouth, Illinois.
She wrote the letter from a newly-settled farm near
Monmouth, Oregon, on June 24, 1854.

This young woman was an example of many emigrants of
1853 who traveled overland to the Pacific coast as part of
various groups devoted to religious principles. Elizabeth
was one of a community of Disciples of Christ who sought a
new country where they might practice their faith in their
own way. The plan was to form a church, a town, and a
school in the name of the Christian Church.

Of the seven wagon trains covered in this volume, four of
them launched out over the western trails with such a
purpose in mind. It was natural, of course, for Hannah
King, a Mormon lady from England, to travel to the Utah
promised land as a culmination of a deep devotion. Celinda
Hines was one of a group of Methodists who traveled west to
their new Canaan in the Willamette Valley of Oregon. They
followed in the wake of the Reverend Jason Lee, who had
formed a germ of a settlement and named it Salem as a
mission station in work with the Indians. Rachel Taylor was
a member of a Methodist "Preachers' Wagon Train," led by
the Reverend William Royal and two sons and their families
to southern Oregon.

The backdrop against which the American westward

movement took place during 1853 and 1854 was the
anticipation of the opening of the vast Indian territory
beyond the Missouri River.

A bill to set up a Nebraska Territory failed in March
1853. It had passed the House of Representatives, but it was
blocked by the Senate. Thus for the time being the vast
Indian territory would continue to be unavailable for
settlement by Americans. According to the "Indian
Intercourse Act" of 1834, settlers were forbidden in that
region, subject to removal by the military if necessary.[1]
Besides the fur-trading forts (Bridger, Laramie, Hall), there
were only occasional trading posts set up by French
Canadians or by Louisiana Frenchmen, or by American
traders, who, with their Indian wives and half-breed
children, were not subject to removal.

In the minds of most Americans the belief in a "Great
American Desert" kept down interest in settling that part of
the continent.[2] They assumed that the Great Plains lacked
water, wood, and communication with the outside world to
be viable for farmers. This idea was re-enforced by those who
traveled through the grassy lands of Nebraska and Kansas
and on through the sage-brush country of the Great Basin.
The land had to wait for the railroad, barbed wire, and
irrigation for effective settlement to take place.[3]

The discussion about the extension of territories and
states beyond the Missouri took place in Congress in the
winter and spring of 1853-54. Talk and pressure continued,
much of it centered around the person of that dynamic U.S.

---

[1] Dorothy Weyer Creigh, *Nebraska: A Bicentennial History* (New York, 1977), pp.
46-50.

[2] Everett Dick, *Conquering the Great American Desert*, Nebraska State Historical
Society Publications, Vol. XXVII (Lincoln, 1975), *passim*; Ralph C. Morris, "The
Notion of a Great American Desert East of the Rockies," *Mississippi Valley Hist. Rev.*,
XXX, No. 2 (Sept., 1926), pp. 190-200.

[3] Walter Prescott Webb, *The Great Plains* (Boston, 1931), *passim.*

Senator from Illinois, Stephen A. Douglas, who had a vision of Chicago as the center of a huge railroad system in mid-continent. On December 14, 1853, a new bill was introduced which laid out the trans-Missouri extension into two territories: Kansas and Nebraska. Kansas, in effect, extended westward from a slave-holding state, Missouri; Nebraska extended west from the free state of Iowa. The Kansas-Nebraska Bill got the reluctant support of the southern legislators. It declared that "all questions pertaining to slavery are to be left to the decision of the people residing there." It was signed into law by President Franklin Pierce on May 30, 1854, too late for the news to reach the overlanders of that year. Both of the new territories extended all the way to the Rocky Mountains, and Nebraska reached northward to the Canadian boundary.[4]

One interesting aspect of the 1853-1854 diaries is that the women, especially those of 1854, took notice of the increased presence of the occasional trading post or "grocery." These were the first germs of settlement at such places as Wood River (Nebraska) and Green River (Wyoming). Real settlement in large numbers, however, had to await the laying of the railroad in the 1860's.

For those who have not read the introduction to the first volume of this series, we reiterate some salient points which have been used to guide the editorial hand. It is a major purpose to let the writers tell their own story in their own words with as little scholarly trimming as possible. The intent in this publication of primary sources is to transcribe each word or phrase as accurately as possible, leaving misspellings and grammatical errors as written in the original.

Two gestures have been made for the sake of clarity:

---

[4] Creigh, *op. cit.*, pp. 46-61; Roy F. Nichols, "The Kansas-Nebraska Act: A Century of Historiography," *Mississippi Valley Hist. Rev.*, XLIII, No. 2 (Sept., 1956), pp. 187-212.

1. We have added space where phrases or sentences ended and no punctuation appeared in the original.

2. We have put the daily journals into diary format even though the original may have been written continuously line by line because of the writer's shortage of paper.

There are numerous geographic references that are mentioned over and over again in the various accounts. The final volume in the series will include a geographical gazeteer, in addition to an index and bibliography to aid the reader.

The scarce and unusual in overland documents have been sought out. Readily available accounts are not included, but they will be referred to in the final volume along with the bibliography. If the reader knows of such accounts written while on the journey, please let us know. Our goal is to add to the knowledge of all regarding this portion of our history — the story of ordinary people embarked on an extraordinary experience.

KENNETH L. HOLMES

Monmouth, Oregon, 1986

The Diaries, Letters, and Commentaries

❦ 1853 ❧

Letters from the ⸹ Butler Sisters

INTRODUCTION

In the 1830's followers of Alexander Campbell, founder of the church known as Disciples of Christ or the Christian Church, moved from Warren County, Kentucky, to Warren County, Illinois. These followers (sometimes referred to as Campbellites), turned their backs on slavery and founded both a town and a college named for the ancestral home, Monmouth, in Wales. Peter Butler surveyed the town in 1831. After twenty years, many of the members of the church were determined to go even farther west to the great Oregon Country, to establish another town and college devoted to the principles of their faith.

During the late 1840's and early 1850's family meetings were held in the home of Ira and Mary Butler. Generally, women were not as eager for the long journey as were the men. With reluctance they stated that they would move only if there would be a town, a church, and a school. The idea was for families to settle and give portions of their claims for support of the school, and the women insisted that the school be open to both men and women.

An advance migration investigated the land out west in 1850. Elijah and Margaret Davidson, Squire S. and Elizabeth Whitman, Thomas and Sarah Lucas, and their families, as well as a number of single men, headed out on the Oregon Trail. They reached Polk County, Oregon, in August and settled on claims not far from the little river town of Independence, on the west bank of the Willamette. The area was eventually known as the Davidson Settlement.

It was not until April 16, 1852, that another wagon train headed west. John E. and Frances Murphy, Elijah and Sarah (Lucas) Butler, Carter and Elizabeth Davidson, Albert W. and Frances Lucas and William and Margaret (Davidson) Mason made this journey. There were also some single men: teamsters and drovers. They arrived in the Willamette Valley in mid-August. The Monmouth, *Illinois Atlas* on April 16, 1852, described the gathering and departure of this wagon train. In following issues, the newspaper also published several letters written during the trip and in Oregon by John E. Murphy.

The final concerted move of Monmouth, Illinois, families occurred in 1853. The following letters were written after this trip. If the group was known as the Butler wagon train, there was good reason for such a name.

Ira F.M. Butler was the elected leader. His wife, Mary Ann (Davidson) Butler accompanied him. They had been married on August 5, 1835, and five children (three boys and two girls) accompanied them: Newton, age 16; Paradine, (a girl), 14; Asa, 10; Augustus, 8; and Margaret, 1. Ira lived on to become a member of the Oregon legislature for three terms; speaker of the House of Representatives, 1857-8; and Polk County Judge, 1878-82. He and Mary Ann were active in the founding of Monmouth, Oregon, and in the establishment of a college in that city.

Although Ira Butler was the chosen wagon-master of the train, the "old man," Peter Butler, appears to have been the real leader. One descendant remembered that "Not a wheel turned in the morning until all hands had gathered while the old man offered prayer. On Sunday they camped. But, on the unlucky day when the Butler cow was swept away by the North Platte River, to the loss of the Butler breakfast coffee cream, the old man was human enough to 'cuss out' both cow and river..."

Grandmother Rachel (Murphy) Butler was greatly beloved by all. This is evident in the Elizabeth Hutchinson letters below. In a note on June 24, 1854, Elizabeth says "Mother is grieving herself to death about leaving home. She has failed so much that she hardly looks like the same person. You must write to her particularly. She feels bad because there is nothing written to her. She thinks if she could write she would not treat you all so. You know, it makes one feel more like they were remembered if their name is mentioned." After the death of Peter (b. March 9, 1789) on June 24, 1856, Elizabeth in Letter III below says, "Your grandmother takes his death very hard and I am afraid She will grieve herself to death." That did not happen, however, and Rachel lived for many more years, dying on January 10, 1874.

A word more about Grandfather Peter Butler. In addition to being a farmer, he was also a surveyor. He had surveyed the new town of Monmouth, Illinois, in 1831 at 22½ cents per lot. At one time he had been asked to survey the new town of Chicago, but refused. He did not think the city possessed a future in the swampy area on Lake Michigan. Ralph B. Eckley, a local historian in today's Monmouth, Illinois, says that when Peter Butler was asked to survey Upper Yellow Banks in Mercer County for a town to be known as New Boston, he was too busy and hired Abraham Lincoln to do the job. Like Lincoln, Peter Butler served as an officer in the Black Hawk War in 1832.

The daughters of Peter and Rachel Butler wrote the letters in the following chapter.

Eliza Butler (Dec. 2, 1816-Dec. 24, 1864) was married to Edward Ground on Oct. 30, 1834, in Warren County, Illinois. They traveled west in 1853 with five children: William, age 17; Robert, 13; Luther, 11; Peter, 5; and Franklin Pierce, 1. The surname is spelled both "Ground" and "Grounds" even by members of the family. They settled in Polk County, Oregon, about five miles south of the new community of Monmouth near a tiny center, Bloomington, on the Luckiamute River. The name of the crossroads was later changed to Parker, its current name. Their neighbors to the north were Eliza's sister, Elizabeth Hutchinson, husband Thomas, and family.

Margaret Butler (Feb. 2, 1822-Dec. 8, 1871) became the wife of Isaac Smith on Dec. 9, 1840. They journeyed overland with their children: Rufus, age 12; Silas Wright, 9; Berryman (a boy) 7; Flora Alice, 5: and Mary Elizabeth, 1. They settled near Bridgeport, 8 miles west of Monmouth at the foot of the Coast Range where they had an abundance of what the overlanders always hoped for: wood, water, and feed for the cattle. In a short

biographical essay published under the title of "Pioneer Bridgeport Families," John J. Brown, a neighbor, described Margaret
thus:

> Mrs. Smith was one of the few women of the Bridgeport
> vicinity who constantly worked in all kinds of weather
> during the Civil war to make the life of the soldier on the
> field of battle more humane and less dreary. She died of
> cancer.

Elizabeth Butler (April 9, 1829-Jan. 2, 1866) married Thomas
H. Hutchinson on July 1, 1851. He was both a bright teacher and
a surveyor and was educated at Abington College in Abington,
Illinois. He eventually became one of the dominant figures in the
founding of the town of Monmouth, Oregon, and of a new college
as well. He surveyed Monmouth, marking out the lots and
streets, in 1855. He was Polk County Clerk at the time of his
death in 1860. On the 1853 overland trek, Elizabeth Hutchinson
traveled with one small child, James, and was also pregnant. The
baby was born as they approached the end of the trail on August
3rd. They had taken the "short cut" — the infamous Barlow
Trail. The baby was born near the incredible Laurel Hill grade,
and was named Robert Cascade in honor of the locale of his birth.
  Once the third migration from Illinois to the "Davidson
Settlement" in Polk County, Oregon, was complete, these devout
families began working out their plans.
  During a meeting, Ira F.M. Butler cast the deciding vote that
named the new community Monmouth, rather than Dover. The
town was founded under a condition that it would forfeit its
charter if any place of business was granted a liquor license.
Several gave portions of land. Sixty persons and/or families made
gifts of cash ranging from $5 to $300 for the establishment of
"Monmouth University." The first educational building, also
used as a church, measured twenty by thirty feet. Generally the
same persons supported all endeavors. In addition to surveying
the new city, Thomas Hutchinson served as secretary of the
university's board. The school later became a state institution.

The sequence of names that followed was Christian College, Oregon State Normal School, Oregon College of Education, and Western Oregon State College.

The men promised the women that a school would be a place "where men and women alike might be schooled in the science of living and in the fundamental principles of religion."

These letters do not spend a great deal of time on the journey to Oregon, but dwell line by line on the destination. We, however, feel that the destination and the reaction to it was an important aspect of the journey. Such letters either encouraged people in the east to make the long journey west, or discouraged them from the trek.

The documents here reproduced are from a large collection of Butler letters in the possession of Mrs. Iris Powell of Monmouth, Oregon. Mrs. Powell is a family historian, and has been most helpful in this project. At the time these typed transcripts were made, the originals were with Miss Edith Butler of Monmouth, Illinois. This lady is now Mrs. Edith Brooks, still living in the Illinois community at age 91. She remembers that many years ago she loaned the originals to someone who made typewritten copies. We have not been able to locate the handwritten originals. Several others have aided our search: Larry Butler of Atcheson, Kansas; Jill Butler Smith of Burlington, Iowa; President Bruce Haywood of Monmouth College, and Alice Martin, an Archivist of that institution.

SOURCES

Principal sources for the Butler Wagon Trains have been as follows:

The voluminous Butler family papers in the hands of Mrs. Iris Powell, Monmouth, Oregon.

Ellis A. Stebbins, *The OCE Story* (Monmouth, Oregon, 1973).

Helen Butler Jones, *The Contribution of Certain Leaders to the Development of the Oregon Normal School, 1850-1930*, Thesis, Master of Science in Education, University of Oregon, June, 1947.

The columns of Ralph B. Eckley in the *Daily Review Atlas* of Monmouth, Illinois, over many years.

"Autobiography of George Miller West," manuscript in the library of the University of Oregon. West traveled with the Butler Wagon Train.

Wesley L.J. Mullenneix, *Plymouth Rock to the Pacific* (Yakima, Washington, 1983). This involves particularly the Butler Wagon Train.

Monmouth *Illinois Atlas* for the year 1852. This involves the letters of John E. Murphy and the 1852 journey.

ELIZA A. GROUND: LETTER I

Bloomington Dec the 25 1853

Dear Brother and Sister

we all arived at oregon safe and sound   we was somewhat tired but we are a giting a little restid   we are all well and harty. the children all look hearty esspeceily peter   he is as fat as a pig   his cheeks is red as a rose and his eyes as black and bright as you please   the trip was tolerably tiresom but knot so mutch so as I expected to find it   I was well the most of the way through though I did not have to lay down to rest any time whilst I was a geting breakfast that was more than I could do in the spring and summer at home or feeling like it at least   I was verry weak along on snake river   the fore part of the trip is nothing if the weather was warme and pleasant   the weather was verry cold and wet for a long time after we started   the latter part of the trip is hard   there is so many long steep hills to climb up and down. crossing the cascade mountains used me up wors than all the rest of the trip. we saw a great many curiositys on the road. we did not suffer mutch for the want of wood and water   we filled our water kegs where we did knot expect to find water and we sacked up wood anough to do us two hundred miles. there was no timber in that distance except one lone tree so we had

wood and sage brush all the way to cook with   we found a
great many currants on the way   they was verry exceptable
they was the best I ever tasted   there was red yellow and
black ones in the mountains   we found rasberry dew berrys
and thimble berrys   we live close to a lake   thare are
hundreds of geese and ducks swimming in it   our folks kills
one every once in a while and sometimes a pheasant.   we
have all of the Cabbages beets squashes and such things as we
can use   one of our neighbours tells us to send to his garden
and help our selves   he wants the cabbage cut off ove the
stalks so that he can raise a nother crop on the same
stalks   they have excellent cabbage and beets here. I think
that people can have plenty to live onn with but very little
work though I cannot help thinking a great deal about old
illinois   I would like to see it about this time. the
connection are all well. thomas hutcheson is gone to the
umqua [Umpqua] with his brother robert[1] to look at the
country   he has been gone over a month   mack timmons[2]
lives three or fore miles from here   they say he is rich   he
has seven sones   charles wells[3] lives out here   one of his
sones was at our house yesterday. hendrilks[4] lives in oregon
the singing teacher   this is a great place for wild roses   the
prairies are red with the berrys at this time   the snow drop

---

[1] Robert Hutchinson, brother of Thomas, and his wife, also named Elizabeth, settled
in Douglas County, OR. Their claim, #1707, was filed at the Roseburg office. They
traveled the trail in 1850. *Genealogical Material in Oregon Donation Land Claims*, III
(Portland, 1962), p. 122. This reference will hereafter be abbreviated as *Genealogical
Material*.

[2] This was Lambert McTimmonds, a 56-year-old Scotsman farmer. He was born in
Ireland and had a wife, Ann. They arrived via the Oregon Trail from Missouri in 1845.
The 1870 census lists them as having seven children. *Genealogical Material*, II, #4524,
p. 100.

[3] Charles and Elizabeth Wells made the western trek in 1852 and settled in Benton
County, OR. *Genealogical Material*, II, #3883, p. 71.

[4] This was probably Samuel E. and Sarah Cordelia Hendricks, who traveled to
Oregon in 1852 to settle in the Salem area. His birthplace was Warren County, KY,
where the Butlers resided at one time. *Genealogical Material*, II, #4420, p. 96.

groes wild here thousands of them. we want you to write to
us   we allway like to hare from you all and all the old
neighbours. give my best respects to matilda smith James
and mary Butler and all inquireing friends and tell them to
write

Eliza A Ground

John M & Eliza Butler

MARGARET B. SMITH: LETTER I

Bridge Port O T   Feb 8th 1854

Dear brother and sister

I have waited a long time very impatient for a letter from
you but have come to the conclusion we never shall so I will
write a few lines to let you know we still exist amonst the
living   we are all well except Berryman[5]   he has a sore
throat   they is a great deal more sickness here than I
expected to find   they has bin a good menny children dyed
this winter with a sore throat   I have heard of a good menny
Deaths since we got in the vally   our children has been
some what healthier than usial   my health is some better
but grieve so much about you all and my native land I cannot
gain very fast   I cannot tell you much about the rest of the
folks   they was all well the last I heard except Lissy
[Hutchinson]   she has had the rheumatism very bad two or
three weeks but she is better   they are at Fathers as usial
and have bin for some time   John I would like to see you
very much   it would do my very soul good to see you all and
talk with you   I could talk so much better than I can
write   the children talk a great deal about you all and
contrive a great menny ways to git to go back   Lavina you

---

[5] Berryman was the 8-year-old son of the Smiths, born in Warren Co., IL, in 1850.
He became a farmer like his father and later, a pharmacist. H. O. Lang, *History of the
Willammette Valley* (Portland, 1885), p. 819.

must write to them often   they are very lonesome   they
have no associates here   little Mary[6] can talk so plain and
sweete she implys some their time   I wish you could hear
her say Uncle Johhny aunt Matilda and tell me to get a chair
and give her titty   tell Mary if she could see her she would
be willing to own the name. you siad John Crawford wife and
Nancy Lomax had gone to Kentucky on a visit   I want you
to write to me the particulars about their visit   write all
about the Knox folks and evry boddy els   I want you to
write all about my old home   I want to know evry little
improvement they have made   I want to know where the
clock stands cupboard and so on   I shall not tell you
ennything about the winter   I will leave that for Mr Smith
as he likes O T better than I do   he will give the
trouth   we went to Lides[7] a few weeks ago   they was not at
home so we went to Mr Haleys[8]   they was all well and Miss
Haley said I must send her respects to you   she likes
O[regon] very much   Sarah[9] is at Portland   they tore the
blanket as they come to O and she does not live at home nor
Monroe.[10] I have cut and the Boys a coat   I had to rip up
Wrights[11] cotton coat and cut all by it evry body has to be
their own Tailor here   I have made six pair of pants five
aprons five sheets three bed frills two white ones and one
calico one dress pillow slips and tablecloths   I have a great
deal of sewing to do yet   I went to the store the other day

---

[6] Mary Elizabeth was born to Margaret Smith in 1852. She died on Octobr 10, 1858, at age 6. Addie Dyal, "Davidson Cemetery in Polk County, Oregon," *Beaver Briefs*, XI, No. 1, p. 12.

[7] Unidentified, probably a nickname.

[8] Two Haley brothers and their wives crossed the plains with the Butler wagon train in 1853: Bedford and Mary; Patrick R. and Jane. They settled southwest of Independence in Polk Co. *Genealogical Material*, II, #4624, p. 105, and IV, #7790, p. 26.

[9] This Sarah who "tore the blanket," i.e. separated from her husband, is so far unidentified.

[10] Monroe is also unidentified.

[11] Silas Wright Smith was the Smiths' second son, age 10.

and bought nine yards of calico a pair of stockings for Mary one paper of pins with four dozen eggs   the children has three dozen more   they are fifty cents a dozen   butter is five bits a pound socks one dollar a pair   Tilda I would like to know what you are about that you cant write   the next time I see you I will pull your ears good   tell Mary Jimmy I want to see them as bad as I can   tell them to write often and kiss little Teldon for me   give my love to all of my old neighbours especially Betty Lucas and Ellin and Ann P   the mail goes out today so I must come to a close   write soon and often   so good by John Eliza and Matilda
                                          Margaret B. Smith

ELIZABETH M. B. HUTCHINSON: LETTER I
                                   Luckamute   Apr   1854

Dear Elisa;

It is a little more than a year, since we left home, and you, and all the rest of our dear friends, and started on that almost endless journey, to this great land of *Redskins*, and *wild cat.*

But luckily we all reached in safety, as you have long since heard; no doubt. This great journey with its numerous inconveniences, and dangers; take man, and beast, through a material change. yea and even women — it seems to arouse, and set to work all the selfish and beastly passions, a natural consequence, when all restrictions are taken from over them

We reached Elija's[12] on the 10th day of Aug with our two little ones. Robert was just a week old, he was born on the Cascade Mts on the 3d of Aug

We stayed with Elijah 3 weeks and then started up

---

[12] Elijah D. Butler was Elizabeth Hutchinson's older brother. He and his wife, Sarah, had crossed the plains in 1852. Helen Butler Jones, *The Contribution of Certain Leaders to the Development of the Oregon Normal School, 1850 to 1930*, Master of Science Thesis, Education, University of Oregon, Eugene, June 1947. p. 9.

country about (excuse this blot for I was killing a *musketo* on my hand and made the pen give down a little too much ink) two days drive from E's   while on the road Mr. Hutchinson took the ague and a few days after we stopped I took it also. there we were both sick with our little babe four weeks old and living in a house without door floor or chimney and cracks in the wall large enough for a dog to creep through. Well I had several hard shakes and then got well, but Mr. Hutchinson had it five months

June 24 1854

Dear Eliza

You see by the previous page that I have in days of yore commenced a letter to you. But I have almost forgotten what I had intended to write, no difference, all has probably been written previous to the date of that, and this, even the crying of the babes of trouble.

Excuse me for taking the same sheet, poverty told me to   You wonder what the reason is that we do not write more positive and tell you all about the country and how each one is satisfied. Well, one reason is we dare not write the truth and conscience wont let us write lies. So we write nothing. Perhaps I am mistaken, may be we dont know the whole truth and are afraid to write a part, lest we be mistaken and thrown in the lie. But Eliza what I am now going to say to you, pray take for the truth, to the best of my judgement.

We are all well and all of the kin folks except Berry Smith.   he has had something like a white swelling on one of his legs   his doctor says it is worse if such a thing can be. I have not heard from him since a week ago last Monday. Eliza Mother and I went to see him   we think it doubtful whether he ever gets well   Mother told me that he said if he died he did not want to buried here and if he ever gets well he intends to go back to Illinois. Mother is grieving herself to

death about leaving home   She has failed so much that she
hardly looks like the same person. You must write to her
particularly. She feels bad because there is nothing written to
her. She thinks if she could write she would not treat you all
so. You know, it makes one feel more like they were
remembered if their name is mentioned. I am shure this
letter will do you more good, than if your names had not been
mentioned. The day before yesterday Mary Ann[13] came to
see us for the first time. She talked so much about
Monmouth Illinois and the folks there that I could almost
think myself there. She is the worst whipped woman you
ever saw — She says she wonders — that she could be so
blinded to her own interest. She says if they do not go back to
Monmouth it will be Ira's fault. Pauline[14] has grown more
since she left home than she had for several years before. She
looks considerably like a woman and every hair on her head
is full of ambition. She begins to talk of *Silks, Spanish side
Saddles young Lawyers* etc. But But Giee's giees as the red
man says are ad Swampus non comatum that is men of the
first standing.[15] I must tell you something about the Mrs of
Oregon[16]   they are from eleven to twenty years old, from
eight to twelve hands high, and some a lilly white, others a
light chesnut sorrel and dark brown hair. dressed in all sorts

[13] Mary Ann (Davidson) was the wife of Ira Francis Marion Butler, son of Peter and
Rachel Butler. The following obituary appeared in the *Polk County Observer* of
Monmouth on July 7, 1888: "Mary A. Butler, wife of Judge Ira F. M. Butler, died at
her home in Monmouth surrounded by family and friends, one o'clock Friday morning,
June 29, 1888. Mrs. Butler was born in Warren county, Ky., Apr. 22, 1814, married
Nov. 5, 1835 in Ill., crossed the plains in 1853, settled in Polk county where she has
resided ever since, till the day of her death..."

[14] This is probably a misspelling of Paradine, 15-year-old daughter of Ira and Mary
Ann Butler.

[15] This conglomeration of words is probably a localized form or distortion of the
Chinook jargon, trade language of the Pacific Northwest Indians. None of the Chinook
authorities, however, list any of them.

[16] Due to the shortage of women, many were married as young teenagers, and are
sometimes referred to as "child brides." They were both white and Indian.

of pretty prints, from Geise and dirt — made in bright to come about half way between the *wire bender* and their delicate walkers. just below each wire bender is tied a part of the leg of their dady's breeches or something similar. Now, when all this rigging gets under good headway of a moderate walk — it presents an aspect worthy of note.

now in my next, (if you do not chastize me for this) I will tell you about the Silks and nicer things. I have omitted to give a specimen of their knowledge. I will state one case which came immediately under my own eye.

One evening while sitting in the presence of one of the afore mentioned personages, it came about that I asked her how old she was. She said she did not know though she thought she was about sixteen. her husband spoke and told what year she was born. She was near twenty I think Oregon will sometime be a very pleasant place to live. the folks will very soon become aristocratic though on account of the wealth and beauty of the valley, there are a great many rich men here

It appears we are destined for years to mingle in one common herd with the sap heads of every country and clime — schools and society are in the lowest degree. The climate is very different to what I expected it has been very cold this summer we have been obliged to keep a good fire all the time and sleep under three or four covers every night. Our gardens are backward. we have not had any vegetables yet except lettuce. times are very hard, there is very little money in circulation. this makes it very hard for new comers to take a start. I must tell you about our camp meeting which commenced two weeks ago last Thursday and lasted until the next tuesday morning we heard some good Sermons though there was but very few conversions. they were cumberland Presbyterians. there is more of that denomina-

tion than any other in this vicinity, though I speak with
some uncertainty, for I have never heard the numbers of any
but they seem to be in the lead. if you ever get this letter I
wish you would answer it and tell us all the news   tell me all
about what you are doing what improvements the children
have made   tell Lavina to write to me   tell me what has
become of Nancy G

Your affectionate Sister
Elizabeth M. B. Hutchinson

ELIZABETH M. B. HUTCHINSON: LETTER II

Oregon   Aug 26/1855

Dear John & Eliza;

I have just been thinking how well I could enjoy myself if
I were at your house to day but of this pleasure I cannot
partake at present. We must wait patiently until the God of
mammon renders himself propitious, and then I hope to
partake freely of this pleasure. I suppose we have a small
claim on Illinois yet, and this pleasure. I feel very much like
holding on to it. We would be very glad if you would tell us
all about our place when you write again. Mr. Hutchinson
has been wanting to write to you for some time but has been
hindered by sickness and many other unavoidable occur-
rences. I think he will write to you in a few weeks, he is very
busy now and will be fore some time. he is away from home
all the time except now and then a day or so that he has a very
poor chance to write to you or even think on any subject
except that pertaining to his business. We are about two
hundred dollars in debt which must all be paid this fall. he
has not collected but very little money yet for surveying
money is very hard to get at this time.

We have 19 head of cattle two mares and colts I dont
know how many hogs two dogs and two children, so this is

the amount of live stock   Eliza you must write to us when
you feel like it and I would be glad if these feelings would
come on you very often   tell us all about Lavinia for I see
she cant afford [to] tell us anything herself. We want to hear
about the little boys also   give my respects to all who
enquire after and would be pleased to hear from me.

Your loving Sister
E.M.B. Hutchinson

As there is some blank paper left I thought I would ask you
whether you and James think it would be better for me to sell
a part of the timbered land off or sell it all together. likewise
whither you think the price of land will rise or is it at a
stand   if you think that land will rise, then maby I had
better not sell the old place for a while. I want you to write to
me whither you think Wilson will pay off that note when it is
due   if I had it I could makout for a while especially if you
can sell the place I got of Isaac. Isaac is very anxious for you
to sell the place near your uncle Wms   Also Hutchinsons
wants it sold   we want you to write to us what you think the
chance will be to sell it   write what was done with
Hutchinsons farm East of Isaacs last year   Also what you
have done with both of them this year

Your father
Peter Butler

ELIZABETH M. B. HUTCHINSON: LETTER III

Bloomington Polk Co. Oregon
Aug. 3d 1856

Dear Niece;

I have delayed writing to you for some time owing to
Sickness trouble and some other things which are not
profitable to mention. I have written a long letter to your
Father in which I gave a full discription of the sickness and

death of your good grandfather[17]   he is no more   his Spirit
has gone to him who gave it and his body layed in the damp
cold grave   it seems as though he had been preparing for
this and Some time previous to its coming he has lately read
the New testament through twice and was reading the Old
But I think he did not quite finish it previous to his death.
he seemed to be much more patient in the latter part of his
life, than he was in his younger days   he Said to us while
lying sick that he had probably done many wrongs to us in
his life time but he could not see it at the time   he said he
wanted us all to forgive him as far as we could   Your
Grandmother takes his death very hard and I am afraid She
will grieve herself to death   She wants us to get tombstones
and put to his grave   tell your Father if we dont get some at
San Francisco we will Send back there for some and he must
see that the largest and *very finest quality* are procured   we
went to get a good deal of writing put on them. Lavinia I
want you to go to that little hickory grove on the west of the
old home and pick two of the nicest oak leaves you can find
and send them in your next letter also two hickory ones at
different times along. I wish you would continue to send
until you send every kind of leaf that grows in the old granate
State   Send me a leaf off Grand Ma's favorite walnut also
one off the rose bush by the front door   your letter of the
(20 Jan) I believe was the first I have ever received from you
but I hope you will not make it the last   the children are all
pretty well though they have all been sick with colds   there
are a great many children dying with the flux   the lung
fever is raging in Oregon at this time   I received a big fine
and interesting letter from P. M. Murphy some days
since   give my respects to all and believe me as ever

loving Aunt
Lissie

---

[17] Peter Butler.

Afternoon

Dear little Erastus your very pretty little letter came safe to hand   it is indeed a neat letter   I will save the card until the baby gets old enough to take care of it himself   he is truly a little treasure   his face is as sweet as the honey dew and his eyes are a pearly brightness   I want to have his miniature taken this summer and send back to Illinois   I dont know but I will have to beg off from the name as his Pa asked for the name before he started to the war[18]   We have concluded to call him Thomas Otis   we think the name you selected was a very pretty one and would be pleased to the little judge by patronizing his name   Jimmy sends his love to you   Robert is out in the orchard singing at the top of his voice or else he would send his love   you must write to them again

Your Aunt
Lissie

Now Grandville

you and Isaac are last but not least   we would be just as glad to see your little faces as if you were as large as Jarvis   be good boys and write us a letter as soon as you can   When they get the great Pacific railroad done we will go to see you

Good Bye

Tell Aunt Nancy Butler if she dont answer my letter she need not expect another

Tell your mother she must take this letter as written to her   also give my respect to all

Your Aunt Lissy

Our territorial meeting commences this week at Monmouth there is great preparations being made for it and I hope much good will be done.

---

[18] The mid-1850's were years of Indian-White conflict in the Pacific Northwest.

AMELIA KNIGHT
Used with the permission of the Oregon Historical Society.

Iowa to the Columbia River

ॳ Amelia Knight

INTRODUCTION

Saturday, Sept. 17 — In camp yet. Still raining. *Noon.* It has cleared off and we are all ready for a start again for some place we don't know where. *Evening.* Came 6 miles and have encamped in a fence corner by a Mr. Lambert's about 7 miles from Milwaukie. Turn our stock out to tolerably good feed.

A few days later my eighth child was born. After this we picked up and ferried across the Columbia River, utilizing a skiff, canoes and flatboat. It took 3 days. Here husband traded 2 yoke of oxen for a half section of land with ½ acre planted to potatoes, a small log cabin and lean-to with no windows. This is the journey's end.

The above quotation from Amelia Knight's "diary" was used by us in the introduction to this set of books in Volume I, page 12. We used it to illustrate the fact of pregnancy in the lives of women traveling overland, and it has been one of the most quoted statements about the overland journey by others as well. We estimate that we have used it in 80-some speeches. It is magnificent! It is also incorrect.

The second paragraph in the quotation simply does not appear in the original manuscript which is in the University of Washington Library; however it is to be found in all heretofore printed copies.[1] This means that some time between September 17, 1853, and 1928, when it was printed in the *Transactions* of the Oregon Pioneer Association, the extra paragraph was added.

The question arises, "Who wrote it?" We think it was not Amelia Knight herself because of all people she would know that

---

[1] *Transactions* of the Oreg. Pioneer Assoc., 56th Annual Reunion (Portland, 1928), pp. 38-54; *Clark County Sun*, Vancouver, Wash., Oct. 24, 31; Nov. 28; Dec. 5, 12, 19, 26, 1930; Fort Vancouver Hist. Soc., *Clark County History*, VI (1965), pp. 36-56.

the baby was born not "a few days later," but the very next day, on September 18, 1853.

This corrected rendering of the diary in no way denigrates Lillian Schlissel's statement: "What is not mentioned at all is the fact of another pregnancy. The diary must be read with this unstated fact in mind."[2]

The lesson for all of us who do serious research in history is that one must always seek the original of any document. A copy, either in typescript or in print, cannot take the place of the actual primary document, whether diary or letter.

Amelia Stewart was a young lady from Boston, who, at age 17 met a young English-born medical student, age 26. They were married on September 18, 1834. Joel Knight had worked for some years as a traveling hatter when he decided to become a doctor.

Over the following years the family made two great moves westward: First they moved to the vicinity of Vernon, Van Buren County, Iowa, in March 1837. Their farm was on the south shore of the Des Moines River near the southeast corner of Iowa, which became a new state in 1846. They lived a short distance north of what became the Mormon Trail from Koekuk to Council Bluffs (Kanesville), i.e. from the Mississippi to the Missouri rivers. They must have seen thousands of travelers with their wagons on the trail in the years that they lived in Van Buren County.

When Amelia wrote her first journal entry on Saturday, April 1, 1853, the family was just beginning the long journey from the south shore of the Des Moines River to the north shore of the Columbia in the newly-named Territory of Washington. This new political entity was established by Act of Congress on February 10, 1853. The Knights began their journey west by following what was already called "The Old Mormon Trail."

When Joel and Amelia settled on their new claim in Iowa in 1837, they already had one child, Plutarch, who was born in Boston on October 21, 1836. Over the next sixteen years in their

<hr>

[2] Lillian Schlissel, *Women's Diaries of the Westward Journey*, (New York, 1982), pp. 199-200.

new midwest home six more children were born. There were seven, therefore, who traveled over the Oregon Trail. When Amelia made her first diary entry on April 9th, she was three months pregnant. One might say that she had her hands full.

We are grateful to the University of Washington Library for making a photocopy of Amelia Knight's original diary available to us. The firm, clear handwriting is so easy to read that we could copy it directly. There is a note with the photocopied diary from Dr. Edmond S. Meany, Professor of History, written to Chatfield Knight, telling him how careful the University would be with such an original manuscript. This note is dated October 13, 1934. There is another handwritten note appended which says "Chat Knight — aged 84, died 1934 — requested that diary and desk be given to the University of Wash, in response to letter written by Prof. Meany in 1934."

We would also like to thank the Clark County Historical Museum, Vancouver, Washington, and particularly David Freece, museum director, and Lesla Scott, librarian, who have both been helpful.

Mrs. Mary Craine of Vancouver, a descendant of the Knights, has been encouraging and has gladly approved of our publishing of Amelia Knight's journal.

CHILDREN WHO WENT WEST
WITH AMELIA AND JOEL KNIGHT:

Plutarch Stewart Knight (Oct. 21, 1836-Jan. 29, 1915), was age 17 in 1853. He was a big help to his father with the work of the wagon train. He attended Willamette University in Salem and later became a well-known Congregational minister. He was pastor of the First Congregational Church in Salem from 1867 to 1883. Knight Memorial Church in Salem is named after him. He and Eleanor Smith were married on April 21, 1861. He served as editor of the *Oregon Statesman* newspaper for a period. He also was Director of the Oregon School for the Deaf. *Oregon Statesman Illustrated Annual*, (Salem, 1893), p. 17; H.O. Lang, *History of the Willamette Valley* (Portland, 1885), p. 809.

Seneca Knight (1838-Jan. 8, 1873), was age 15 in 1853. Amelia
  characterizes him with the words, "Seneca, dont stand there, with
  your hands in your pockets, get your saddles and be ready." He
  became a farmer and stockman. He was evidently a single man and
  died at the home of his mother.

Frances Amelia Knight (1841-April 1, 1927), was 14-years-old in 1853.
  She married a widower, Nathan Pearcy, a Virginian, in 1865. There
  were two small children by his first wife, Fanny. They were Fanny,
  age 7, and Nathan, Jr., age 5. Pearcy moved her into his beautiful
  home on Pearcy Island, at the confluence of the Willamette and
  Columbia rivers. They lived there until moving to Portland in
  "about 1879." They had famous peach orchards and livestock on
  their river-bottom with its rich alluvial soil. But the floods came, and
  the homestead went back to bulrushes. There was still enough of the
  house left in 1928 for the Portland *Oregonian* to run a story in its
  Mar. 25 edition, "Old, Forlorn Pearcy Home Once Scene of
  Happiness." Nathan died in Portland on May 30, 1903. Frances
  lived on for another 24 years, and died also in Portland.

Jefferson Knight (1842-Oct. 18, 1867), was 11-years-old in 1853. He
  took up farming with his father on their donation land claim on the
  north bank of the Columbia, ten miles up the river from Vancouver,
  Wash. He died of drowning in the river near the homestead.

Lucy Jane Knight (1845-May 15, 1877), was age 8 in 1853. She started
  the long journey with the mumps (entry for April 11). Lucy and
  Almira were filled with fear when they saw the first Indians on Apr.
  29 and ran to hide in the wagon. She was lost on Aug. 8, having
  wandered behind the wagon train. Emigrants in another train picked
  her up and returned the frightened little girl to her family. In 1865
  Lucy married an energetic Swiss steamboatman and boat builder,
  John Jacob Wintler, who came to the Vancouver area via the
  Panama Canal route in 1857. She lived for only 12 years after her
  marriage. In that time she bore 6 children.

Almira L. Knight (1848-?), age 5 in 1853; grew up in Clark Co., Wash.;
  married W.B. Patterson.

Chatfield Knight (1851-Dec. 27, 1934), age 2. Received much
  attention from his mother on the westward journey. She mentions
  him being sick and how he "fell out of the wagon, but did not get
  hurt much," (July 17). He lived a long life in Washington State and
  donated the diary to the University of Washington, Library.

Wilson Carl Knight (Sept. 18, 1853-Sept. 6, 1886), was the baby born
near the Lambert farm, just out of Milwaukie, Oreg., at the end of
the westward journey. There is a handwritten note in the Clark
County, Washington, Historical Museum saying that he had been
of delicate health over much of his early life and went to New York
for special treatment. It seemed to help as his health improved. In
New York State he married Esther Nelson. He inherited the family
homestead on the bank of the Columbia, ten miles upstream from
Vancouver. He died of consumption on Sept. 6, 1886.

There was another son, Adam, who was born in 1855 and lived until
1928.

THE DIARY

Saturday April 9th 1853. Started from home about 11
oclock, and travel 8 miles and camp in an old house, night
cold and frosty —

10, Sunday M, Cool and pleasant, roads hard and dusty,
evening came 18½ miles and camp close to Mr Fulkersons
house

11, M. morn, Cloudy and signs of rain, about 10 o'clock it
begins to rain, at noon it rains so hard we turn out, and camp
in a School house after traveling 11½ miles, rains all the
afternoon, and all night   very unpleasant, Jefferson and
Lucy have the mumps, poor cattle bawl all night

12, T, morn, Warm and sultry, still cloudy, road, very
muddy, travel 10 miles and camp in Soap creek bottom
creek bank full, have to wait till it falls —

13 W, Noon, Fair weather, have to overhaul all the wagons
and dry things, Evening still in camp

14th   Quite cold   little one crying with cold feet, sixteen
wagons all getting ready to cross the creek, hurry and bustle
and get breakfast over, feed the cattle, and tumble things

into the wagons, hurrah boys all ready, we will be the first to cross the creek this morning, gee up tip and tyler[1] and away we go the sun just rising Evening we have traveled 24 miles to day, and are about to camp in a large prairie without wood, cold and chilly east wind, the men have pitched the tent, and are hunting something to make a fire, to get supper, I have the sick headache and must leave the boys to get it themselves the best they can —

15th Cold and cloudy wind still east bad luck last night, three of our horses get away, supper   they have gone back, one of the boys have gone back after them, and we are going on slowly Evening Henry has come back with the horses all right again, came 17 miles to day roads very bad and muddy cold and cloudy all day   it is begining to rain, the boys have pitched the tent. and I must get supper —

16th   Campt last night 3 miles east of Chariton point in the prairie. made our beds down in the tent in the wet and mud, bed clothes nearly spoiled. Cold and cloudy this morning, and every body out of humour, Seneca is half sick, Plutarch has broke his saddle girth, Husband is scolding, and hurriing all hands (and the cook) and Almira says She wishes she was home, and I say ditto, Home sweet home — Evening we passed a small town this morning called Charitan point, the sun shone a little this affternoon   came 24 miles to day, and have pitched our tent in the prairie again, and have some hay to put under our beds, corn one dollar per bushel, feed for our stock cost 16 dol, to night —

17th Sunday   It is warm and pleasant, we are on our way again traveling over some very pretty rolling prairie, corn is up to 3 dollars a bushel, travel 20 miles to day, and have

[1] Oxen were often given names. Here they were named for the battle cry of the 1840 election of President William Henry Harrison and Vice-President John Tyler: "Tippecanoe and Tyler Too."

campt in the prarie, no wood to cook with, have to eat cold supper, have the good luck to find corn at 80 cts a bushel

18th, Cold breakfast the first thing, very disagreeable weather, wind east, cold and rainy, no fire, we are on a very large prarie, no timber to be seen as far as the eye can reach,   Evening have crossed several very bad streams to day, and more than once have been stuck in the mud, we pass Pisga this afternoon, and have just crossed Grand river, and will camp in a little bottom, plenty of wood, and we will have some warm supper I guess   came 22 miles to day, my head aches, but the fire is kindled and I must make some tea, that will help it, if not cure it —

19th, Still damp and cloudy, corn very scarce and high travel 20 miles and camp.

20th   Cloudy, We are creeping along slowly, one wagon after another, the same old gait, and the same thing over out of one mud hole and into another all day   crossed a branch where the water run into the wagons, no corn to be had within 75 miles, came 18 miles and camp

21st   Rained all night, is still raining   I have just counted 17 wagons traveling ahead of us in the mud and water, no feed for our poor stock to be got at any price, have to feed them flour and meal   travel 22 miles today —

22nd   Still bad weather, no sun, traveling on mile after mile in the mud, travel 21 miles and cross Nishnabotna and camp on the bank of it

23rd   Still in camp, it rained hard all night, and blew a hurrican almost, all the tents were blown down, and some wagons capsized, Evening it has been raining hard all day, every thing is wet and muddy, One of the oxen missing, the boys have been hunting him all day. Dreary times, wet and muddy, and crowded in the tent, cold and wet and uncomfortable in the wagon   no place for the poor children, I have been busy cooking, roasting coffe &c to day, and have came into the wagon to write this and make our bed —

24th   Sunday, The rain has ceased, and the sun shines a little, must stay in camp and dry the bed clothes   no feed for the stock but what little grass they can pick, after noon found the ox, and lost our muley cow   must wait and find her

25th   Rather cold but the sun shines once more, still feeding the cattle and horses on flour, one of our horses badly foundered, On our way again at last, found our cow with a young calf, had to leave the calf behind then travel on a while, and came to a very bad sideling bridge to cross over a creek, came 18 miles —

26th   Cold and clear   found corn last night at 2 dollars a bushel, paid 12 dollars for about half a feed for our stock,   I can count 20 wagons winding up the hill ahead of us, travel 20 miles and camp —

27th   A nice spring morning, warm and pleasant   the road is covered with wagons and cattle, paid $2, 40cts for crossing a bridge, travel 25 miles to day and camp on a creek (called keg) about 10 miles from the Bluffs —

28th   Still in camp, pleasant weather, we will stay here a few days to rest and recruit our cattle, wash cook ect.

29th   Cool and pleasant, saw the first indians to day Lucy and almira afraid and run into the wagon to hide, Done some washing and sewing to day —

30th   Fine weather   spent this day in washing, baking and overhauling the wagons,   several more wagons have campt around us

Sunday May 1st   Still fine weather, wash and scrub all the Children

2nd   Pleasant evening, have been cooking, and packing things away for an early start in the morning, threw away several jars, some wooden buckets, and all our pickels   too unhandy to carry, Indians came to our camp every day begging money and something to eat   children are getting used to them

3rd   Fine weather, Leave Loudenback and his team this morning, and are on our way again, travel 6 or 7 miles and camp on pony creek, here Plutarch is taken sick

4th   Weather fair, travel 4 miles to day   passed through Kanesvill, and camp in a lane, not far from the Missouri river, and wait our turn to cross   no feed for the stock, have to buy flour at 3½ per hundred to feed them

5th   We crossed the river this morning on a large steamboat called the Hindoo,[2] after a great deal of hurrahing and trouble to get the cattle all aboard, one ox jumpt overboard, and swam across the river, and come out like a drowned rat   The river is even with its banks, and the timber in it, which is mostly cotton wood is quite green, Cost us 15 dollars to cross, after bidding Iowa a kind farewell, we travel 8 miles and camp about noon among the old ruins of the Mormon Town[3]   we here join another company, which will make in all 24 men, 10 wagons, and a large drove of cattle   have appointed a Captain, and are

---

[2] According to the *Missouri Republican* of St. Louis in its edition of May 11, 1853, the *Hindoo* was "still engaged in ferrying emigrants across the river at Council Bluffs," but the "larger portion" had set out for the West. The *Hindoo* left for St. Louis on May 13. Louise Barry, *The Beginning of the West* (Topeka, 1972), p. 1146.

[3] In the fall of 1846 the great migration of Mormons had crossed the Missouri and spent the cold months at their "Winter Quarters," now part of greater Omaha, Nebr. Leonard J. Arrington and Davis Bitton, *The Mormon Experience* (New York, 1979), pp. 97-98.

now prepared to guard the stock, 4 men watch 2 hours, and then call up 4 more, to take their places, so by that means no person can sleep about the camp, such a wild noisy set was never heard.

6th   Pleasant, we have just passed the Mormon graveyard,[4] there is a great number of graves on it, the road is covered with wagons and cattle, here we passed a train of wagons on their way back, the head man had been drowned a few days before, in a river called Elk horn while getting some cattle across, and his wife was lying in the wagon quite sick, and children were mourning for a father gone and with sadness, and pitty, I passed those who perhaps a few days before had been well and happy as ourselves, came 20 miles to day, —

7th   Cold morning, thermometer down to 48 in the wagon   no wood, only enough to boil some coffee, good grass for the stock, we have just crossed a small creek, with a narrow indian bridge across it, paid the indians 75 cnts too, my hands are numb with cold — Evening travel 23 miles and camp on Elk horn bottom close to the river, it is very high and dangerous to cross --

8th   Sunday morning. Still in camp waiting to cross, there are three hundred or more wagons in sight, and as far as the eye can reach, the bottom is covered, on each side of the river, with cattle and horses, there is no ferry here, and the men will have to make one out of the tightest wagon bed, (every camp should have a water proof wagon bed for this purpose) every thing must now be hauled out of the way head over heels (and he that knows where to find any thirg will be a smart fellow) then the wagons must be all taken to pieces, and then by means of a strong rope stretched across the river, with the tight wagon bed atached to the middle of it, the rope must be long enough to pull from one side to the

---

[4] *Ibid.* Some 200 persons had died at the 1846-1847 Mormon Winter Quarters.

other, with men on each side of the river to pull it, and in this
way we have to cross every thing a little at a time, women and
children last, and then swim the cattle and horses, there were
three horses and some cattle drowned at this place yesterday
while crossing, It is quite lively and merry here this morning,
and the weather fine, we are campt on a large bottom, with
the broad deep river on one side of us, and a high bluff on the
other

9th   Morning cold within 4 degrees of freezing, we are all
on the right side of the river this morning   it took the men
all day yesterday to get every thing across which they did all
safe by working hard, we are now on our way again   Evening we have driven a good ways out of the road to find grass
and camp after traveling 22 miles

10th   Cold   thermometer down to 30 in the wagon
ground froze last night, came 20 miles and camp.

11th   Evening, it has been very dusty, yesterday and to
day   the men all have their false eyes[5] to keep the dust out,
we are traveling up platte river bottom, the north side   we
have been near the river several times, it is a beautiful river
about a mile across, full of Islands and sand bars   as far as
the eye can reach the road is covered with teams   Plutarch
is well and able to drive, came 23 miles

12th   Thursday noon, beautiful weather, but very dusty,
we are campt on the bank of Loop [Loup] fork waiting our
turn to cross, there are 2 ferry boats running, and a number
of wagons ahead of us, all waiting to cross, have to pay 3 dol a
wagon, 3 wagons, and swim the stock, travel 12 miles to day,
we hear there are seven hundred teams on the road ahead of
us, evening wash, and cook this afternoon, —

13th   It is thundering and bids fair for rain, crossed the

[5] Goggles

river very early this morning before breakfast, got breakfast over after a fashion, sand all around us ankle deep, wind blowing, no matter hurry it over, them that eat the most breakfast, eat the most sand, we are all moving again slowly — Evening came 24 miles to day, finding we can get along faster and more comfortable alone, we left all company this morning and have campt alone, our company passed us while at supper and said good evening, and campt a little ahead of us —

14th   Had a fine rain last night, laid the dust, cool, and the sun shines this morning, we see very few indians, did not see more than a dozen Pawnees, we are now in the Souis country, passed the sand bluffs, travel 5 miles and obliged to stop and camp on the prairie near a large pond of watter, on acount of the high winds and some rain, wind so high that we dare not make a fire, impossible to pitch the tent, the wagons can hardly stand the wind, all that can find room are crowded into the wagons, those that cant have to stay out in the storm, some of the boys lost their hats

15th   Sunday morn, Cool and pleasant after such a storm, travel 18 miles and camp —

16th   Evening we have had all kinds of weather to day   this morning was dry dusty and sandy, this afternoon it rained hailed and the wind was very high, have been traveling all the afternoon in mud and water up to the hubs, broke chains, and stuck in the mud several times, the men and boys are all wet and muddy, hard times but they say misery loves company, we are not alone on the bare plaines, it is covered with cattle and wagons, we have come to another muddy branch, we will cross it and find a camping place, good grass for the stock and thats one good luck we have, travel about 20 miles, the wind is getting higher

17th   Tuesday morning. we had a dreadful storm of rain

and hail last night, and very sharp lightning, it killed 2
oxen for one man, we had just encampt on a large flat
prairie, when the storm commenced in all its fury, and in
two minuets after the cattle were taken from the wagons,
every brute was gone out of sight, cows, calves, horses all
gone before the storm like so many wild beasts. I never saw
such a storm the wind was so high, I thought is would tear
the wagons to pieces, nothing but the stoutest covers could
stand it, the rain beat into the wagons so that every thing
was wet, and in less than two hours, the water was a foot
deep all over our camping ground, as we could have no tent
pitched, all hands had to crowd into the wagons and sleep
in wet beds, with their wet clothes on, without supper, the
wind blew hard all night, and this morning presents a
dreary prospect, surrounded by water, and our saddles have
been soaking in it all night and are almost spoiled, had little
or nothing for breakfast our cow (rose) came up to be
milked, the men took her track, and found the stock about
4 miles from camp, start on, and travel about two miles,
and came to dry creek, so called because it is dry most of
the year   I should call it water creek now, as it is out of its
banks and we will have to wait till it falls, no wood within 8
miles, raining by spells, —

18th   Wen [Wed.], Still in camp, very high winds again
last night   blew some of the tents over, Cold and windy this
morning and not a stick of wood to make a fire, trying to dry
the bed clothes between showers, the creek is falling —

19th   Thurs, morn, Clear, all getting ready to cross the
creek afternoon   crossed dry creek this morning and have
traveled 10 miles, and come to wood creek, and are up a
stump again, it is also very high, and we will have to cross it
as we did Elkhorn, in a wagon bed, and swim the stock, just
got things packed away nice this morning, now they must all

be tumbled out again, well, there is plenty of wood, and I will spend the afternoon in cooking —

20th   Friday morn, crossed wood creek last night, and got loaded up a little after dark, and drove out 3 or 4 miles where we found a good camping place, We are now traveling between Platte river and wood creek, plenty of water and grass, not much wood and that cotton wood   travel 21 miles.

21st   Sat, We have just crossed deep dry creek, it had a little muddy water in it, Very warm   it is the first day the cattle have lolled, thermometer up to 92 in the wagon, good grass, bad water, and no wood, came 20 miles

22nd, Sunday, fine weather, crossing branches, and mud holes all day, traveled about 18 miles —

23rd, Monday   the road is covered with droves of cattle, and wagons, no end to them, dry and dusty all day, travel 20 miles and camp on the bank of Platte river, plenty of wood, by wading across to the islands for it,

24th   Stay in camp to day, to wash and cook, as we have a good camping ground, plenty of wood, and water & good grass   weather pleasant, I had the sick headache all night, some better this morning, must do a days work, husband went back a piece this morning in search of our dog, which he found, with some rascles who were trying to keep him, —

25th   Wendsday, It is raining, we have got our washing, and some cooking done, and with a bunch of wood tied on each wagon (for the purpose of making coffee, as we will not see wood again soon) we are ready for a start as soon as the rain holds up — evening it has been cold and rainy all day, only travel 12 miles and camp, —

26th Thursday   Evening it rained all the fornoon, cleared off at noon, we started and traveled about 14 miles over marshy wet ground, while the team were creeping along I went up on a high bluff, and had a splendid view of platte and her beautiful timbered Islands

27th   Friday   Cloudy and wind cont. we are now traveling along the edge of platte, it is so wide here, we can just see timber the other side, it must be 2 miles across   travel 20 miles to day —

28th   Saturday   travel 18 miles to day, over very sandy ground   passed a lot of men skining a buffalo, we got a mess and cooked some for supper, it was very good and tender   it is the first we have seen, dead or alive, —

29th Sunday   quite warm, came 15 miles   very sandy, and bad traveling for the cattle, it will be 175 miles before we see timber again, we haul a little dry wood along to make coffee and tea, —

30th Monday   it has been cloudy and cool to day, and better roads, traveled 23 miles

31st   Tuesday evening, travel 25 miles to day, when we started this morning, there were 2 large droves of cattle and about 50 wagons ahead of us, and we either had to stay poking behind them in the dust, or hurry up and drive past them, which was no fool of a job to be mixed up with several hundred head of cattle, and only one road to travel in, and the drivers threating to drive their cattle over you if you attempted to pass them, they even took out their pistols, husband came up just as one man held his pistol at Wilson Carl,[6] and saw what the fuss was, and he said boys follow me, and he drove our team out of the road entierly, and the cattle

---

[6] Wilson Carl was a single man, a wagoneer for the Knights. He settled in Yamhill Co., Oreg., an accomplished carpenter. Some say the town of Carlton was named for him, but there is some disagreement about this. On May 26, 1856, he and Mary Stout were married. Joseph Gaston, *Centennial History of Oregon*, II (Chicago, 1912), pp. 906-911. The Knights thought enough of him to name their son, born on September 18, 1853, on their arrival in the Portland area, for him, Wilson Carl Knight. *See* Introduction, above, p. 34.

seemed to understand it all, for they went in the trot most of
the way,   the rest of the boys followed with their teams, and
the rest of the stock,   I had rather a rough ride to be sure,
but was glad to get away from such a lawless set, which we did
by noon. the head teamster done his best by whiping and
holloing to his cattle, he found it was no use and got up into
his wagon to take it easy, we left some swearing men behind
us, we drove a good ways ahead, and stopt to rest the cattle
and eat some dinner, while we were eating we saw them
coming, all hands jumpt for their teams, thinking saying
they had earned the road too dearly to let them pass us again,
and in a few moments we were all on the go again.   very
warm to day, thermomenter at 98 in the wagon at one
oclock,   toward evening there came up a light thunder
storm which cooled the air down to 60,   we are now within
100 miles of ft. Laramie, —

June 1st   It has been raining all day long, and we have been
traveling in it, so as to [be] able to keep ahead of the large
droves, the men and boys are all soaking wet and look sad
and comfortless, the little ones and myself are shut up in the
wagons from the rain. still it will find its way in, and many
things are wet, and take us all together we are a poor looking
set and all this for *Oregon.* I am thinking while I write,
Oh Oregon you must be a lovely country,   came 18 miles
to day

2nd   Thursday morning. It has cleared off pleasant after
the rain and all hands seem bright and cheerful again, we are
going along the same old gait. Evening traveled 27 miles to
day passed Court house rock, and chimney rock, both
situated on the other side of the river, and have been in sight
for several days, we have campt oposite chimney rock —

3rd Friday morn. We had another hard blow, and rain last
night, looks some like clearing off this morning, Evening

came 21 miles to day and have campt about oposite to Scotts bluffs, water very bad, have to use out of platte most of the time, it is very high and muddy —

4th   Saturday   More rain last night, is raining some to day, the roads are very bad, nothing but mud and water, came 16 m

5th   Sunday   Very warm. Slow traveling, several of the oxen have sore necks, caused by traveling in the rain, came 18 miles to day, and are campt near platte, where we have wood, and plenty of grass for the stock —

6th   Monday. Still in camp, husband and myself being sick (caused we suppose by Drinking the river water, as it looks more like dirty suds, than anything else)   we concluded to stay in camp, and each take a vomit, which we did, and are much better; the boys and myself have been washing some to day, the prickly pear grows in great abundance along this platte river road. —

7th Tuesday. Rained some last night, quite warm to day. Just passed fort Laramie, situated on the opposite side of the river; This afternoon we passed a large villiage of Siou indians, numbers of them came round our wagons, some of the women had moccasins, and beads, which they wanted to trade for bread. I gave the women and children all the cakes I had baked. husband traded a big indian a lot of hard crackers for a pair of moccasins, and after we had started on, he came up with us again, making a great fuss, and wanting them back (they had eat part of the crackers) he did not seem to be satisfied or else he wished to cause us some trouble, or perhaps get into a fight, however we handed the moccasins to him in a hurry, and drove away from them as soon as possible, several lingered along watching our horses that we tied behind the wagons, no doubt with the view of stealing them, but our folks kept a sharp lookout, till they left, we had a thunder storm of rain and hail, and a hard blow this afternoon, have traveled 18 miles, and are campt among the black hills, they are covered with Cedar, and pine wood, sand stone, lime stone, and pure water —

8th   Wendsday   It is a pleasant morning after the rain, every thing looks fresh and green, we are traveling through the black hills, over rocks, and stones. there is some splendid scenery here, beautiful vallies, and dark green clad hills, with their ledges of rock, and then far away over them you can see Larimie peak, with her snow capt top; evening came 16 miles to day, had another shower this afternoon, and have campt in a lovely spot, plenty of wood, water, and good grass

9th   Thursday, came 18 miles to day; weather warm, had a slight shower in the afternoon, campt without wood or water, but good grass. —

10th   Friday   It has been very warm to day thermometer up to 99 at noon, traveled 21 miles over a very rough road, and have campt on the bank of the platte river, wild sage brush to burn, which makes a very good fire, when dry, very poor grass, here one of our hands left us (Benjamine Hughs)

11th   Saturday, The last of the black hills, we traveled this forenoon over the roughest and most desolate piece of ground that was ever made (called by some the Devils grater) not a drop of water, not a spear of grass to be seen, nothing but barren hills, bare broken rocks, sand and dust. quite a contrast to the first part of these hills   we reached platte river about noon, and our cattle were so crazy for water, that some of them plunged headlong into the river with their yokes on, travel 18 miles and camp —

12th   Sunday morn, we are traveling on in the sand and dust   it is very dusty, and the road is covered with teams and droves of cattle, the grass is very poor, mostly gone to seed — Evening came about 17 miles and have campt near the bank of platte, the boys have driven the cattle on to an Island where they can get grass, and I have just washed the dust out of my eyes so that I can see to get supper, —

13th Monday evening. This has been a long, hard days travel   came 30 miles through sand and dust, and have campt opposite the old upper ferry on platte, tomorrow we will come to the first poison water, there will be no more good water for about 25 miles, we will also leave platte river in the morning for good —

14th Tuesday evening   we started this morning at day break to travel our long, dry, dusty days travel, the dust and sand has been very bad — passed the Avenue rocks this afternoon, traveled 31 miles and are about to camp, there is not less than 150 wagons campt around us, but we have left most of the droves behind, and no end to the teams, had a great deal of trouble to keep the stock from drinking the poison or alkali water, it is almost sure to kill man or beast who drink it —

15th   Wendsday came 19 miles to day, passed Independence rock this afternoon, and crossed Sweet water river on a bridge   paid 3 dollars a wagon and swam the stock across,   the river is very high and swift, there is cattle and horses drowned there every day; one cow went under the bridge and was drowned, while we were crossing belonging to another company, the bridge is very rickety and must soon break down. we are campt 2 miles this side of the bridge near the river. —

16th   Thursday   We are now traveling up sweet water valley between two mountains, one of them being covered with snow, sweet water is a clear cool and beautiful stream, and close to its margin lies the road, this morning we passed the devils gate, came 16 miles, and have campt on the bank of Sweet water, no wood, nor grass, on this side of the river

17th   Friday   Concluded to stay in camp and rest the cattle a day or two, swum the cattle and horses across the river where there is plenty of good feed, we also get our wood from the other side, the best swimmers go over, and cut a light cedar log, and swim back with it, have been sewing and cooking to day. the mosquitoes are very bad here   cut the first cheese to day

18th   Saturday   Still in camp, overhauling the wagons, cooking sewing patching, ect, ect, had a very hard blow and a slight sprinkle of rain this afternoon —

19th   Sunday. On our way again, traveling in the sand and dust   sand ankle deep, hard traveling, came 18 miles and camp on the bank of sweet water again, and swim the cattle over to feed —

20th   Monday evening. came 22 miles to day, passed good water once, passed a good deal of poison water, and have campt in the mountains   weather warm and pleasant —

21st   Tuesday evening, we have traveled over a very rough rocky road to day, over mountains, close to banks of snow. — had plenty of snow water to drink, husband brought me a large bunch of flowers, which he said was growing close to the snow, which was about six feet deep. travel 16 miles to day, and have campt on the mountains about seven miles from the summit, we are traveling through the south pass, the wind river mountains are off to our right, among them is Fremonts peak, they look romantic covered with snow.

22nd   Wendsday morning, very cold   water froze over in the buckets,   thermometer down to 30, the boys have on their overcoats and mittens, Evening it snowed a little through the day, the road has been very dusty, but smooth and level as a turnpike   came 18 miles and camp about ½ mile from the pacific springs   we left sweet water this morning —

23rd   Thursday, cold again this morning. water froze over, came 27 miles and campt on the bank [of] little Sandy river after dark

24th   Friday noon, came from little Sandy, to big Sandy, 7 miles, and camp for a day or two to rest the stock, good grass, and water here, Henry Miller[7] left us this morning   we started with five hands, and have only two left —

25th   Saturday   Still in camp, washing, cooking, and sewing &c. Weather very pleasant —

26th   Sunday morning, we are on our way again traveling in the dusty dust, we must go 17 miles or more without water or grass, evening all hands came into camp tired and out of heart, husband and myself sick, no feed for the stock, one ox lame, camp on the bank of big Sandy again —

27th   Monday morn, Cold cloudy and very windy, more like November than June, I am not well enough to get out of the wagon this morning, the men have just got their breakfast over, and drove up the stock, all hurry and bustle, to get things in order, its children milk the cows all hands help yoke these cattle the d---ls in them, Plutarch: I cant   I must hold the tent up, its blowing away, hurrah boys, who tends these horses; Seneca, dont stand there, with your hands in your pockets, get your saddles and be ready   Evening, traveled 18 miles to day, and have campt on the bank of Green river, and must wait our turn to cross on a ferry boat, no grass for the poor cattle, all hands discouraged, We have

---

[7] Henry Miller was a 21-year-old man from Ohio. He settled on a claim in Coos Co., Oreg., on June 10, 1854. He was still single at that time. *Genealogical Material in Oregon Donation Land Claims*, III (Portland, 1962), #1831, p. 131.

taken in 2 new hands to day, which will make us full handed again, —

28th Tuesday evening, still in camp, waiting to cross nothing for the stock to eat, as far as the eye can reach it is nothing but a sandy desert, and the road is strewed with dead cattle, and the stench is awful, one of our best oxen too lame to travel, have to sell him for what we can get, to a native for 15 dollars; (all along this road we see white men living with the indians, many of them have trading posts, they are mostly french, and have squaw wives,) have to yoke up our muley cow in the ox's place —

29th Wendsday morn, Cold and cloudy, the wagons are all crowded up to the ferry, waiting with impatience to cross, there are thirty or more to cross before us, have to cross one at a time, have to pay 8 dollars a wagon, 1 do for a horse or cow, we swim all our stock, Evening we crossed the river about 3 oclock, then traveled 10 miles, and campt close to slate creek, it is cold enough to sit by the fire —

30th Thursday evening. Traveled 20 miles to day, and have campt in the mountains, near a clear cold spring of good water, grass plenty, and dry sage brush to burn, the children have climed a mountain to see the sun set

July 1st Friday, We had a fine shower last night, which laid the dust and freshened the grass, it is cold this morning, almost freezing, We are now ascending a steep mountain, now we are at the top — all around us we can see the snowy mountains, and down below is a beautiful green valley, and a small Indian villiage. Evening travel 18 miles to day, crossed hams fork of Green river this afternoon, and have campt half way up a steep mountain

2nd Saturday evening we have been traveling up and down steep mountains all day   came about 15 miles, and camp, within 2 miles of Bear river close to a good spring. —

3rd Sunday Bad luck this morning, soon after starting one of our best oxen took sick, and in less than an hour he was dead, suppose he was poisoned with alkali water, or weeds. turned out the old ox and started on. crossed Smiths fork of Bear river on a bridge paid 1 dollar a wagon, it is a very rappid stream, and hard to swim stock over. we then came over some very rough ground, the worst we have seen, nothing but rocks to travel over, close under a steep mountain, water and grass plenty, also wood, we will stay here till after the fourth, two of oxen quite lame. —

4th of July, Monday it has been very warm to day, thermometer up to 110 and yet we can see banks of snow almost within reach, I never saw the mosquitoes as bad as they are here Chat has been sick all day with fever, partly caused by mosquitoe bites, the men have been shoeing one of the lame oxen the first one they have tried to shoe the other ones foot is too much swelled.

5th Tuesday Noon, we are campt on top of a mountain to noon and rest awhile, it is warm, but there is a good breeze up here, Chatfield is sick yet had fever all night, Evening crossed 2 creeks to day, one with a bridge over paid 1 dollar a wagon to cross, travel 15 miles over a very hilly road and camp near the sulpher springs situated in a small prairie, surrounded by mountains

6th Wendsday evening traveled 20 miles to day and camp near a spring (in mosquito valley) there is plenty of good grass all along Bear river valley traded a cow and calf to day for a steer to yoke up with the odd one, and find after useing him half a day, that we have been cheated, as he cant stand it to travel —

7th Thursday evening, We have traveled 20 miles to day, all up hill and down, it has been very warm and dusty. we have campt about half a mile off from the road close to a splendid spring of limestone water, in a beautiful pine and cedar grove, while I am writing we are haveing a fine little shower, which is a great treat, our poor dog gave out with the heat and sand so that he could not travel, the boys have gone back after him, it has cleared off and I must get supper —

8th   Friday morn. Verry pleasant. found our dog last night; we have just left the Soda Springs, after regaling ourselves and quite romantic, we then come on a few miles and stopt at Steamboat Spring, a great curiosity, situated near the bank of Bear river, it spouts up about a foot and a half, out of a hole in the solid rock   it is about warm enough to wash in, I put my hankerchief in to wash, and it drew it under, in a moment it came up again, and I took better care of it, Afternoon after traveling 14 miles, we have campt near a spring, to rest a lame man, and a sick man, a lame Ox, and a lame dog, ect, grass plenty   left Bear river this forenoon —

9th   Saturday   We passed the forks of the emigrant road yesterday noon, after leaving the California road, we find the grass much better, as most of the large droves are bound for California; Noon came 10 miles and have campt on Shoshanee creek, in this part of the country the water is all hard   not fit to wash with, got our thermometer broke here —

10th   Sunday evening, Travel 9 miles this forenoon, and came to Port neuf creek, paid 1 dollar for crossing it on a very rough bridge, then we stopt awhile to noon in a small bottom then travel 8 miles up a mountain, and camp near the top close to a very large spring of clear cold water, running from under a snowy mountain, —

11th   Monday morn, We will now descend the mountain, pleasant weather, but the roads dusty, evening we have forded Rosses creek, and one more small creek to day, came 15 miles and camp by a small creek. —

12th   Tuesday Noon, came 12 miles, crossed Rosses creek again this morning, on a bridge, paid 25 cents a wagon and we have just crossed Port neuf river on a ferry boat, paid 2 dollars a wagon, and swam the stock, we are now in sight of the the three Butes, Evening came 10 miles this afternoon, crossed Panack [Bannock] creek, and have campt this side of it, we are now traveling down the bank of Snake river. —

13   Wendsday afternoon, we have just been spending an hour at the American Falls on Snake river, there are several falls on this river, the river is wide, and deep, and very swift in places, we should cross it and keep down on the other side, but there is no ferry boat, and we have no way to cross it, therfore we must keep down on this side, with very little grass, while on the other side there is plenty. travel 22 miles and camp. —

14th   Thursday   It is dusty from morning till night, with now and then a sprinkling of gnats and mosquitoes, and as far as the eye can reach it is nothing but a sandy desert, covered with wild sage brush, dried up with the heat, however it makes good fire wood; evening I have not felt well to day, and the road has been very tedious to me, I have ridden in the wagon and taken care of Chatfield till I got tired, then I got out and walked in the sand, and stinking Sage brush till I gave out, and I feel thankful that we are about to camp after traveling 22 miles; on the bank of Raft river, about dark. river high. —

15th   Friday evening, last night I helpt get supper, and went to bed, to sick to eat any myself, had fever all night, and all day. it is sundown, and the fever has left me, and I am able to creep round and look at things, and brighten up a little, the sun has been very hot to day, remained in camp nearly all day waiting for the river to fall, we forded the river late this afternoon by raising the wagon beds a foot, to prevent the water from running in, we have encamped about half a mile from the same place, the bottom here is full of poison water.

16th   Saturday   evening we came 16 miles over a very rough rocky road, without water, then rested 2 hours, and travel 4 more, and have campt near Swamp creek. —

17th   Sunday, we are traveling through the digger Indians country but have not seen any yet, we crossed Swamp creek this forenoon, and Goose creek this afternoon, goose creek is almost straight down, and then straight up again, several things pitched out of the wagons into the creek, travel over some very rocky ground, here Chat fell out of the wagon, but did not get hurt much. came 26 miles to day, and camp after dark near the bank or Snake river

18th   Monday   traveled 22 miles   crossed one small creek, and here campt on one called Rock creek   it is here the indians are so troublesome, this creek is covered with small timber and thick under brush, a great hiding place, and while in this part of the country the men have to guard the stock all night. one man traveling ahead of us, had all his horses stolen and never found them as we know of. (I was very much frightened while at this camp, and lie awake all night — I expected every minite we would all be killed, however we all found our scalps on in the morning). there is people killed at this place every year.

19th   Tuesday   came 15 miles crossed Rock creek about noon in the midst of all the dust, we had a nice little shower, which laid the dust, and made the traveling much better, campt about 3 oclock, close to a Canon in Rock creek.

20th   Wendsday evening, dry traveling to day, no grass, water very scarce, stopt at noon to water at a very bad place on Snake river, 1½ mile or more a steep bank or precipice, the cattle looked like little dogs down there, and after all the trouble of getting the poor things down there, they were so tired they could not drink and was obliged to travel back, and take the dusty road again, we are still traveling on in search of water, water

21st Thursday morn, very warm, traveled 25 miles yesterday and campt after dark ½ mile from Snake river — Crossed Salmon river about noon to day, and are now traveling down Snake river, till we reach the ferry afternoon came 12 miles, and have campt close to the ferry, our turn will come to cross in the night, have to pay 4 dollars a wagon, cross on a ferry boat, and swim the Stock which is a very hard job, on such a large river, Indians all round our wagons.

22nd Friday, crossed the river before daybreak, and found the smell of carrion so bad, that we left as soon as possible the dead cattle were lying in every direction. still there were a good many getting their breakfast among all the fags, I walked of among the rocks, while the men were getting the cattle ready, then we drove a mile or so, and halted to get breakfast; here Chat had a very narrow escape, from being run over, Just as we were all getting ready to start Chatfield the rascal came round the forward wheel to get into the wagon, and at that moment the cattle started, and he fell under the wagon, somehow he kept from under the wheels, and escaped with only a good, or I should say bad scare, I never was so much frightened in my life, I was in the wagon at the time putting things in order, and supposed Frances was taken care of him. After traveling 6 miles, we have encampt for the day, on the bank of a creek, full of springs, a fine place to wash, and rest the cattle, plenty of good grass. afternoon rained some. —

23rd   Saturday, We took a fresh start this morning with every thing in order, for a good days drive, travel about 5 miles, and here we are, up a stump again, with a worse place than we have every had before us, to be crossed, called Bridge creek. I presume it takes its name from a natural bridge which crosses it, this bridge is only wide enough to admit one person at a time, a frightful place, with the water roarring and tumbling ten or 15 feet below it   this bridge is composed of rocks and all round us, it is only place to cross over and is nothing but a solid mass of rocks, with the water ripping and tearing over them   here we have to unload all the wagons and pack every thing across by hand, and then we are only on an Island there is a worse place to cross yet, a branch of the same, have to stay on the Island all night, and wait our turn to cross, there is a good many campt on the Island, and there are camps on each side of it. there is no chance to pitch a tent, as this Island is a solid rock, so we must sleep the best way we can, with the water roaring on each side of us; The empty wagons, cattle, and horses, have to be taken further up the river and crossed by means of chaines and ropes, the way we cross this branch, is to climb down about six feet on rocks, and then a wagon bed bottom will just reach across, from rocks to rocks, it must then be fastened at each end, with ropes on chains, so that you can cross on it, and then we climb up the rocks on the other side, and in this way every thing has to be taken across   some take their wagons to pieces, and take them over in this way —

24th   Sunday evening, crossed the river this morning, and got loaded up, then traveled 16½ miles without water, then we came to a creek of poisen water in the bottom, did not dare to stay there, came on a mile and a half, to a spring in the bottom and have campt, the Indians are very bad here, have to keep watch all night.

25th   Monday morning. Bad luck this morning to start with, a calf took sick and died before breakfast, soon after starting one of our best cows was taken sick and died in a short time, presume they were both poisened with water or weeds, left our poor cow for the wolves, and started on, Evening it has been very warm to day, traveled 18 miles and have campt right on top of a high round sand hill, a fine mark for the indians, we have also got on to a place, that is full of rattlesnakes. one of our oxen sick.

26th   Tuesday   very warm, and terrible dusty, we raised a long tedious mountain this forenoon, crossed one little creek about noon, all the water we have seen to day, it is near night, and we are still traveling on, and urging our poor tired cattle on till we find water, it looks as if it never rained in this region, it is so dry and dusty, we have been jumping and jolting over rocks all day, and are now about to camp near a creek of clear cold water   traveled 17 miles —

27th of July Wendsday, another fine cow died this afternoon. came 15 miles to day, and have campt at the boiling Springs, a great curiosity, they bubble up out of the earth boiling hot, I have only to pour water on my tea and it is made; there is no cold water in this part, — (This band and myself, wandered far down this branch, as far as we dare, to find it cool enough to bath in, it was still very hot, and I believe I never spent such an unesy, sleepless night, in my life, I felt as if I was in the bad place, I still believe it was not very far off — I was glad when morning came and we left.)

28th   Thursday noon Filled all the empty vessles last night with water, to cool for the stock, have traveled 12 miles to day, and have campt in the prairie, 5 or 6 miles from water, Chat is quite sick with Scarlet fever.

29th   Friday   came 18 miles over some very rocky road and camp by a spring, Chat is some better —

30th   Saturday   Travel 16 miles over a very hilly, but good road, and camp by a stream of water and good grass, it has been very warm to day.

31st   Sunday morning, cool and pleasant, but very dusty, came 12 miles and camp about 1 oclock not far from Boise river, we will stay here a day or two and rest, and recruit our cattle —

August 1st   Monday   Still in camp, have been washing all day, and all hands, have had all the wild currants we could eat, they grow in great abundance along this river, there are three kinds, red, black, and yellow, this evening another of our best milk cows died, cattle are dying off very fast all along this road, we are hardly ever out of sight of dead cattle on this side of Snake river, this cow was well and fat an hour before she died. — Cut the second cheese to day —

2nd   Tuesday noon traveled 12 miles to day, and have just campt on the bank of the Boise river, the boys have all crossed the river, to gather currants, this river is a beautiful clear stream of water running over a stony bottom, I think it the prettiest river I have seen as yet, the timber on it is balm of gilead,[8] made a nice lot of currant pies this aftenoon.

3rd   Wendsday evening, traveled 18 miles, and have campt about one half mile from the river, plenty of good grass.

4th   Thursday evening. We have just crossed Boise or Reids river, it is deep fording, but by raising the wagon beds about a foot, and being very careful we are all landed safe, and about to camp not far from the bank of the river, have

---

[8] This was the black cottonwood, a poplar. Charles R. Ross in *Trees to Know in Oregon* (Corvallis, 1967), p. 61, describes it as a "friend of the pioneers." He says, "To pioneers on the Old Oregon Trail the cottonwood was the most important tree. For nearly 1000 miles of their journey it was the only shade tree to be found." It was called "Balm of Gilead because when the spring buds burst, it emits a refreshing balmy odor. *See* fn. 13, p. 298, Volume V of this series.

traveled 20 miles to day, have also seen a good many Indians and bought fish of them, they all seem peaceable and friendly. —

5th   Friday, We have just bid the beautiful Boise river with her green timber, and rich currants farewell, and are now on our way to the ferry on Snake river; evening traveled 18 miles to day, and have just reached Fort Boise, and campt, our turn will come to cross, sometime tomorrow, there is one small ferry boat running here, owned by the Hudsons Bay Company   have to pay 8 dollars a wagon, our worst trouble at these large rivers, is swiming the stock over, often after swimming nearly half way over, the poor things, will turn and come out again, at this place however, there are indians who swim the river from morning till night   it is fun for them, there is many a drove of cattle that could not be got over without their help, by paying them a small sum, they will take a horse by the bridle or halter, and swim over with him, the rest of the horses all follow, and by driving and hurraing to the cattle they will most always follow the horses, sometimes they fail and turn back; this fort Boise is nothing more than three mud buildings, its inhabitants, the Hudsons bay company a few french men, some half naked indians, half breeds &c

6th   Saturday afternoon, got all safe across the river by noon, and it being 15 miles, and have just reached Malheur river and campt, the roads have been very dusty, no water, nothing but dust, and dead cattle all day, the air filled with the odor from dead cattle,

Augst 8th   Monday morn, we have to make a drive of 22 miles, without water to day, have our cans filled (here we left unknowingly our Lucy behind, not a soul had missed her untill we had gone some miles, when we stopt awhile to rest the cattle; just then another train drove up behind us, with

Lucy she was terribly frightened and so was some more of us, when we found out what a narrow escape she had run. She said she was sitting under the bank of the river, when we started, busy watching some wagons cross and did not know we were ready. I supposed she was in Mr Carls wagon, as he always took charge of Frances and Lucy and I took care of Myra and Chat, when starting he asked for Lucy, and Frances says "shes in Mother's wagon." as she often came in there to have her hair combed. — it was a lesson to all of us.) Evening it is nearly dark and we are still toiling on till we find a camping place the little ones have curled down, and gone to sleep without supper, wind high, and it is cold enough for a great coat and mittens. —

9th Tuesday morning early, came into camp last night at nine oclock, after traveling 19½ miles, with enough water in our cans to make tea for supper, men all tired and hungry, groped round in the dark, and got a supper over, after a fashion, we are now on our way to Birch creek, which is 2½ miles from our camp, Halted at Birch creek and got breakfast, then started on and traveled as far as Burnt river 17 miles and camp...

10th Wendsday, traveled 12 miles, crossed burnt river 5 times, and have campt on the bank of it about 4 oclock in the aftenoon, to repare the wagons some — Evening cold.

11th Thursday, frost this morning, three of our hands got discontented, and left us this morning to pack through, I am pleased as we shall get along just as well without them, and I shall have three less to wait on, — Evening came 10 miles to day, and crossed burnt river 4 times, and have campt near a small spring, about 3 miles from the river.

12 Friday, Came 12 miles to day crossed burnt river twice, lost one of our oxen, we were traveling slowly along,

when he dropt dead in the yoke   unyoked and turned out
the odd ox, and drove round the dead one, and so it is all
along this road   we are continually driving round the dead
cattle, and shame on the man who has no pity for the poor
dumb brutes that have to travel, and toil month after month,
on this desolate road. I could hardly help shedding tears,
when we drove round this poor ox who had helped us along
thus far, and had even given us his very last step. We have
campt on a branch of Burnt river. —

13   Saturday   Travel 5 miles this morning, then stopt to
water at a spring; it is near night   we are still traveling on,
through dust and sand, and over rocks, untill we find water,
had none since this morning.

14th   Sunday morn, Campt last night after dark after
traveling 15 miles in a large bottom, near some puddles of
very poor water   found out this morning that it needed
straining   Afternoon, after traveling 10 miles we have
campt on the bank of Powder river about 1 oclock   another
ox sick, we will rest here untill morning —

15th   Monday. traveled 11 miles, crossed Powder river
three times   (Powder river is a small clear stream) and have
campt on a small creek, about 12 miles from the Grand round
Valley. —

16th   Tuesday, Slow traveling on account of our oxen
having sore feet, and the roads being very rocky, passed the
Silvery springs. traveled 12 miles, and now we have a long
steep rocky hill to descend into the Valley   it is a mile long,
very steep and rocky from the top of this hill, we could see a
band of Indian horses in the Valley below, and being mostly
white, they looked like a flock of chickens, after reaching the
bottom of this hill with a good deal of difficulty, we find our
selves in a most lovely Valley, and have campt close to a

spring, which runs through it, there are also two or three trading posts here, and a great many fine looking Kayuse Indians riding round on their handsome ponies. —

17th   Wendsday evening. crossed the Grand round Valley, which is 8 miles across, and have campt close to the foot of the mountain, good water, and feed plenty, there are 50 or more wagons campt around us, Lucy and Myra have their feet and legs poisoned, which gives me a good deal of trouble. bought some fresh Salmon of the Indians this evening, which is quite a treat to us, it is the first we have seen. —

18th   Thursday Morn   Commenced the ascent of the Blue Mountains   it is a lovely morning, and all hands seem to be delighted with the prospect, of being so near the timber again, after weary months of travel, on the dry dusty sage plains, with nothing to relieve the eye; just now the men are holloing, to hear their echo ring through the woods. — Evening travel 10 miles to day up and down steep hills, and have just campt on the bank of Grand round river, in a dense forest of pine Timber, a most beautiful country;

19th   Friday   quite cold morning, water froze over in the buckets; travel 13 miles, over very bad roads, without water   after looking in vain for water, we were about to give up as it was near night, when husband came across a company of friendly Kayuse Indians about to camp who showed him where to find water, half a mile down a steep mountain, and we have all campt together, with plenty of pine timber all around us. the men and boys have driven the cattle down to water and I am waiting for water to get supper, this fornoon we bought a few potatoes of an Indian, which will be a treat for our supper.

20th   Saturday, Cold all day, came 11 miles, and camp about two oclock, in a pine and fir forest close to a small stream of poor water, grass very scarce, 15 miles more and we will leave the blue mountains.

21st   Sunday morn   Cold, after a great deal of trouble to find all our cattle, we got started about 11 oclock and travel 4 miles then stopt to noon, not far from a spring, then travel 3 or 4 miles and turned out to let the cattle feed an hour   feed very scarce, Evening we are descending a long mountain   it is nearly dark   came 12 miles, and still traveling

22nd   Monday morning, I began to think last night we would never get to the foot of the mountain   it was 4 miles long, however we came into camp after nine oclock at night and find ourselves in the Umahtilah Valley, a warmer climate, more like summer, no feed for the poor stock, we are now traveling on the Nez perces plains, warm weather and very dusty, came 12 miles and camp at a spring ½ mile from the Umahtilah river, grass all dead but the stock eat it greedy   for fuel willows and some little sage brush.

23rd   Tuesday   very warm, grass all dead, the dust is worse than ever to day. I can hardly see the toung [tongue] cattle

24   Wendsday Morn, traveled 20 miles yesterday and came into camp after dark on the bank of the Umahtilah river, numbers were campt around us, no feed for the poor stock; it is quite warm, came 5 miles this morning, and have just stopt at the Indian agency to fill our cans at the well, Evening after filling our cans with water, we came on and stopt to noon, and let the cattle pick dry grass as it is too warm to travel in the middle of the day then come 10 miles, and crossed Butter creek then came a mile up the creek, and have encampt near a good spring, and as there is no feed near the road, the men have driven the stock a mile and a half out to dry bunch grass.

25th   Thursday   We will remain in camp to day, to wash,

and rest the cattle. it is 18 miles to the next water, cotton wood and willows to burn. we will start this evening and travel a few miles after dark it is too hot and dusty to travel in the heat of the day. campt about nine oclock in the dry prairie

26th   Friday afternoon, came 6 miles last night and 12 to day, and have just reached a small spring, where we can only water one ox at a time, by dipping up buckets full, this spring seems to rise out of the ground, and then fall again right off. we will camp here, and drive the cattle a mile to feed, a good many Indians campt around us, bought Salmon of them for supper and breakfast, sage brush to burn,

27th   Saturday, Came 5 miles and stopt at the well spring about noon, and watered the stock, then drove them out to grass, this well spring is not much better than a mud hole. we will remain in camp till evening, our cattle are weak and in order to save them, we travel slowly and rest during the heat of the day. 15 miles to the next water.

28th   Sunday, Started last night about sun down, and drove 5 miles, and found tolerable good grass, to turn the cattle out to. Started very early this morning and drove as far as Willow creek, 10 miles and camp again till evening, plenty of willows to burn, but no running water it is standing in holes along the creek and very poor. it will be 22 miles before we get water again.

29th   Monday, traveled 10 miles last night, and 12 to day and have campt about 1 oclock on Rock creek weather very warm, and dust bad.

30th   Tuesday. travel 7 miles this morning, crossed Rock creek 4 times, and have just crossed John Days river, and encampt on the bank of it about 1 oclock, not far from a trading post, here husband sold an ox that was unable to work for 25 do., we will make the best of this river, as it is 25 miles to the next, Our camp is in a very pretty Valley, or glade, surrounded by hills and our cattle and horses are feeding among the hills, a mile or two distant, and close to us lies the river, a beautiful clear stream, running over a gravelly bottom.

31st Wendsday morn   Still in camp, it was too stormy to start out last evening, as intended, the wind was very high all the afternoon, and the dust a fine sand so bad we could hardly see   thundered, and rained a little in the evening. it rained and blew very hard all night, is still raining this morning, the air cold and chilly. it blew so hard last night as to blow our buckets and pans from under the wagons, and this morning we found them (and other things which were not secured) scattered all over the valley. one or two pans came up missing. every thing is packed up ready for a start, the men folks are out hunting the cattle. The children and myself are shivering round and in the wagons, nothing for fires in these parts, and the weather is very disagreeable. Evening got a late start this morning, traveled about a mile and was obliged to stop, and turn the cattle out on account of rain, at noon it cleared off we eat dinner, and started, came up a long, and awful rocky hollow, in danger every moment of smashing our wagons, after traveling 7 miles, we halted in the prairie long enough to cook supper, split up some of the deck boards of our wagons, to make fire, got supper over, and are on our way again. cloudy and quite cold all day —

Sept 1st   Thursday morn, traveled 8 miles last night, and encampt in the prairie without wood or water — Afternoon after traveling 11 miles and descending on a long hill, we have encampt not far from the Columbia river, made a nice dinner off of fried Salmon, quite a number of Indians are campt around us, for the purpose of selling Salmon to the emigrants —

2   Friday   Came 5 miles this morning, and are now

crossing the Fall (or Deshutes as it is called here) river on a ferry boat, pay 3 dollars a wagon, and swim the stock, this river is very swift and full of rapids. Evening travel 5 miles this afternoon   ascended and descended a long steep hill, crossed Olneys creek and have campt on the hill close to it, cold weather, and no wood, pretty good grass —

3rd   Saturday Morn   cool and pleasant   had a fine shower last night which laid the dust and makes the traveling much better — here husband (being run out of money) sold his sorrel mare (Fan) for 125 dollars, Evening Traveled 17 miles to day   crossed Olneys (or the 15 mile creek) 7 times and have encampt on the bank of it   we are near the timber once more...

4th   Sunday Morning   Clear and bright. had a fine view of Mount Hood, St Hellens and Jefferson this evening traveled 15 miles to day without water, after descending a long, steep, rocky, and very tedious hill we have campt in a Valley on the bank of Indian creek, near some French men who have a trading post, there are also a good many indians encampt around us   no feed for the cattle to night. 15 miles more will take us to the foot of the mountains.

5th   Monday forenoon, passed a sleepless night last night, as a good many of the indians campt around us were drunk and noisy and kept up a continual racket, which made all hands uneasy, and kept our poor dog on the watch all night, I say poor dog because he is nearly worn out with traveling through the day, and should rest all night, but he hates an Indian and will not let one come near the wagons if he can help it, and doubtless they would have done some mischief but for him. ascended a long steep hill this morning which was very hard on the cattle, and also on my self as I thought I never should get to the top although I rested two or three times. after traveling about two miles over some very pretty rolling prairie, we have turned our cattle out to feed awhile, as they had nothing last night — Evening traveled about 12 miles to day and have encampt on a bra[n]ch of Deschutes, and turned our cattle and horses out to tolerable good bunch grass —

6th   Tuesday   Still in camp, washing and overhauling the wagons to make them as light as possible to cross the mountains   Evening after throwing away a good many things and burning up most of the deck boards of our wagons so as to lighten them, got my washing and some cooking done, and started on again   crossed 2 branches, traveled 3 miles, and have campt near the gate, or foot of the Cascades Mountains, (here I was sick all night caused by my washing and working too hard)

Septbr   7th   Wendsday, first day in the mountains   came 16 miles to day, crossed Deshutes or a branch of it 4 times and have encampt on the bank of it, bought flour at 20 cts per pound to feed the stock —

8th   Thursday   Traveled 14 miles over the worst road that was ever made   up and down very steep rough and rocky hills, through mud holes, twisting and winding round stumps, logs, and fallen trees. now we are on the end of a log, now bounce down in a mud hole, now over a big root of a tree, or rock, then bang goes the other side of the wagon and woe to be whatever is inside, (there is very little chance to turn out of this road, on account of the timber and fallen trees, for these mountains are a dense forest of pine, fir, white cedar, or redwood, the handsomest timber in the world must be here in these Cascades Mountains) many of the trees are 300 feet high and so dense as to almost excude the light of heaven and for my own part I dare not look to the top of them for fear of breaking my neck — we have campt on a little stream called Sandy, no feed for the stock except flour and by driving them a mile or so, they can get a little swamp grass, or pick brush —

9th   Friday, Came 8½ miles   crossed Sandy 4 times, came over corduroy roads, through swamps, over rocks and hommochs, and the worst road that could be immagined or thought of, and have encampt about 1 oclock in a little opening near the road, the men have driven the cattle a mile off from the road to try and find grass, and rest them till morning. we hear the road is still worse on ahead; There is a great deal of laurel growing here which will poison the stock if they eat it, (there is no end to the wagons, buggys ox yokes, chains, ect that are lying all along this road   some splendid good wagons just left standing, perhaps with the owners name on them; and many are the poor horses and mules, oxen, cows, &c, that are lying dead in these mountains, afternoon, slight shower —

10th   Saturday   pleasant, Noon we have just halted in a little valley at the foot of Big Laurel hill to rest ourselves and poor weary cattle an hour or so   we dare not rest long in these mountains for fear of a storm, which would be almost certain to kill off all our stock, although the poor things need it bad enough, after what they have gone through with this forenoon,   it would be useless for me with my pencil to describe the awful road we have just passed over (let fancy picture a train of wagons and cattle passing through a crooked chimney, and we have big laurel hill) after decending several bad hills, one called little laurel hill, which I thought as bad as could be but in reality it was nothing to this last one called Big Laurel, it is something more than ½ mile long, very rocky all the way, quite steep, winding, sideling deep down and muddy, made so by a spring running the entire length of the road, and this road is cut down so deep that at times the cattle and wagons are

almost out of sight, with no room for the drivers except on
the bank, a very difficult place to drive also dangerous, and
to make the matter worse, there was a slow poking train ahead
of us, which kept stopping every five minuits, and another
behind us which kept swearing, and hurrying our folks on,
and there they all were, with the poor cattle all on the strain
holding back the heavy wagons on the slippery road. (the
men and boys all had their hands full, and I was oblidged to
take care of myself and the little ones as best I could, there
being no path or road except the one where the teams
traveled, we kept as near the road as we could, winding
round the fallen timber and brush, climbing over logs,
creeping under fallen timber, sometimes lifting and carrying
Chat, at others holding my nose to keep from smelling the
carrion.) I must quit as all hands are getting ready to travel
again — Evening   came 10 miles to day   crossed Sandy
river once and have campt by it about dark   fed the stock
flour, and cut down Alder for them to browse on   nothing
else for them, *poor things*, kept them yoked and tied all night.
(here I was sick all night and not able to get out of the wagon
in the morning.) —

11th   Sunday evening   traveled 12 miles to day, crossed
Sandy (or Zig Zag) river once and have encampt close to a
spring branch, and drive the cattle ½ mile from the road to
feed on swamp grass, the road has been a very little better to
day although we came down some very bad hills, also
through mud holes —

12th   Monday evening   came 12 miles to day, crossed
Sandy once ascended thru very steep hills, passed over the
devils back bone, they call it here — We also passed over
some very pretty country to day, we stoped to noon at a
beautiful spot, it was prairie interspersed with strips of pretty
fir timber, with their branches sweeping the ground, to the

left of us was a deep ravine, with a clear stream of water meandering through it, (this pretty place was along towards the end of the old *fellows* back bone)   passed one new made claim this evening, and have encampt near a small stream of clear water — it is three miles to the first farm —

13th   Tuesday Noon, ascended three very steep muddy hills this morning, drove over some muddy mirey ground, and through mud holes, and have just halted at the first farm to noon, and rest awhile, and buy feed for the stock; paid 1½ dollars per hundred for hay; — price of fresh beef 16 and 18 cts per pound butter ditto 1 dollar, eggs 1 dollar a dozen; onions 4 and 5 dollars per bushel, all too dear for poor folks so we have treated ourselves to some small turnips at the rate of 25 cts per dozen, got rested and are now ready to travel again — Evening traveled 14 miles to day, crossed Deep creek, and have encampt on the bank of it, a very dull looking place, grass very scarse, We may now call ourselves through, they say; and here we are in Oregon making our camp in an ugly bottom, with no home, except our wagons and tent,   it is drizzling and the weather looks dark and gloomy. here old man Fuller[9] left us, and Wilson Carl remains —

14th   Wednesday   still   in   camp,   raining   and   quite disagreeable

15th   Still in camp, and still raining. I was sick all night

16th   Still in camp, rain in the forenoon, and clear in the afternoon — wash some this forenoon —

17th   Saturday morning   in camp yet, still raining — Noon it has cleared off and we are all ready for a start again,

---

[9]Several Fullers traveled overland in 1853. The only one, according to land records, who might be termed an "old man" would have been Joel Fuller, born in 1803. His wife was Rebecca. They had been married on Jan. 1, 1824. They brought with them a family of several children and settled on Claim #3148 in Marion Co. *Genealogical Material, op. cit.,* II (Portland, 1959), p. 34.

for some place we dont know where Evening came 6 miles, and have encampt in a fence corner by a Mr Lamberts[10] about seven miles from Milwaukie, turned our stock out to tolerable good feed —

Oregon T Saturday evening Sept. 17th, *1853*.

---

[10] Joseph H. and Mary Lambert lived near Milwaukie, Oreg., on the west bank of the Willamette, several miles southeast of Portland. He was a noted nurseryman and originated the Lambert Cherry. Howard M. Corning, *Dictionary of Oregon History* (Portland, 1956), p. 140.

Life and Death on the Oregon Trail

⸙ Celinda Hines

INTRODUCTION

> [August] 20th   Saturday... 10 Oclock   Saw a commet very
> plain in the SW...
> [August] 23   Tuesday... The commet shown very brilliantly in
> the evening...

It took the perceptive eye of a bright young woman to see what
few others observed in the August sky in 1853. Celinda Hines was
in what is now southern Idaho.

One other woman mentioned it in her diary: Hannah King
jotted down on August 28th: "Memo, first saw a Splendid
bearded Comet on the 22nd of August — 1853." [See page 217.]

Another 1853 journal writer, William Hoffman, noted on
August 25th, "A comet has appeared in the west for a week past
having a considerably long tail. At times it appears very
brilliant."[1]

There were four observable comets in 1853. This one is
designated by astronomers as "1853 III." It was scientifically
described by Wilhelm Klinkerfues of Gottingen University. In
late August it could be seen by the naked eye with a tail reaching
over twelve degrees in length. It is known as "The great comet of
1853."[2] One wonders why more wagoneers did not observe and
mention this phenomenon.

---

[1] A.S. Taylor and W.M. McKinney, "Squire Hoffman's Comet," *Idaho Yesterdays*,
III, No. 2 (Summer, 1959), pp. 2-4.

[2] Gary W. Kronk, *Comets, A Descriptive Catalogue* (Washington, D.C., 1984), p. 44.
Professor Donald B. Brownlee, Astronomy Department, University of Washington,
Seattle, correspondence.

The Celinda Hines diary was published in the *Transactions* of
the 46th Annual Reunion of the Oregon Pioneer Association in
1918.[3] Since then it has been quoted often in articles and books
about the overland trail. The original handwritten document is in
the Beinecke Rare Book and Manuscript Library of Yale
University. We are grateful for the permission to use it. The
reader will note that there are many gaps of several words at a time
throughout the document. According to George H. Himes,
Secretary of the Oregon Pioneer Association, in a note at the end
of the published diary, it "was almost destroyed by fire many years
ago before it was placed in my custody."[4] The 1918 printed
edition is also at odds when compared with the original
manuscript. We have deferred to the original manuscript and
sought to copy it as accurately as possible.

The Hines overland party was basically a family affair. Three
Hines brothers: Gustavus, Jedediah and Harvey, and their
families, headed for Oregon from New York State in the spring of
1853.

Another brother, Joseph Wilkinson Hines, and his wife,
Elizabeth, went by sea, sailing from New York and crossing the
Isthmus of Panama. They then sailed north to San Francisco
and on to Portland.[5]

The elected leader of the overland party was Gustavus Hines.
His wife was Lydia (Graves) Hines. Accompanying them were
Lucy Ann Lee, the 11-year-old orphaned daughter of the late
Reverend Jason and Lucy Lee, pioneer Methodist missionaries
to the Pacific Northwest.[6]

The youngest brother was Harvey Kimball Hines. His wife
was Elizabeth (Graves) Hines. She and Lydia (Gustavus' wife),
had the same maiden name, but were not sisters.[7]

---

[3] (Portland, 1918), pp. 69-125.

[4] *Ibid.*, p. 125.

[5] Joseph Wilkinson Hines, *Touching Incidents in the Life and Labors of a Pioneer on
the Pacific Coast Since 1853,* (San Jose, California, 1911), *passim.*

[6] "Rev. Gustavus Hines," Howard M. Corning, *Dictionary of Oregon History*
(Portland, 1956), p. 114.

[7] *Ibid.*, "Rev. Harvey K. Hines," pp. 114-15.

The oldest of the brothers was Jedediah (Diah) Hines. He and his wife Eliza were the parents of Celinda, the author of the diary. Celinda describes vividly her father's death (he drowned in the Snake River in present-day southern Idaho).[8] Eliza Hines was now a widow. Four years after her arrival in Oregon, the *Oregon Statesman* of Salem announced her marriage to Fielding Lewis of Linn County, Oregon, on August 18, 1857. The same newspaper reported her death on January 26, 1859, at age 49.[10]

Two young women, Martha & Julia, are often mentioned in Celinda's diary. She went for numerous walks with them. Martha and Julia were sisters of the Hines wives. Martha Graves was the 19-year-old sister of Elizabeth (Mrs. Harvey) Hines. Julia Graves was the 17-year-old sister of Lydia (Mrs. Gustavus) Hines. In Oregon, both women met their future husbands: Martha was married in January 1854 to a well-known carpenter-builder of Portland, Abram Walts.[11] Julia became the wife of an attorney, Chester A. Terry.[12]

Celinda, herself, mentions a "Mr. Shipley" in the last pages of her diary. She met him in Portland at the newly-founded Methodist Academy and Female Seminary.[13] She writes on October 3rd, "Mr. S. is principal of the academy here." She never mentions that the same day was her 27th birthday. Then on October 7th she writes, "Attended singing school in the evening. Mr. Shipley teacher   Pleasant." They were both members for the next months in the choir of the Methodist Church. She was a soprano, and he had sung bass in a traveling singing group in the east called "The Ohioans."[14] Adam Randolph Shipley and

---

[8] See entry for August 26, below, pp. 115.

[9] September 8, 1857, p. 3, col. 6.

[10] *Ibid.*, Feb. 22, 1859, p. 3, col. 1.

[11] "Abram Walts," Obituary, giving facts of life and family, *Pacific Christian Advocate*, Dec. 23, 1886.

[12] The Chester Terrys are listed in the Marion Co., OR, federal censuses for 1860 and 1870.

[13] "Pioneer Seat of Learning: The Portland Academy and Female Seminary," *Oregon Native Son*, II (Nov., 1900), pp. 286-94.

[14] The story of the Methodist choir is told in Joseph Gaston, *Portland, Oregon, Its History and Its Builders* (Chicago, 1911), pp. 408-10.

Celinda Elvira Hines became man and wife on September 30, 1854.[15] He became United States Postmaster of Portland on November 4, 1854.[16] Celinda resigned as teacher at the Portland Academy after her marriage.

Adam Shipley and Calvin S. Kingsley conducted a commercial enterprise, "Adam R. Shipley, and Company," dealing in books and stationery from 1852 to 1862,[17] when the Shipleys sold out and moved to a 1000-acre farm they purchased just south of Oswego (now Lake Oswego) in Clackamas County.[18] Their farm stretched out from the Tualatin River northward for a mile among rough, rolling, timbered hills. The land was not suited to large acreages of grain, but it was fine for growing fruit trees and grapes in particular. They also kept bee hives in quantity.[19]

Adam was a well-known horticulturist. He became the principal authority on grape culture in Oregon. In the 1860's he imported from the eastern states some 45 varieties of American and European grapes. When asked by a friend in the Horticul-

---

[15] *Oregon Statesman*, Oct. 10, 1854, p. 3, col. 1.

[16] Lewis A. McArthur, "Earliest Oregon Postoffices as Recorded at Washington," *Oregon Hist. Qtly.*, XLI (March, 1940), p. 57.

[17] The Adam R. Shipley and Co., papers: correspondence, invoices and legal documents, 1852-63, are in the University of Oregon Library, Ms. 947.

[18] There is a reference to this in a fascinating collection of documents that describe the lives of the Shipley family. This collection is in the Oregon State Supreme Court Records in the State Archives in Salem Case No. 02426. In 1872, German-born neighbor, John Franke, visited them. He was talking to Adam and Celinda in the "library" of their house when he brought up the subject of wanting Adam to help him to write a will. Adam agreed to do so, and, when he had finished writing the first part with a form book, he asked John who would receive the property. John answered that he trusted the Shipleys the most, and all was to go to them. Reluctantly Adam wrote up the will, and Celinda and several others invited signed as witnesses. Upon the death of John Franke on Dec. 10, 1889, the will was probated. Then in 1892, Franke's brother, Adolph Franke from Prussia, appeared and challenged the will, claiming Franke was not mentally sound when the will was made. The case was tried in the "County Court of the State of Oregon for the County of Clackamas," and the will was found valid. It was appealed in the Oregon Supreme Court, which also allowed it to stand. This record has been most useful in dealing with dates and other aspects of the Shipley family's life. Both Celinda and Adam said they moved to the farm in 1862. For the Supreme Court decision see *Oregon Reports*, XXII (San Francisco, 1926), pp. 104-05.

[19] *Ibid.*

ture Society to name the best three varieties for the Willamette Valley he said, "If I were setting out three hundred grapes to-day, I would first set one hundred Concords, then another one hundred Concords, then another one hundred Concords," adding, "that is, to make money."[20] Celinda Shipley supposedly developed a method for preserving grapes in pottery jars: The hot fruit was sealed with sealing wax.[21] Of course, preserves and jelly, as well as raisins, were also produced.

This pioneer couple had eight children, two of whom died at birth. The six who lived were Milton K., b. 1858; Cora E. (Struble), b. 1860; Lester A., b. 1862; Celinda A. (Miller), b. 1865; Alphonso W., b. 1868; and Randolph C., b. 1873.[22]

Adam Randolph Shipley died on July 14, 1893;[23] Celinda Elvira Hines Shipley died on March 10, 1905, age 78.

THE DIARY

5th [May] thursday Very pleasant. All right at the camp. It took almost all day to ferry the teams & cattle across   Some of the cattle swam the river & one cow got mired but at length we were all safely landed in Nebraska at Little St Louis. I purchased a pair of shoes as cheap as I could in NY. We went out a mile & camped for the night plenty of grass   good water. Julia sick   all the others well.

6th friday   A M.   pleasant   P M rainy. Some cattle of Mr. Leonard's[1] & one of our mules gone. We started on &

---

[20] J.R. Cardwell, "First Fruits of the Land: A Brief History of Early Horticulture in Oregon," *Oregon Hist. Qtly.*, VII (March, 1906), pp. 28-51, especially p. 31.

[21] Mary Goodall, *Oregon's Iron Dream, A Story of Old Oswego* (Portland, 1958), pp. 123-24.

[22] *Ibid.*, see also L. and W. Brown, *Genealogical Index to the Clackamas County, Oregon, Probate Records from 1845 to 1910* (Oregon City, 1974), p. 107.

[23] *Ibid.*

[1] Joseph and Mary Leonard settled in Linn Co., Oregon. He was a "shoe-maker, plasterer, farmer." Leah Collins Menefee, Comp., *Immigration Rosters of the Elliott Cut-Off: 1853 & 1854* (Albany, Or., 1984), p. 36

left them   Uncle H & pa remained   Mr. Stateler[2] who by
the way is a missionary at West Port[3] & brother in law of Mr
Leonard — and his wife having come so far with us & Mr S'
horse having gone off with the mule   Mrs S & pa remained
with the wagons   Uncle H. & Mr. S. hunted for the
lost   Mr. S did not return at night & Mrs. S. Uncle H. &
pa stayed all night in the wagon having no supper nor any
covering except the wagon cover although it was very cold &
rainy. We went out on the prairie about six miles ahead &
pitched our tents. Water & no wood

7th saturday   Pleasant, but cold as winter   Uncle H
came   no news as yet. He went back with pa's breakfast and
with the intention should not the mule be found to go back
to the Shawnee mission[4] & purchase another but during his
absence the indian White Crow had bought him back. They
payed him $1.00 & then came to the camp. Mr. L had not
yet found his cattle   A very intelligent Delaware chief came
to the camp. He wore a beautiful wampum belt exceeding
every thing I had ever seen of the kind. He advised us to
take the divide route instead of the government road by Ft
Leavenworth as it is they say a better road. Uncle G captain

8 Sunday   Weather cold. Some Californians camped near
Jonny Cakes[5] house   lost one of men

[2] The Rev. Lerner B. Stateler and his wife, Melinda, were teachers at the Shawnee
Methodist Mission. Louise Barry, *The Beginning of the West* (Topeka, Kansas, 1972),
p. 334.

[3] Westport Landing, Mo., had been established as a fur trading post at the
confluence of the Kansas and Missouri rivers in 1821. It was incorporated as the town of
Kansas in 1850, later to be Kansas City.

[4] Within a few miles west and northwest of Westport were three missions to the
Shawnee Indians. They represented three denominations: Methodist, Baptist, and
Society of Friends (Quakers).

[5] Solomon Johnnycake was an influential Delaware Indian leader, Barry, *op. cit.*, p.
225.

9th Monday   Cold. Started about half past eight. Found the road bad. Collins wagon got almost tipped over   Julia Martha & I rode Charles wagon. M jumped out every bad place. We went about 15 m camped in a beautiful place   Crossed the [unreadable]

10th Tuesday   Pleasant   Found some bad road in the morning   afterwards it was good   Scenery delightful   went about 13 miles. wood & w

11th Wednesday   Pleasant. road good except crossing ravines   scenery delightful

12th Thursday   Rainy   Crossed the Grasshopper in a ferry. The wagons had to be unloaded & let down the bank with ropes it being too steep and high on both sides and the river so deep that we could not ford it. It took all day to cross it. It rained most of the time. We stopped at an indian house. The woman was very good looking. She wore a broad-cloth blanket round her for a skirt [shirt?] a calico sash round her waist & broad cloth pants trimmed with ribands. Her feet were small & she wore what looked to be tin ornaments for dress & steel ones — in her ears which resembled eight or ten small keys

13th Friday   One cow not to be found   Passed over a level prairie   good road most of the way   camped near a ravine   Plenty of wood & water

14th Saturday   Pleasant. Road good with the exception of a number of ravines which we had to cross before noon. We were obliged to stop at one while the men constructed a bridge as we could not cross without. In the P M. we were on a level prairie   road good. Just before night we intersected the southern road which crosses the Kansas at the upper ferry   camped near the junction.

15th Sunday   Very pleasant. The Co. all but Mr. Leonard wishing to camp over Sunday did so but Mr. L left He having a good many cattle & but three men & two wagons   none at least expressed sorrow at his departure In the P M Martha Julia Charles & myself walked out   had a very pleasant time. All were alarmed at our prolonged stay

16th Monday   rained in the P M & hailed the largest I ever saw   Pleasant. Passed the catholic mission of the Pottawatamies⁶   Found there to our surprise quite a pleasant looking village there. Country — rolling prairie consequently many ravines. The worst one bridged. Went about 17 miles (Cross creek)

17th Tuesday   Warm. Crossed the Vermillion bridged — Overtook a Co. of Californians: one lady & maid in the Co. & a drove of cattle. Camped in a delightful place near which was a grave   The bones have been dug up. H. A. Blinn Michigan died [unreadable] 27 1852 — three marks on the board [unreadable] was very rainy

18th Wednesday   Very cold   Country uneven   Crossed the Little Vermillion   See dead cattle every day along the road. Saw two men who were 50 miles behind their Co.   gave them some sea bread. Overtook another Co. of Californians with a drove   Camped near a ravine   Traveled 24 miles

19th Thursday   Very pleasant & warm. Saw Mr. Leonard about a mile & a half ahead [crossed?] Salt creek the banks of which are very high. The oxen were not detached from the wagons but ropes were hitched to the wagons to let them down. All crossed over in safety   Soon after we arrived at

---

⁶ The Catholic Mission of the Pottawatamies was founded in 1848 at the site of present St. Marys, KS. On the grounds were two half-finished log houses. Barry, *op. cit.*, pp. 773-74.

the Middle Fork of the Blue. Aunt Lydia, Julia Lucy Ann
& myself were in Charles wagon as we were going down the
bank   the wagon tipped over   none were much hurt but L
A & myself being behind the others & the things coming
upon us we could not move   I could stir neither hand nor
foot. Julia & Aunt jumped out in the mud & water. L A. & I
remained until the cover was removed & some of the things
taken out   Every one was very much frightened. Some
Californians were near & assisted us. The wagon was injured
a little   The contents of the provision chest were mostly
emptyed into the stream. But on the whole but little damage
was done   The wagon was reloaded & we proceeded
Camped near the Blue   Made the acquaintence of a Mr
Ferguson[7] a Santa Fe trader who had lived ten years in
Mexico & crossed the plains six times. We could not cross
the river for high water   Mr F's Co. were making a raft.

20th Friday   Thirteen head of cattle were missing   7 of
our work oxen   They were found P M. Mr F's raft went
down stream. River continued to rise. We washed in a
ravine. People camped [unreadable] direction waiting for the
water to fall   Impossible to cross unless it did

21st Saturday   Very warm   Concluded to go north to the
ferry about 7 miles   came to a ravine which we could not
cross   went round   came to a crossing   I rode Mr. F's
pony across the water   Charles wagon run against a tree in
consequence of the breaking of a chain. Detained a little but
no damage done   Mr. F's Co with us   I drove loose stock
part of the way   Camped about two miles from the ferry in a
beautiful place   This week our route has been over a rolling
prairie beautiful to behold. We frequently see wolves or
those who guard do & 7 rattle snakes have been seen by the

---

[7] This was probably J.M. Ferguson. Barry, p. 1005. *Op. cit.*

Co since we started   We find Leeach [leek?] lillies & star of
Bethlehem wild here   Wagon run over Mrs Bryant's[8] foot

22nd Sunday   It rained hard in the night   We got up
[unreadable] tent   Morning cold   Martha & Mr Miner[9]
& I took a walk after noon

23rd Monday   Remained in camp because our turn had
not yet come to cross the Blue   Many camps in sight. Mr
Jones Co from Kansas has arrived

24th Tuesday   Struck our tents & went to the ferry. Many
wagons were before us some who were booked before us &
some who were not   I should think there were a hundred
wagons in sight during the day   The river was falling but
yet very high   It was almost impossible to swim cattle but
we had no difficulty with ours   we all crossed in safety &
camped on the other side   We were now in the Pawnee
country

25 Wednesday   Pleasant   Started early & traveled about
24 miles across a rolling prairie   Passed four graves. Mr
Jones Co joined us in the morning   five wagons   Mr
Collins left at noon   Uncle Harvey drove his team. He was
angry at Uncle Gustavus   Camped on [unreadable] prairie
Saw 2 wolves a. m.

26 Thursday   It rained some in the night   Morning

---

[8] Mary, wife of Charles Wesley Bryant. They were from Wyoming Co., N.Y. They
settled near present-day Lake Oswego and had two children, Alta and Lee. The Bryants
lived to celebrate their 60th wedding anniversary. He is reputed to have brought the
first red clover seed to Oregon on his 1853 journey. *Genealogical Material in Oregon
Donation Land Claims*, II (Portland, 1959), claim #3250, p. 39 (Hereafter designated at
Genealogical Material). Leslie Scott, *History of the Oregon Country*, III (Cambridge,
Mass., 1924), p. 342. Wedding anniversary noted in undated clipping in scrap book,
Oregon Hist. Soc.

[9] In a "List of Immigrants to Oregon," printed in the Portland *Oregonian* on Oct. 29,
1853, B. and J. A. Minor are mentioned. The list had been sent to the newspaper by
Thomas K. Williams at the "Utilla [Umatilla] Agency," just east of present Pendleton.

pleasant & warm. Crossed a number of ravines   Passed
them all in safety. Camped after crossing a very bad place
where we saw a wagon which was broken. Two companies in
sight   Saw three graves

27th Friday   Very pleasant & warm   Crossed Otter creek
A M. In the P M. crossed Little Sandy having about noon
crossed the Big Sandy   Saw five graves   See dead cattle
often. Saw some elk hornes   Encamped [unreadable] the
Little Sandy   Heard a pack of wolves barking near
by   Two camps in sight

28th Saturday   Cloudy   Crossed some 15 ravines before
noon when in crossing one one of the hind wheels to Uncles
large wagon broke all of the spokes coming out   No other
damage was done   On examination it was found that the
spokes in all the wheels were loose. We camped to repair
it   Some timber was found not far off which was thought
would answer the purpose

29th Sunday   About ten at night I was awakened by a
violent storm of rain   Water poured in torrents & we were
soon drenching with rain. We succeeded in keeping some of
our clothes & bedding comfortably dry   After about an
hour the rain abated in a measure (although it continued
raining some all night) after which we lie down as best we
could & I slept most of the time till morning which the storm
having ceased   was cold & cloudy   Mr Long[10] who was a
wagon maker went to work at the wheel the others assisting
as much as they could. Mr Jones being a blacksmith set the
tire & before night all was repaired   Many trains passed
during the day   After tea M J & myself went to see a
grave   It was a young lady   The body had been dug up by

---

[10] This was Charles Long, who is usually called simply "Charles" by Celinda. His
name is in no Oregon records that we have seen. Possibly he went on north or south as
was often the case with single men.

wolves   Bones & clothing were scattered around. Prickley pears wild

30th Monday   Pleasant   Arrived at the Blue or rather the Republican Fork   Our route lies up the river 50 miles. The country is level but we have as many ravines as we did where the prairie was more rolling   Saw two antelopes A M.

31st Tuesday   Rainy. Mr. Jones Co & ours came to the conclusion that we could go faster & get along better separate so our Co. that is Mr. Judson, Mr Bryant and their families together with ourselves went on & left them   It stopped raining before noon. At noon Mr Jones Co. came up   The country is rather level   Camped near the river

June 1st Wednesday   We had a stampede in the night but they went only a short distance   It rained in the night   I rode on horse back all the A M.   like it much   Crossed a very bad stream   all got over well   Camped near it Rained very hard during supper

2nd Thursday   Cold   Two young men of Messrs Martin & Miner's acquaintance on their way to California came They had lost six horses worth about 1400 $ We traveled about 25 miles   Country level. Roads good. Camped within sight of the Platte or rather the forest skirting it.

3rd Friday [unreadable] pleasant   Rains some after noon. Passed Ft Kearny about four O'clock   Camped about 2 miles beyond. People are forbidden to camp within three miles of the Ft. No wood & nothing but rain water standing in puddles on the prairie.

4th Saturday   The men went to the Ft. in the morning to shoe the horses & mules. Government has a blacksmith shop there for the accommodation of emigrants but at present there is no smith   Aunt E. M. J. and I went with pa in the [unreadable]   There are four [unreadable] two small ones built of wood   The barracks are made of mud   There is a store where they sell about the same as in Kansas. There are sixty soldiers there   They have no fortifications & it was probably built more for the accommodation of emigrants & to awe the indians than for a defence. The seargeant invited us to his house where we were pleasantly entertained. The captain[11] informed pa that there had passed here 85000 head of cattle & 8000 men who were crossing the plains this year also that most of the emigration [unreadable] Oregon Took up camp after dinner & started up the Platte   Our route lies up the river to South Fork on the south side   Many go on the north   The road is level being between the bluffs & the river.   The Bluffs are very high & picturesque   The river ranks among the first class as to width but is very shallow as indicated by the many islands with which it is filled. The water partakes of the same laxative properties of the Mo. & Miss.

5th Sunday   Road not very [unreadable] water but from the river   Camped about the middle of the P M. I rode on horseback   It rained & was very windy   I saw five snakes

6th Monday   Pleasant   Saw some of the most beautiful Cactus I had ever seen   Camped near the river in a very pretty place

7th Tuesday   Pleasant   Road leads along by the river. Scenery pleasant   Camped not far from the river. No wood

8th Wednesday   It rained in the night and we got very wet   Scenery pretty   Camped near the bluffs   After tea

---

[11] This would have been Capt. Henry W. Wharton, 6th Infantry. He was in command at Ft. Kearny from 1851-57, serving "with distinction." Merrill J. Mattes, *The Great Platte River Road*, Neb. State Hist. Soc. Pubs., XXV (Lincoln, 1969), pp. 207-08, 224.

we went out on to a very high one. Scenery delightful   The
[unreadable] in a chain but each [unreadable] be a mountain
by itself being disconnected from its neighbor while between
& around lie the sweetest little vales imaginable   From the
summit of the one we ascended the river is to be seen for
miles   No scenery I had ever beheld bears any comparison
to it. They seem to be of sand formation with neither rocks or
stones to be seen. On the perpendicular side of one we saw
many names written   Saw a new kind of cactus.

9th Thursday   Pleasant   Road very good. The Bluffs are
now on the other side of the river   We drove to the crossing
of the South Fork   Camped by a very good spring
preparatory to crossing the river   Many were camped
Among the rest [unreadable] We took another [unreadable]

BOOK 2

June 10th 1853   Made preparation to cross the Platt by
fording or rather the South Fork   The river is about a mile
& a quarter wide in low water   it is shallow but now it was
high water   Yet it was thought that we could cross without
raising the wagon beds as was usual in such times   We
drove to the river & as our turn came — for there were many
waiting   They put all the oxen on the wagons   Ten yokes
were attached to one of our wagons   Mr Long and Martha,
Julia & myself rode across   Water came into the box some
but we had no difficulty in getting across. The men waded to
drive the teams   They went back with them & hitched on
to the other wagons. Pa following with the mules   In the
river a chain broke which detention caused the mules to
become so restless as to be almost unmanageable & in the
meantime a team which had been trying to get ahead ran
against the carriage & almost upset it. They however got

through without any very serious difficulty   We drove on about five miles & camped near a good spring. We unpacked the wagon & dry out the things as they needed airing much   Saw the first drive of sheep I had seen   Pa packed our wagon so that our family might sleep in it   We did so & found it very comfortable

11th Saturday   Our road lie along by the river & was very good   At noon we came where there had been two buffalo killed   The head of one was there   it was very *large*. In the P. M. Mr Miner came hurrying to us with news that he had killed one buffalo & wounded another   The women got out of the carriage & took out the things & the men started for some buffalo meat   They did not get up to the camp until nearly dark   Mr Smithers killed a badger & as our camp was in a prairie dog village some one killed a dog   Their bark resembles that of a puppy but they look more rats   Mother & I washed [In margin:] Before noon a fine buffalo came near   I saw him distinctly

12th Sunday   Arrangements were made for us girls to ride in the other wagon so we arranged our seats accordingly Road very good   We had no water for dinner   In the night it rained and hailed

13th Monday   In the A. M. the road lay along by the river   P M. arrived at a good spring   the road soon leaves the bottom & leads upon the bluffs which are here of a rocky formation which seems to be a mixture of sand & lime   In about three miles we came to Ash hollow so called from the ash trees which grow there. We had looked to this place as one where we should have *plenty* of wood & water   Another road comes in here & we saw some companies which we had not before. Every Co but Mr Caulie's which we had seen were now behind us   The glen is very picturesque   rocks

rise almost perpendicular two hundred ft or more   We had
scarcely encamped in a prettier place

14th Tuesday   Warm & pleasant   The men set the tire on
one wagon wheel before starting   The road lies along by the
river   We see many trains on the other side who started
from Council Bluffs   In the afternoon we came into a
hollow & saw many trains just before us   Camped near the
river. after tea Martha Julia, Lucy Anna, Gustavus &
myself went on the bluffs   It was some distance and they
were hard to ascend but the scene which was unfolded to our
view amply repaid us for our fatigue. We saw three antelopes
& two wolves   Castle Bluff was near but we had not time to
visit it & we thought by the looks that we could not ascend
the dome if we were to go there

15th Wednesday   Our route was mostly near the river & in
the A M. the road was very sandy   In the P M. it was
better   We passed a number of trains   Weather very
pleasant   Came in sight of some trees but did not near
them   Camped on the bank of a stream   Had a fine time
washing

16th Thursday   The weather was fair   We soon came in
sight of Courthouse rock   About noon we came near it &
within about 4 miles the nearest point where the road
approaches to it   It is a massive pile of rocks on the level
prairie & not even a stone in miles of it   It is very
appropriately named from its appearance   We soon after
came near a Sioux village. It consisted of 25 Lodges made of
buffalo hides with poles projecting at the top   Many of the
inhabitants came out to see us. Most of the males had no
clothing but a sort of apron. They are the most pleasant
agreeable looking indians I have ever seen. They can not talk
with us. At night we came to Chimney rock which had been
visible to us for 15 miles. It is a pillar of rock & sand 250 ft. in

hight & wholly detached from the neighboring hills. We camped near the river about two miles from the rock. After tea uncles, Mr Long, Julia Martha & I went to see it by moonlight   The sight was awfully sublime   The sides of the base on which the pillar rests are so steep that it was with the utmost difficulty we could climb up it at all. We however succeeded in climbing up some distance. We found it covered with names   We got back to the camp about 10 O'clock

17th Friday Warm. All day the scenery was most enchanting intirely surpassing in loveliness & originality any thing I had ever beheld. Bluffs the most picturesque and resembling to the life some old castle of ancient times. About noon we came to Scotts Bluff which much resembles an old fortification   It takes its name from the circumstance of a Mr. Scott & Co. traders who were robbed by the indians Mr S was wounded. On reaching this place he was unable to travel farther. His companions remained with him until they could stay no longer   They & he Knew that he could survive but a short time. He begged them to leave him & they did so. Afterwards human bones were found there, supposed to be his remains. Went up the valley about 6 miles & camped in a most romantic spot near a spring brook. Martha & I went to find a spring   Mr. Martin & Mr. Long went with us. We went on up the ravine expecting any moment to find the spring   at length we came upon what we supposed to have once been a trading post   There were several log buildings connected together   in them were remnants of wagons & other things which emigrants would want   In one had been a blacksmith shop. The whole was now deserted. Near by was one of the most beautiful springs I have ever seen. The scenery here is most romantical. At length we tore ourselves away from this delightful retreat &

returned to camp. Our people had been much concerned about us. They knew not that *the men* were with us & thought perhaps we were lost.

18th Saturday   Very warm   Drove to Horse creek Over a high valley   Passed some indian villages   Camped near one. Pear cactus very thick & troublesome

19th Sunday   Rained some in the night   P M Saw some indians chasing buffalos. It was said that there were 50 in the herd. They succeeded in killing a number of them   The chase was very interesting to us. [In left margin:] Remained in camp

The indians had nothing but halters on their horses. One was killed a little way across the creek from us   We went to see it   Mr. Martin & Mr Long carried us across   A very small boy insisted in swimming it seemingly an expert as his father   We examined some bows & arrows with which they killed them   The Sioux gave Charles a quarter & offered him another but he took but one. Martha & I took off our shoes and waded back. Many Sioux came to the camp that day for food. I wrote a letter to cousin Licotta Higgins   Mr Martin wrote in my album   Our horses were stampeded but they got them again

20th Monday   Pleasant   Passed some sioux villages & also some trading posts mostly temporary ones   Camped near a gorge. We have had no water but river water & no wood since leaving the cold spring near the old trading post

[June] 21st Tuesday   Warm & pleasant. Went to within two miles of Laramie Fork which we could not ferry as there were 150 wagons ahead of us in waiting. Camped near the river

22nd Wednesday   Cold & windy   Hailed some   Remained in camp all day   Uncles exchanged the mules for a heavy wagon, three yokes of oxen & two cows giving $200 to boot. Uncle G took the new wagon, Harvey the broken one & fixed their beds in them

23 Thursday   Went to the ferry   Uncles sold the carriage & harness. We crossed without difficulty — Made the acquaintance of a Mr. Donaldson of St. Louis going to California. Soon arrived at the Ft. Stopped for noon near it. It is on the north Side of Laramie river & is overlooked on the north by a hill where stands the burying ground   I visited the Ft. & was much surprised at seeing no fortifucations. There are at present 64 soldiers   We made an acquaintance of the quarter-master Mr Flemming[12] a young gent but 9 months from West Point — a native of Erie Pa. He walked to the camp with us making himself very agreeable   I received 3 letters one from Marie Wightman one from R E Prescott & one from R E Robinson. Camped near a pond of water

[June] 24 Friday   Warm   Came to the Black Hills   Laramie Peak has been in sight for a week   Some of the road was very rough, some very good. Landscape wild & romantic   On the bluffs we were by cedar & pine trees. Was advised by a trader to take a cut off thereby shunning the Black Hills & also 20 miles where there was neither wood or water. He represented that by going this new way we should have good water at intervals of 4 or 5 miles also a better road & 30 miles nearer. We took it   At noon a man gave us some ice   We camped near a small clear stream in a bed of larkspur the most beautiful

Saturday   Warm. Country peculiar   Passed Horse creek a beautiful stream before noon. Heard a waterfall near the the crossing   I walked about 5 miles P M   Passed a place

---

[12] This was Lt. Hugh B. Fleming. LeRoy R. Hafen, *Fort Laramie and the Pageant of the West, 1834-1890* (Glendale, Ca., 1938) pp. 210, 233-34.

where the Platte passes through the mountains. Camped
near the river about 2½ miles from the gorge

26 Sunday   Pleasant   Some of our neighbors (Traders)
killed an antelope   Charles went and got some meat. After
dinner We went to see the gorge. The scenery surpasses for
grandeur sublimity & peculiarity any thing we have yet seen
on the road   The river passes through what seems to be a
natural fissure in the earth I should think 700 feet in
height   We went to the top of the bluff. How grand how
magnificant   Several miles of the road with teams & camps.
The river & its various windings with its valley & bluffs on
either side   Laramie Peak in the distance with its snow
capped crest was before us in all the grandeur of which a
landscape can be possessed   We returned to camp & found
we had an addition to our company in a little boy named
Labonte Judson[13]   Mr Leonard had arrived   He had left
his company   they were all right

[June] 27th Monday   Morning pleasant. We went out to
the hills. The wind soon commenced blowing a perfect gale.
Sand blew with such violence as to be painful even to our
hands. We were almost blinded. The country was a barren
waste of sand hills covered with short stunted grass.
Towards night passed the Labonte   Were much refreshed
at the sight of trees & water   Went 4 miles & camped near a
beautiful stream skirted by trees.

28 Tuesday   Pleasant   Not so windy as yesterday. Country barren   Shall be very glad to get through the Black
Hills. Camped at noon by a beautiful stream   Camped at
night in a retired place by a stream   Gustavus came near

---

[13] Phoebe Judson, this baby's mother, told the story of the event in her own
reminiscent book, *A Pioneer's Search for an Ideal Home* (Bellingham, Wash., 1925) pp.
39-42. Her words are quoted in full in an epilogue following this diary.

being lost. He went after a pail of water & lost the camp

29th Wednesday   Pleasant   Came on to the river. Have got through the Black Hills. The road is better now Camped near the river. Uncle H caught a rabbit & a [unreadable]

[June] 30 Thursday   Warm. I rode on horseback A M. Crossed some very bad places. Snow in sight on the bluffs all day. Camped near a ravine. Uncles, Mr Martin & Mr Miner went on to the bluffs & stayed all night   Passed Mud creek [unreadable]   We heard wolves howling in the night nearer & Louder than I had ever before heard.

1st July Friday   Warm   I engraved my name on a rock near our camp. Hunters return unsuccessful. Crossed the North Platte on a bridge paying six dollars a wagon & 1 shilling a head for loose stock. 5 miles very sandy   some of the time we could not see the heads of the oxen   Camped near the Platte

2nd Saturday   Pleasant. Passed the Rocky pass about noon. afterwards passed alkali swamps   Camped near the Willow springs

3rd Sunday   Warm & pleasant. I rode on horse back in the A M. Mr. Miner & Mr Martin for company. P M crossed Wire creek also Greese wood creek. Like wise Bad slue & Alkali region   Camped near Independence rock.

[July] 4th Monday   Very warm   Saw a buffalo chase in the morning   The water in a ravine near by seems to proceed from snow in the mountains as it flows by day and ceases by night   We got up an independence dinner all the company eating together   Very pleasant.

5th Tuesday   Warm & pleasant but for the dust   6 miles

from camp came to Independence rock which is a large oval mass of primitive rock alone on the prairie 6 miles from this is the Devils Gate the place where the Sweet Water river passes through the mountains which are composed of solid primitive rock. The passage is nearly straight through the mountain. The rocks on either side are Between three & 400 ft. in height perpendicular. How the water ever found a passage through this granite is very strange Our road lies up the Sweet Water We camped on the southern bank having crossed it in the morning near Independence rock. Fuel Grease Wood

6th Wednesday Warm Road up the river Very sandy. Country barren Sweet Water mountains lie parallel with the river on the north & near it. On the south they are farther off They are one continued chain of granite rock Camped near the river. Drove the cattle on the other side. Fuel sage The men went over the river on the mountains, made a fire. Alkali all around south of the river

7th Thursday Pleasant Men caught some fish in the morning & we had some for dinner. Crossed the Sweet Water three times in the P M. The first time the crossing was good. but at the next we had to raise the things in the wagon & the next was still worse Mr. Bryant came near upsetting his wagon Camped near the river where we were nearly encompassed by mountains of granite We were on the north side of the river — on the south side the mountains are of a different formation sand I should think

8th Friday Rather cold & windy Camped at noon at Ice Springs. It is said that by digging two or three ft. under ground ice may be found. It rained very hard during our stay there so no one tried it. Before noon we came in full view of the Rocky mountains. Some of the Co. had seen them two days before. We camped at night on the south side of the river having crossed it in the morning. We were in sight of the mountains

9th Saturday   Warm & pleasant   Crossed the river once. The bluffs on either side of the river are of a grand formation & seem to have been thrown up by water   We made but one drive & camped on the north side of the river in a beautiful glen

[July] 10th Sonday   Warm & pleasant. Uncle Gustavus preached at 2 O'clock   After tea all but Mr. & Mrs Judson & Messrs Miner & Nelson[14] went on an adjacent bluff to view the scenery   The valley was at our feet with its river so serpentine that although near yet we could not trace its various windings   Many camps were strewed along its banks   Bluffs the most picturesque reared themselves on every hand while the snow capped Rocky mountains pierced the clouds in the distance

11 Monday   Pleasant   Passed one Co. who had lost two persons a man & a woman who left an infant also lost 88 head of cattle. And another company who by the sinking of a boat lost 3 wagons & all their provisions & some of their clothing & have since broke two wagons one yesterday. Camped at noon at Strawberry creek   Saw strawberries in Bloom   Passed Willow creek in P M.   Camped on the Sweet Water for the last time   after crossing some indians came to the camp. One came riding up to another & pitched upon him seemingly with the intention of doing him harm — pulling his hair & threatening him with an axe above his head   We thought that perhaps it was but a maneuvre to attract our attention so that others might have an opportunity to steal   Mr. Bryant interfering they soon went

[14] *Ibid.*, pp. 6-7. Phoebe Judson tells how her husband, Holden A. Judson, hired a "young Scandinavian" to help drive the team, but neither she nor Celinda Hines ever give anything but his last name, "Nelson."

away. The men guarded the cattle all night so we are among the Black Feet having left the Crows. Wolves howled terribly near camp.

12th Tuesday   Pleasant but windy. Went 10 miles to South Pass then 3 to Pacific Springs near which we camped for dinner   Road good all the way   Soon after dinner a wagon just ahead of our train was upset but no material damage done. The same train have had two men killed by lightning. We drove till late without finding water but at length Came to Dry Sandy where we found some water & camped. Fuel sage Uncle H & Mr Bryant drove the cattle away to feed & remained with them all night. The water is very poor

13th   Warm & pleasant. Road good but sandy soil much of it has been. producing nothing but sage. We have seen no grass of any consequence since we left Ft Laramie on the road passed. Little sandy P M 12 miles from where we started   Camped on the Big Sandy 4 miles further   In the P M saw some mountains in the distance covered with snow

14th Thursday   Warm & pleasant   Were detained in the morning by the cattle crossing the river   Took the road leading down the river although it is some farther; on account of the Green river desert Which by the most direct road is 50 miles across & no water   Down the river it is 17 miles   We went 27 miles & camped on Big Sandy   Charles, Mr. Miner & Nelson went away with the cattle & stayed all night. The Desert is a rolling prairie producing nothing but sage

[July] 15 Friday   Pleasant. Went to Green or Colorado river over the desert   Camped near a slew from the river   no grass for the cattle which have had nothing to eat since morning   Saw a N Y. Co.

16th Saturday   Pleasant   Crossed the river on the ferry paying $6.00 a wagon. They had to drive the cattle some ways up the river to swim them   They were loth to swim & it was necessary to drive them in with a drove to get them across consequently we were detained a good part of the day. But notwithstanding the cattle were very tired & hungry having traveled at least 27 miles the day before   we were under the necessity of driving 10 miles before camping in order to find grass   Camped on Slate creek

[July] 17th Sunday   Went about 4 miles & camped for the day on the creek   Passed the day very pleasantly   Towards night it rained a little but it soon cleared off very pleasantly   Found some very pretty specimens of petrified wood

18th   Monday   Pleasant   Concluded to take into our Co a family with one wagon who had been with us two days   Another Co of two wagons wished admission but our Co declines. In the P M. uncle G went to find a camp   he came back with the report that there was trouble with the indians ahead   The story went thus: Two packers from Oregon to the states were overtaken & followed by 8 indians or people disguised as such who tried to entice them away into a ravine by saying there were emigrants there who wished to see them,   being unsuccessful in their efforts they attempted to drive off one of their pack mules   One of the white men told them that they must desist & stop following them. The indians said they would not & followed them for ten miles   One of the indians drew a pistol which the white man saw & dexterously aiming his rifle shot but not till after the ball which the indian shot grazed his breast — On firing the packer saw the blood spirt from the indians side & the other packer fired but they supposed without doubt that the first shot mortally wounded him   The indians rode off &

the packers came & it was said that 800 or more were in pursuit & people were going on as far as possible to camp for fear of them. We camped near a small stream on a side hill. several camps being near thinking if we were attacked we could all combine & resist it as we supposed the indians would take revenge on the emigrants as we were among the Snakes who are a blood thirsty nation. Soon after our stop these same packers came up & wished shelter & protection for the night   Some were in favor of retaining them & some were not but uncle concluded on the whole as there were a number of women & children & few men in the train it was best not to keep them but had no objections to them remaining at either of the other camps if they were willing to keep them   It seems the story was in the main true except that there were not more than 12 in pursuit   Yet it was expected that the whole nation would soon be in arms   A camp near by kept the packers & all prepared to resist should an attack be made. No women but 20 men in the camp

19th Tuesday   We woke pleasantly surprised to find ourselves so happy & that we had not been molested. Mr. Judson was well acquainted with one of the packers. He went in the same Co when Mr J crossed the plains 2 years ago   He says that the packer is a fine man & would harm no one without provocation   Several of the emigrants saw the affray & justify the packers   They concluded to return with the emigrants at least until they should meet others with whom they could join so as to make it safe to proceed. Indians came around in the morning spying to find where they were & soon after starting others came up   Our road was hilly just before noon   they had to double team to ascend a very steep hill   I went around to get some snow & saw one of the packers. He appeared rather disconsolate but

fearless & very pretty. In the P M. we ascended Quaking
asp hill also passed Poplar grove on the top of the Green
river mountains   The Co in which the 2 men had taken
refuge was near us. The Co. consisted of 21 men well armed
& no ladies

[July] 20th Wednesday   Weather good   Road hilly
Two long hills to go up & 2 very bad ones to descend. I
walked almost all day   Camped near Bear river. Some indians came to camp & peeked into the wagons to see if the
two men were there. a trader came after they went away he
told us that the indians would not tell him what they were
around for but that doubtless they were spies & that their
object was to kill these men if they could find them. He also
said that indians were coming together from different parts
& that they were numerous as two or three tribes had joined
together & they would visit every train as they had
understood they were returning — until they found them &
that any one in the tribe would know them if they should see
them   We knew not whether the trader was sincere or
whether he was trying to get some information. The packers
camped near

21st Thursday   Warm & pleasant   No one molested last
night   Crossed the river on a bridge also three other
streams. Road very hilly but not as bad as yesterday   Near
night we had a long hill to ascend & then to descend. the
descent was so bad in one place that they had to find a road
for themselves   We went a short distance & camped by the
river   We were annoyed very much by mosquetoes which
were the largest I had ever seen. I do not remember where we
have camped before when other camps were not in sight

22nd Friday   Remained in camp till near noon to recruit
the cattle. A company of packers came along & we

ascertained that the two fugitives had joined them & as the
Co is large we think they are out of danger   Uncle &
Charles having a few words   Charles left & went to Mr.
Bryants. Mr. Martin took his place — We went on & it
looking like rain campèd near a slou   it soon rained a
perfect torrent. We had to strain the water before using
it   Grass was excellent. No wood

23 Saturday   Pleasant   Crossed some bad slues from the
river   Part of one road was hilly   Camped at noon near a
fine spring Called I believe White Mound spring   It
commencing to rain we camped near the river in a very
pleasant place

[July] 24 Sunday   Pleasant   Remained in camp all day.
Uncle H preached at 4 oclock. it commenced raining &
rained a few minutes   After tea Charles left to find another
Co for Oregon

25th Monday   Pleasant   Our road was up the basin   we
had a number of slues to cross & at about 11 Oclock we
arrived at the far famed Soda Springs   The first one we
visited was clear & the water equalled the best soda
water   it was very strong   It boiled up out of the
solid rock — as they all do — & in its ebullitiouns resembles
the slakeing of lime   Placing the face near the surface the
vapor has the same effect which the inhaling of hartshorn[15]
produces. Two other springs were near which resembles the
other except for the color of the water which is of another
color. Two hills of soda are near. We camped for noon two
miles ahead near the steam boat springs. We passed one
spring on the bank of the river   Steam-boat spring is so
called from the noise of its ebullitions resembling that of a
steam boat pipe — as some fancy — This one is very clear

---

[15] Ammonium carbonate, an ingredient of smelling salts, was made by chemically
breaking down stag antlers and subsequent distillation. Hence the term "hartshorn."

and boils up about a foot above the surface   it is strong with soda   Near this is another small one the waters of which does not at present run over the surface consequently it is dirty   it is said to resemble steam boat whistle   These springs are near the river. They all come out of a basin of solid rock which where the water flows over is of a copperas color   Many rocks around are of a deep yellow color   In the P. M. we passed the basin spring   Soda water bubbles up into a natural reservoir of stone which is a great curiosity   P M. passed through a volcanic region. There were large holes in the ground & rocks had been thrown up some times for rods in length. small one   Near here the California route leaves the Oregon trail but some of the California emigrants go up to Ft Hall   We went up the bottom & camped near a small stream   we drove till after dark for water

[Written in margin] We camped near a place stones looked as if they had been burned

26 Tuesday   Road yet leads up the basin   Passed a great many slews   Camped near a stream near the termination of the valley. This basin is productive. Have seen very little sage since we have been in it

27th Wednesday   Pleasant   Our road led through a kanyon over the dividing ridge between the waters of Salt lake & those of the Columbia   The road to the summit was through a grove of poplar trees & shrubbery   The trees were small but the grove was the largest we have seen for a long time   The road in the main was good but there were a great many bad places to cross. The descent was better. There were few trees & the grass in some places was a perfect meadow   Large rocks were seen on the sides of the mountains perfectly isolated with grass all around them Mr. Martin came near upsetting uncle G's wagon in crossing a stream   Some of the streams were large & very bad to cross. Springs would gush out of the mountains & large streams would flow from them   we camped on the bottom near a stream   Grass wood & water plenty —

28th Thursday. Left Ft Hall about 19 miles to the north thereby saving 16 miles — it is said that the road is better   We were in sight of the Three Butes all day   They are three mountain peaks rising high above the chain. We almost suffered with dust & want of water   Near night we came to the Port Neuf river which we had to ford   it is large & deep   we had to raise our wagon beds. Ft Hall trading post is near

The commander of the Ft. Mr. McArthur[16] is very agreeable   We camped about a mile on near a fine spring   The men from the post came to see us   Chas. Co were near

29 Friday   Our road was through sage brush   Before noon it lead along the Port Neuf river sometimes over hills & then along the river bottom   Crossed the Bannoc. Went down into the bottom & camped near the river by a spring. The Ohio Co & the Co where Charles is camped with us. The mosquitoes were very annoying. Heard the Falls

[July] 30 Saturday   Pleasant but very dusty. Road lay along by Lewis River a good deal of the way   Before noon we came to the American Falls of Lewis river. The falls are not perpendicular but the water dashes & foams down rocks making a grand sight   After noon we crossed Falls creek so named from the many cascades in it   Some very pretty ones are in sight of the road   We traveled in Co. with Charles

---

[16] Neill McArthur managed Fort Hall for the Hudson's Bay Co. from 1851 to 1854. The fort was abandoned in 1856. Louis S. Grant, "Fort Hall Under the Hudson's Bay Company, 1837-1856," *Ore. Hist. Qtly.* XLI, No. 1 (Mar. 1940), 34-39.

Co. P M.   Towards night we crossed Rock creek   Crossing very bad & rocky. The creek is very rocky   Camped near Lewis river   Some very pretty cedar trees were near Different from any I had ever seen. Grass was very poor —

31st Sunday   Pleasant   Went a few miles & camped not far from the river between some hills   Martha Julia & myself went upon a hill under some trees by ourselves This is the first day since we came in sight of the Rocky mountains that we have not seen snow & I think the first since we came in sight of Laramie Peak.

1st Aug. Monday   Pleasant   Camped at noon at Raft River   Went a mile on the bottom in the morning & then went on to the second bottom trees except on the mountains & no shrubs but sage only on Raft river   After noon went over a desert of sage   Stopped for tea about 5 Oclock went on until dark but found no water. We had water for ordinary purposes but the cattle had had none since noon & it had been very dusty   Found good grass & camped among the sage   not a tree or shrub in sight   Very warm   [Note in margin:] On Raft river the last Californa trail leaves the Oregon road.

2nd Tuesday   Pleasant   By getting some water of Mr Beak[17] got breakfast before starting but could not wash the dishes   Went on through the desert which is 16 miles long   Came to a creek & camped   Remained two or three hours baking — getting dinner &c. Found a wagon there   P M. went on towards night after going I believe about 11 miles came to the river which is here very

---

[17] Although she definitely spells it "Beak" here, on Aug. 10 it appears as "Beal." This was Tavenor Beale, who arrived with his wife, Judith M. (Hutchins) in Oregon on Nov. 1, 1853. Their Donation Land Claim was #1462, in Linn Co. *Genealogical Material*, III (Portland, 1962), p. 104. *See also* Leah C. Menefee, *Immigration Rosters of the Elliott Cut-Off: 1853 & 1854* (Albany, Or., 1984), p. 3.

large   went on a ways & camped off from the river   No
water except from the river & what we had in our
casks   Saw snow

3 Wednesday   Pleasant with a very refreshing breeze   It
would be very pleasant riding but for the dust. Sage part of
the way but in the flat of Goose creek Grass willows &
rushes. Stopped for noon near Goose creek   Camped for
night on the river

[August] 4 Thursday   Road rocky some of the way
Warm & very dusty   Camped for noon on Dry branch for
night on Rocky creek   The banks are rocky & look like a
great chasm or crevice in the earth   Some packers camped
with us   one from Hastings   Mr. Holcomb[18] —

5th Friday   Suffered much with the dust   Camped on
Rocky creek for dinner   Crossed the creek here   crossing
good. Camped on the creek at night. Aunt Lydia was very
sick

Saturday   Very dusty — Camped for noon on Lewis
river   The banks are very steep   Also on the river at
night. A great ways to water & down a very steep bank. Some
rapids near. Wolves howl

Sunday   Pleasant   remained in camp all day   almost
impossible to get water on acount of the banks of the river
being so high & difficult to ascend. The river seems to have
worn away the sand & dirt & to have formed a channel far
below the surface of the ground. There were some very fine
rapids above & below us. Martha Julia & myself went down
to the river to cook   Mr Martin went with us   Indians
were around almost all day. We bought some very [unread-

---

[18] Thomas Holcomb and his wife, Susan, arrived in Oregon in September and settled
on claim #4181 in Polk Co. on April 15, 1854. They were from North Carolina.
Genealogical Material, II (1959), p. 84.

able] of them. They dry [unreadable] very bad but we were obliged to remain to rest the cattle.

8th Monday   Went about five miles to a creek & camped. Good grass about two miles on the bluff. Good water handy to get at. Julia Martha & I went to the creek to wash There was a warm spring about half a mile up the ravine   Mister Long came to see us   A family camped near us — one wagon. some fine rapids were near in the river

[unreadable] Tuesday   Remained in camp [unreadable] the men put [unreadable] the wagon wheel of uncle Harveys wagon which was broken before Pa found a cow. One of Mr Bryants oxen died   They did not know he was sick   We went about 7 miles & camped on the river. Some part of the road was dangerous   Saw some very fine falls from streams on the north side of the river   the first was a perpendicular fall of many feet in height   most of the others issued out of the banks of the river & falling several ft. flowed [into?] the river. There were [unreadable] of them   all [unreadable] interesting [unreadable]   Saw some large lizards.

10th Wednesday   Went to the ferry a short distance. This family that were with us Mr. Russel lost an ox in the morning   Mr. Beal left our company. Mr Russel had 3 yokes of oxen & one span of horses   Their Ladies have walked nearly all of the way. Saw at the ferry a horse which had been bitten by scorpions dying. A short distance below the ferry is Salmon Falls   They are perpendicular [unreadable] but not very high [unreadable] very scraggy [unreadable] very pretty and interesting. Crossed the ferry paying $6.00 per wagon   They paid $10.00 to some men for swimming the cattle over on account of the difficulty of doing so for the swiftness of the current and the width of the river & also the weakness of the cattle   Went about 4 miles

& camped in a valley by a small stream   very beautiful sage wood & water   [in margin:] Bad & rocky road

[August] 11th Thursday   Pleasant. Remained in camp until after noon [unreadable] very well. Alta[19] very sick. I stayed with them last night. Julia & I washed for Mrs. B[ryant] & Martha baked for her. Went about 6 miles road hilly   went down a very fast hill then up one. Camped on Rock creek   Did not get into camp till after dark. Road — through sage brush.

12th Friday   Crossed the two Rocky creeks   The ladies went below where a natural bridge crosses the south creek. The banks of the stream are perpendicular [unreadable] I should think   water comes down in a waterfall just above the bridge and then foams & dashes over under & between huge rocks making a grand sight. The water is nearly 20 ft. deep   I should judge   Just below the bridge the other stream comes in. We went a short distance & crossed by the assistance of Mr. Long who was with us. Traveled about 15 miles & camped near a small stream   Grass excellent   I sat up with aunt Elizabeth to cook & slept with [unreadable]

13th Saturday   Warm & dusty [unreadable] stream Good grass & water Willows for fuel. Mountain wheat higher than my head   Captain Brant[20] [Grant] & co. from Ft. Vancouver called & made us a visit. Captain took tea with us. He had been to Ft Hall to dispose of some government property — Also to Salt Lake   He brought us a few potatoes

    [19] This was the child of Charles and Mary Bryant. *See* fn. 8.

    [20] The best portrayal of the life of this colorful Hudson's Bay Co. trader is in Merle Wells' *The Mountain Men and the Fur Trade* (Glendale, Ca., 1972), Vol. IX, pp. 165-86. Richard Grant had just retired from a life of service to the "Great Company." He had been in charge of Ft. Hall for ten years and was planning to set up as an independent trader at Ft. Loring, a former army post not far from Ft. Hall.

14th Sunday   Warm & pleasant   Remained in camp. In
the P M. one wagon came & camped near [unreadable] of
the ladies was [unreadable] Miss Harrison [unreadable]
many seasons in Oswego & its society. Towards eve a Mr.
Rowley[21] & a Mr. Cook from a Ohio train came & made us a
visit   Mr. C. has formerly lived in Adams. Gustavus sick

[August] 15 Monday   Warm & dusty   I rode on horse
back in the AM. for Gustavus who was not much better than
yesterday. Several trains traveled near us   in one was a lady
who was recently married. her husband had near Pacific
springs I hear set her out of the [unreadable] giving her her
[unreadable]   Another Co took her in & like her very
much   The husband says she was ugly to his children she
being his second wife. Went through sage 8 miles   Stopped
for noon in a bad place on a high hill. Had to go down a steep
long hill for water. Went about 4 miles & camped in a
valley   Grass good. also water. Charly came to see us. They
have lost 4 yokes of oxen in 3 days. Mr. Bryants
[unreadable] sick yet   Two of our [unreadable] rattle
snakes in the vicinity   [In margin:] Nelson found [unread-
able] scorpions by his

[August 16, Tuesday] Pleasant. Before noon went up some
very long hills   Numerous hills were in sight which were
very precipitous & flat on the top   The top strata seemed to
be of rock which looked as if it was laid up by the hand of
man on the sides & on the top & with equal thickness. The
hills were very high & seemed as if formed of [unreadable]
Our road was the [unreadable] Camped for night [unread-
able] 6 miles before [unreadable]   Saw some trees which
were a welcome sight to us. They were the black thorn

---

[21] Henry and Rosetta P. Rowley from Ohio arrived in Oregon in October and settled
on claim #1557 in Clackamas Co. on Jan. 10, 1855. *Genealogical Material*, I (1957), p.
63.

berries sweet   where the heat was almost intolerable   several camps were very near. Went about 4 miles   Gustavus was sick. I rode for him   the horse stumbled & threw me off. Camped in the vicinity of numerous pools which I should think proceeded from a stream underground Sprinkkled some in the PM.

17th Wednesday   Some part of the day was [unreadable] & very pleasant. It [unreadable] some. From all [unreadable] could get we supposed   we had two 15 mile drives before us & we were much surprised at noon on coming to a fine stream   Camped late near a sulphur spring. Other springs were near. It rained in the evening.

[August] 18th Thursday   In about 4 miles we came to some hot springs. The water was boiling hot. It was with difficulty we succeeded in washing our hands   There were [unreadable] and streams flowed from them. They were to us a great curiosity. Camped for dinner near a fine stream. A violent shower of rain came on to gladden our hearts. Camped for night near Barrel spring   Valley beautiful. Very high bluffs were on either side   The stream delightful   Black thorn trees a little up the gorge   Grass good. Valley covered with mountain wheat   Have seen [unreadable] or train for two [unreadable] some Road [unreadable]

19th Friday   Road hilly   stony in the morning but good the rest of the day. The hills were very peculiar   Huge rocks being on the top of the ground each one seemingly disdaining the acquaintance of his neighbor. Some were I should think nearly 50 ft. in height. The hills all day were of this character   Camped for noon [unreadable] no water. [unreadable] covered with snow on the south west. Passed through less sage & more grass   camped for night near a number of springs   Some were impregnated with iron

Grass up the kenyon eleven ft. in highth. Mountain wheat hear very high

20th Saturday   The road for almost two miles was through kenyon [unreadable] willow & rose bushes   Very pleasant. Passed two fine streams before noon   Road hilly   Hills covered with grass. Much prefer a hilly road as it is not so monotonous. We are anxiously looking forward to see where the road goes & what we are coming to next. Camped for noon near some springs   A Co. came & camped near Glad to have company again. Went [unreadable] Boise river [unreadable] did not [unreadable] went about 15 miles   10 Oclock Saw a commet very plain in the SW   Found a scorpion near our fire

21st Sunday   Pleasant   Started on before breakfast as we had no water. Crossed over three bottoms before reaching the river   The first is covered with sage. The second with sage. The second with woods   The 3 with grass. The river is skirted most of the way with Balm of Gilead Poplar & [unreadable] trees & bushes of [unreadable] We were truly refreshed by the sight of a grove of trees again. Went about 6 miles before reaching the river. On camping we moved our cooking utensils, victuals &c to an adjacent grove where were plenty of wood & water & withal a delightful shade which none know better how to appreciate than those who have traveled in dust & sage   their eyes [unreadable] by the sight of a tree for weeks [unreadable] if they chance to see one it is on some adjacent mountain   O we enjoyed this beautiful retreat. Taking grass, wood, water & every thing into consideration   I think we have never had a more pleasant camp. From the invitation of a gentleman uncles went to a neighboring camp to hold meeting in the evening   We went with them [unreadable] 60 persons were [unreadable] Had a very pleasant [unreadable]

[August] 22 Monday   Went about 10 miles down the river
before dinner road good but dusty — P M went about 6
more   Met Mr Marsh from Michigan, brother in law of L
F Devendorf. He & another gentleman Mr Walter have a
cart & one span of horses. Camped by the river in a beautiful
place   grass excellent [In margin:] Road through grass

23 Tuesday   Pleasant. Mr. Marsh came to see us in the
[unreadable] bad hill to ascend in the morning   Road went
along on the bluffs until noon then struck down on to the
river thence on the bluff & down to the river at night. On the
bluffs were some sage & some weeds & some grass. Our camp
at night was the best we have had on the road. Grass grew
luxuriously all about. We were close to the river as pretty a
stream [unreadable] ever saw with a [unreadable] as clear as
crystal. Mr Marsh came & took tea with us & Mr Walter
also. The commet shown very brilliantly in the evening [In
margin:] indians came to the camp at noon   we bought
some fish of them

24 Wednesday   Pleasant but uncomfortably warm as it has
been since we have been on the Boissee. In the morning a
great many indians came to camp with fish which they
wished to exchange for clothing. We bought a number. The
Salmon [unreadable] here are [unreadable] indians (the
Diggers) cannot understand the Eng. language. They
understand & use the words swap & no swap, which words
they make use of in trading. We occasionally meet one with
whom Uncle G & his family can converse in the Chinook
dialect & jargon used by the indians of western Oregon
These indians are dressed in any old clothing they can
[unreadable] the emigrants   Some [unreadable] others are
fully clad. They seem most anxious to get shirts & socks.
They seem to be better clad than the Sioux but from the fact
of not having seen many with clothing of their own

manufacture which is a shirt — I should think that aside from what they get of emigrants they wear at least no more than that nation. [unreadable] similar to yesterday [unreadable] AM. Camped [unreadable] Went about 9 miles before dinner   Crossed the river after dinner & went down about 6 miles & camped on the north bank (north west) in a very pretty place. It seems so delightful to be among grass & near trees & bushes. Had a fine bath in the river

[August] 25th Thursday   Warm as usual. Much inconvenience from dust   Went about 8 miles before [unreadable] Camped on the river [unreadable] more after dinner and camped on the river. Had a very fine camp. This is the most beautiful river I have seen. In all the distance we have come down it there has not been a single tributary to it

26th Friday   Pleasant. Went about a mile & a half to the ferry. Crossed the wagons in safety But in swimming the cattle we soon found our troubles had but now commenced [unreadable] with much [unreadable] swim at all but at length they were all safely over. Pa who rode a horse, as he had not done before & assisted in driving them By some cause or other he went too far down the river   his horse rared with him & saying 'I must take care of myself' got off   He endeavored to get hold of the horse — as he let go of the bridle — but being on the lower side the currant took him down & the horse swam out of his reach. He [unreadable] to an island but finding [unreadable] strong turned to the [unreadable] dont be scared I am [unreadable] He soon sank [unreadable] in heart   Most of the men were near but none of them dared go in   the danger was too great   Uncle G swam in & got out pa's hat. They had previously hallowed for assistance & some indians went with a canoe but to no purpose   The men came & informed us of

the distressing calamity of which we had heard nothing   I
will not attempt to describe our distress & sorrow for our
great Bereavement[22]   But I know that our loss is his gain
that he is yet [unreadable] & he loves [unreadable] watch
over me & continue to guide me   An indian chief being
with us with whom uncle G could talk in the Chinook dialect
— took several of his men who were expert swimmers &
divers & made every exertion to get the body but were
unsuccessful. With hearts overflowing with sorrow we were
under the necessity of pursuing our journey immediately as
there was no grass for the cattle where we were. Messrs
Marsh & Walter being with [unreadable] services were
engaged [unreadable] Marsh drove our team & went about a
mile   camped on a river   It seems that Pa had a present-
ment that something was to happen as he had often spoken
of his dread of crossing at this crossing   Wolves howled

[August] 27th Saturday   Took water with us & went about
15 miles to Malheur river & camped. road pretty good
mostly through sage   Our camp was in a very pretty place
but all was sadness to me

28th Sunday   Very pleasant   Remained in camp   The
men [unreadable] nearly all [unreadable] The new road
[unreadable] the Willamette valley above Oregon city saving
150 miles distance leaves the old trail near this place. But
from all we can learn it is not at present a feasible route
except for packers because no wagons have been through. A
trading post is near kept by a Mr Turner. He went to
Oregon two years ago in the same co with Mr Judson. They
wintered at Salt Lake. The mormons got something against
him & he was obliged to hide himself [unreadable] Mr
Judson [unreadable] when no one [unreadable] two of his

---

[22] Another version of this tragedy in the Hines family is in Judson, *A Pioneer's Search
for an Ideal Home, op. cit.*, pp. 58-63. This is quoted in full in our epilogue to the Hines
diary.

associates betrayed him   He was taken back to the city &
tried & was acquitted

29th Monday   Pleasant   Went about 2 miles & crossed
the Malheur river   Took water & went on   Camped for
noon under a bluff. Went on until after dark   some time no
water   after crossing the river in the morning made 25
miles   Road rather hilly   Camped by a small stream

30 Tuesday   Warm & dusty   Went over hills to Burnt
river [unreadable] & in trying to extinguish the flames uncle
G Aunt L & Julia burnt their hands quite bad   Crossed the
river twice after noon   After the first crossing the road led
through under a canopy of bushes which would have been
delightful had we not been looking out for dangerous places
all the time. Went till after dark again   Camped near the
river. It was dark & rainy. Lightning played around the
mountain tops which rose several hundred feet on all sides of
us.

[August] 31 Wednesday   It was cloudy & cool which was
very fortunate on account of hilly bad roads   Stopped for
noon on the river   Crossed the river (Burnt) nine times
Our road was the most intricate of any day since we
started   Sometimes crossing the river & then recrossing
immediately thence through a beautiful grove of poplars &
Balm of Gileads then perhaps over a steep high hill & then to
the river & then through a thicket of bushes Sumach
[unreadable] cherry so dense that [unreadable] through them
[unreadable]   In the PM. towards night we left that branch
of Burnt river which we had been travelling up nearly all the
afternoon & crossed over a very high steep hill & camped on
a small stream. Have heard birds sing occasionally since we
came to the Boise river

1st Sept. Thursday   No so warm as it has been   very

pleasant. Road better than yesterday but hilly   before noon
came on to a flat through which runs Burnt river   Camped
on the river at noon   Went up the valley. Road good
Camped at night in the valley [unreadable] Made about 15
miles [unreadable] crossing of Snake river we [unreadable]
cattle   Many are [unreadable] while some are stopped

2nd Friday   Pleasant with a cool breeze from the mountains. Went up the valley a short distance which had here
become quite narrow   Then taking water struck over the
hills the first of which was long & steep to the valley of
Powder river. When on the hills we first beheld the Blue
mountains proper, Although we had been traveling amid
spurs of them for several days. These mountains are mostly
covered with timber & appeared as we [unreadable] them
even more grand [unreadable] than the Rocky [unreadable]
Camped by a little river among the hills for dinner.
Ascended soon more hills first saw the mountains & after
descending some long ones came on to the valley of Powder
river. There we found sage again   Camped in the valley
where there was some grass but no water. [In margin:] Went
20 miles

3rd Saturday   It rained considerable in the night but it
having ceased we started on before breakfast for water
Mountains looked magnificant   Soon were nearly enveloped in dense clouds while around others smaller clouds
hovered in all a delightful placidity [unreadable] delightful
scenery & but for the casualty which one week ago deprived
me of my only earthly parent, how well might I have enjoyed
it   Went 5 miles to a slue where we breakfasted. We then
went to the river 8 miles & camped for the night. A family
with one wagon came & camped near   The man crossed the
plains 2 years since & getting out of provisions at the first
crossing of Snake river went all the remainder of the way

with nothing but fish & such game as they could [unreadable]
In the evening some indians came of [unreadable] some peas
& potatoes paying $1.00 for 4 qts of peas & the same for one
mess of potatoes. Afterwards two others came of whom we
purchased salmon   These Kayuse indians seem rather
intelligent and often well dressed

[September] 4th   Sunday   Pleasant. Went 10 miles to
water & camped for the day   Road good with some hills.
Mr Gray the gentleman from Oregon[23] whom I first saw at
St Louis came up & camped with us. He had a drove of
sheep. He had a baggage [unreadable] teams & a light wagon
drawn by horses [unreadable] oxen he was obliged to leave
his heavy wagon. He then bought horses & is packing
through & takes his carriage for the ladies. His sheep are
some ways behind.

5th Monday   Pleasant. Went about 7 miles to Grande
Ronde   This is a fertile valley 8 miles across & 20 miles
long entirely encompassed by mountains & watered by
Grande Ronde river   The road comes in from the south &
goes out at the west   Camped for [unreadable] a valley &
near the trading post. We were thronged with indians nearly
all on ponies. It reminded me very forcibly of an old
fashioned general training   They had plenty of money
$50.00 gold pieces which they probably got by selling horses
to emigrants   After dinner we went 8 miles to the other side
of the valley   Camped near a pretty mountain stream.

---

[23] William H. Gray was an old-timer in Pacific Northwest history. He had already
made two overland journeys and returned east. The 1853 journey with the large flock of
sheep here mentiond is best approached through Rebecca Ketchum's journal: "From
Ithaca to Clatsop Plains," *Oregon Hist. Qtly.*, LXII, No. 3 (Sept. 1961), pp. 237-87;
also LXII, No. 4 (Dec. 1961), pp. 337-402. She was an articulate member of the Gray
company. The editors of her journal were L. M. Kaiser and Priscilla Knuth. Gray
planned to take the sheep to Astoria at the mouth of the Columbia, but the vessel
in which he was transporting them capsized, and he lost the entire flock in the Columbia
River.

Indian lodges near. Thronged with indians during our stay.
Some belong to the Kayuses some to the Nez Perces. At our
noon camp [unreadable] perce chief with whom [unreadable]
some acquaintance   He seemed very pleasant & spoke
Eng. with such a pleasing awquardness as to amuse us very
much   Others were there who had seen uncle. Before noon
we met many mostly women on ponies who said they were
travelling to the Shoshone country. They had peas with
them for food which they would swap for flour or bread. One
proposed to swap her baby for, a shirt. These indians here
seem more intelligent & happy than any we have seen

6th Tuesday   Pleasant. Remained in camp till noon   The
men [unreadable] wagon boxes [unreadable] wagon & ours &
lightened loads as much as possible   Uncles bought each of
them a horse with their saddles   One woman wished me to
swap a gold ring for an old brass thimble   We went on after
noon   The road was very hilly. The hills covered with
timber Firs Pines & a little spruce. The trees are some
distance apart   The ground covered with a little grass &
rose bushes &c. Went 8 miles & camped in a ravine. Very
lonesome   Mr Miner left on foot

[September 7] Wednesday [unreadable] Cool breeze every
after noon [unreadable] very delightful with the exception of
being hilly   The road was smooth & nice   The forest
beautiful. The ground is covered with grass. The trees are far
apart Often large places entirely devoid of them. Frequently
small patch of little trees nearly of a size looking very
beautiful. Our night camp was on an open space covered
with little stones & some grass. There was no water but we
had come prepared for our noon camp which [unreadable]
[in margin:] we being alone sounded very lonesome

8 Sept. Thursday   Pleasant   Went twelve miles without

water. Road bad. Very hilly & in some places stony. Forest more interesting   Sometimes the road was very bad winding around trees &c. Camped at night at Lee's Encampment. Ritchie's train near.[24] Mr. Bailey one of the men who was with Mr. Leonard came on   says Mr. L is going through on foot as are many others   We have lost 4 oxen in all up to this time

9th Friday   Pleasant. Some part of the way the road was good but hilly but much better than yesterday. Went 17 miles without water Had no dinner. Before night we came out of timber & were on hills covered with bunch grass   Came on to the Umatilla valley & camped on a branch of that river   Several trains were near also a trading post

10th Saturday   Pleasant   went 5 miles to the river then about 2 miles on where we dined   Went down 8 miles & The road was not on the river but the country is a rolling prairie. Camped on the river at night   Timber a spicies of poplar   Dr Hills train near

11th Sunday   Crossed the river   on starting Uncle H's wagon upset   no one hurt   Nothing injured except some things [unreadable]   Left the river in about 1½ miles and went on to the prairie again   carried water with us   Dined on the prarie about 4½ miles from the river. Went 9 miles on the river again   road good

[September] 12th Monday   Went about 5 miles. crossed

---

[24] The Ritchie clan was special. In charge of the wagons was Matthew D. Ritchie, age 25. He and his wife, Mary, had been living in Iowa and were now headed west with children: Adam, age 3, and Sarah, a baby. But the key family figure was Elizabeth Ritchie, Matthew's mother. According to the land records, her husband had died in February, 1848, in Iowa. "He had several wagons and teams and plans for going to Oregon and she came as soon after that as she could." Another son, James, 25-year-old, accompanied her. *Genealogical Material,* I (1957), claims #508, #1483, and II (1959), #2626. The mother and James settled in Linn Co; Matthew and family in Lane Co.

the river. then struck over to a creek ten miles   Road good.
Camped for noon 6 miles from starting. Saw at the river a
house — The Ind. agency[25] — the first building which
looked like civilization since Laramie   Country rolling

13th Tuesday   Went 18 miles over a rolling country
without water except what we carried for culinary purposes
— Road good   Scenery pretty   Camped for night by a
spring. I have drank more unhealthy water never muddier
[unreadable] camps near. Wind blew very hard all the PM.
Dust very oppressive   Sand blew into the tent during
supper so as to cover the dishes. Rained at night

14th Wednesday   Road very much as yesterday   if any
thing more hilly   Not so windy as yesterday   No water.
Made 18 miles   Camped on a creek. A trading post was
near kept by a gentleman from Oswego County. 18 graves
near   Several camps around. Have passed trading posts
nearly every day since we left Grand Ronde

15th Thursday   Several horses & cattle were missing & we
remained in camp till after dinner when all were found.
Went about 10 miles. Very hilly. Road good. Cold & windy.
Scenery pretty when on the hills. Made a [unreadable]

[September] 16th   Friday   Went about a mile & over hills
& then came into a valley   went up it 9 miles to a spring
then struck over the hills to John Days river   The descent
to the river is steep & rocky in some places but smooth most
of the way   Dined by the river then crossed & ascended a
very bad hill. Very long & rocky much more so than any we
had passed before   The river is about 3 [unreadable] from
the spring. Went two miles from the river & made a dry

[25] The Portland *Oregonian* listed in its Oct. 20, 1853, issue, Thomas K. Williams as
agent at the "Utilla [Umatilla] agency." This was a former Methodist mission a few
miles east of present Pendleton at the western border of today's Umatilla Indian
Reservation. *See* also Edward Hill, *The Office of Indian Affairs, 1824-1880, Historical
Sketches* (New York, N. Y., 1974), pp. 125 & 128.

camp. After ascending the hill we came to two roads one leading to the upper & the other to the lower ferry of the DeShoots river   We took the lower road because the river is sometimes fordable at the lower ferry

17th Saturday   Rather cold. Road hilly but good. Went 15 miles without water   Camped near [unreadable] of very impure water   A trading post near by   flour 25 a pound First came in sight of Mount Rainir

18 Sunday   Pleasant   Went 5 miles to the Columbia down it about 2 then we forded the DeShoots near its mouth. It is a large river & very rapid. Before crossing we very unexpectedly met Uncle Joseph Hines who was sent out as a missionary after we left N Y.[26] he left N Y May 20th with his family who are now near Portland all well. He ascertained from Mr Grey who had arrived at P our whereabouts & came out to meet us. We were almost overjoyed at so unexpected a meeting   Uncle J piloted us across the river (an indian had just done the same for him) The current was so strong that it was almost impossible to guide the oxen & prevent them from going down stream   We came very near upsetting in the river in very deep water & the current was so strong   We went out 4 miles & camped near a stream Our road was very hilly   Mr Marsh left us this morning but is still in the train

19th Monday   Pleasant   Went about 7 miles over hills &

[26] This was a fourth Hines brother, another Methodist minister, who, with his wife, Elizabeth, had come to Oregon by ship in 1853. On June 20 they had sailed on the steamer, *Illinois*, from New York to the Isthmus of Panama. On the Pacific shore they boarded the *Golden Gate* which took them to San Francisco. From there they sailed on the *Columbia* to "the prospective metropolis" of Portland, where they arrived in late July. He went on up the Columbia to The Dalles and on by horseback to the Deschutes River, where he met his brothers and their families. Later the Joseph Hines family moved to San Jose, California, where they lived out their lives. Joseph W. Hines, *Touching Incidents in the Life and Labors of a Pioneer on the Pacific Coast Since 1853* (San Jose, 1911), *passim*.

then down the river 3 to the Dalls. It had been our intention
to cross the cascades but uncle J advised us to go by the Dalls
[unreadable] our wagons & go ourselves down the river and
send the cattle & horses down the pack trail which goes
along near the river. In the eve. we went to a store & found
a Mr Newell with whom Uncle G was acquainted in
Oregon.[27] Dr N was the first man who crossed the plains
with wagons. He said he often wished his wagons would
break so that he might have an excuse for leaving them but
they did not & he came with them. a thing which we have
often spoken of as being impossible. The Dr treated us very
kindly & gave us some apples

[September] 20th Tuesday   Very warm. The men had
engaged a barge to take us to the Cascades & we put our
things on board & went on our selves but it began to leak &
we were obliged to get off also to remove our baggage   Dr
Newell told us if we would leave the baggage until the next
day & go down on the steam boat he would be responsible for
there safe arrival in a day or two. Marsh & Walter with them
[unreadable] Martin Judson   [in margin: Uncle Joseph
went with the cattle]   Accordingly we took what provision
& clothing was necessary & repaired on board the steam boat
Allan[28] which was already crowded with passengers   It is a
poor apology for a boat very small having no cabin & we were
obliged to seat ourselves as best we could on the floor or
whatever we could find to sit upon. This is the only steam

---

[27] This was the famous trapper, Robert Newell. He was called "Doc" not because he
was a real doctor, but because he had a knack for helping those with health problems in
the wilderness, especially in the use of natural herbs. LeRoy R. Hafen, "Robert
Newell," *The Mountain Men and the Fur Trade*, VIII (Glendale, Ca., 1971), pp. 251-
76.

[28] This was a small propeller type steamer brought up the lower Columbia on the deck
of a sailing vessel. She was hauled over the portage at the Cascades and worked the
upper river between there and The Dalles. Celinda's description is quite apt. T. C.
Elliott, "The Dalles-Celilo Portage, Its History and Influence," *Oregon Hist. Qtly.*,
XVI, no. 2 (June, 1914), p. 163.

boat which plies between the Dalls & the Cascades. It was brought here last spring from the Sacramento being the first steam boat which ever run on that river   Were about 7 hours running down (50 miles) The scenery was very romantic indeed. The banks of the river are mostly perpendicular rocks from one to a hundred feet in height. This river is not so wide as the Ohio but much deeper and unlike that river the waters of the Columbia are clear & pure. We landed on a stony beach after dark but succeeded in finding a sandy place & made our camp. We had brought our beds but had no tents so we made our beds under the star-spangled arch of heaven & thought no one could wish a more magnificent canopy

[September] 21st   Wednesday   In the morning we found we were very fortunate in the selection of a camp ground as it is the only place near the landing which is level & uncovered by stones   Many were less fortunate. A boat came in before noon laden with emigrants who camped around us. There are several barges that pass between The Dalls & this place. Few boats except those of the Hudson's Bay Co. run over the Cascades   This Co. run over the Cascades losing it is said about one boat in ten   Our baggage not come

22nd Thursday   Pleasant   Walked out to see the scenery which is very romantic   We are entirely hemmed in by the Cascade Mountains some of the immediate peaks of which some of our party judge to be 1000 ft in heighth. There is a mountain on the north side of the river river some distance from it. The side next to the river of which is perpendicular & clearly shows the action of water & I should think that this perpendicularity was caused by the Columbia's first bursting through the mountains & that the channel of the river was once near its base   All the mountains here are covered with fir trees some very densely others more sparingly. The

Cascades here are rapids nothing in comparison to the rapids at Niagara. The indians say — some of the oldest — that they can remember a time when there were no cascades here & they ran their canoes through the mountains, that they were caused by land-slides from the mountains. There are three stores here a bakery & boarding house & there is a wooden rail road between here & the lower landing 5 miles. At night the steam boat came in towing the barge on which were our wagons & luggage. All were safe. It sprinkled some in the evening

23rd Friday Messrs Judson, Marsh & Walter came with some of the cattle The others were behind — they thought that they would not be here in a day or two as there is so much danger of losing the trail as there are so many diverging from the right one. They had taken provision for but two days the length of time we were informed it would take to come down but we have ascertained it usually takes five but provision is to be obtained at the ferry

24th Saturday It rained in the night & the temporary tent which uncle H had put up leaked & we became very wet not many of our things were wet but the bedding. Called at one of the stores & the merchant gave us some peaches which were truly a rarity as we have been deprived of fruit all summer Some of the emigrants left to day. They make the portage of 5 miles & then take a boat again Uncles G & H started this morning to meet those with the cattle The would [have] went yesterday but were obliged to put the wagon together which had been taken apart at The Dalls

25th Sunday Warm & pleasant I was sick all day. Our party received several calls from gentlemen stopping here & I am informed that the land in this vicinity is nearly all taken

26th Monday   Another barge came in loaded with emigrants. Dr. Hill & Mr Richey among the rest. Messrs Bryant & Judson with their families left this morning About noon Uncle H. & J. came   uncle J has the ague & fever so they came down the river. They think the cattle will be here to day. It seems that they were induced to cross at the upper ferry & the road was so bad that it delayed them two days. They came before dark & a tired Co they were

[September] 27th Tuesday   Very warm. Uncle J had the ague & fever which detained us here to day   Had an invitation to attend a party at the boarding house.

28th Wednesday   Very warm   We started for the lower Cascades early. There is a wooden rail road 2½ miles down. The highway is very bad. We were obliged on that account to go all the way on foot. We arrived there without any accident. The walk down was delightful   Were it not for our anxiety about the teams it would have been truly enchanting. The scenery is exceedingly wild   Mountains towered 100's of feet above us & the river now rolling in terrific madness now as placid as a sleeping infants brow. Camped at the Lower Cascade for the night. A gentleman presented us a water melon   There is one public house here, a two story frame one — Steam boat Multnomah[29] came up [in margin:] Four sail boats were in.

[September 29] Thursday   After dinner went on board the steam boat Peytona[30] on which we had previously conveyed our things & went down 30 miles to Sandy [River]   The

---

[29] This was a 108-foot side wheeler built in Oregon City. It sailed the Columbia below the Cascades. Randall W. Mills, *Stern-Wheelers up the Columbia* (Palo Alto, Ca., 1947), p. 189.

[30] This steam scow operated in 1853 between the Cascades and the mouth of the Sandy River. There was a good wagon road between the Sandy and Oregon City by then. Earl K. Stewart, "Transporting Livestock by Boat," *Oregon Hist. Qtly.*, L, no. 4 (Dec. 1949), p. 252.

trip was delightful   Rocky islands rear their craggy peaks
far above the surface of the water. There is a high rocky
precipice called Cape Horn   The scenery is very beautiful
here. When some more than half way down we were startled
by the intelligence that the boiler was empty. The fire was
immediately put out & the boiler refilled. Had this not been
discovered when it was we should probably been the victims
of an explosion. When nearly down we were somewhat
frightened by the captains rushing up to the pilot in great
agitation who seemed also to be much excited   the cause of
which we knew not [printed copy ends here] but it seemed
the boat struck a snag & was in danger   Camped at the
Sandy   Found a Mr. Crosby[31] there who invited us all to
his house

30th Friday   Mr. C came with oxen to take our wagons &
other things up there   Here we sat in a chair for the second
time since leaving Missions. Slept in our wagons. One of
Uncle Gustavus appointments is here

1st Oct.   Saturday   Very pleasant. We were camped near
Mr. Crosby's. Country very fine   Every kind of vegitable
grows large. Melons plenty. Cattle came this morning   all
well   Concluded to remain over sabbath

2nd Sunday   held meeting   Mother not well   Mr. Martin left for Portland   Went to see Mr. Russels people who
were camped near. Mrs. C[rosby] has taken [unreadable
word: could be "Bonney" or "Benney"] Eliza's horse

3rd Monday   Started for Portland with two wagons & two
yokes of oxen on each   Road not very good on account of

---

    [31] John Crosby was listed in the 1850 census as a "Dr. of Medicine" born in Ireland.
His land claim was in Clackamas Co. He signed it with an "X". He was evidently a
highly educated "physician." *Genealogical Material*, I (1957), claim #729. He had a
wife, Rachel, and two children.

the close proximity of the trees. The land is all taken on the road. We took the things out of the wagons. Went to the parsonage with our baggage   Uncle G had left his at Sandy   There we met Rev C S Kingsley[32] who invited us to his house where we went   were very pleasantly entertained Mr. S[hipley] is principal of the academy here. Mr. & Mrs. Dryer called[33]

4th Tuesday   Remained at Mr. Kingsleys. This is a very pleasant location overlooking the city. Mount Hood rears its snow capped summit in the distance. I engaged to teach for Mr Kingsley [unreadable] a week & board. Went down to the parsonage which is a very fine house. The ship on which our boxes were shipped has arrived and is discharging her cargo. Uncle H's boxes are out now   Mr. Miner came

[October] 5th Wednesday   Aunt Lydia, Julia & Lucy Anna started for Oregon city intending to stop at Mr. Durhams[34] Where aunt Elizabeth is. I went into school Liked it very much. The girls are in my department and the boys in Mr. K's.   Went to singing school

6th Thursday   Pleasant. Like school as well as yesterday. Uncle H's people went to house keeping. I went to prayer meeting in the evening   Uncle Joseph & family are at uncle Harveys   Gustavus earned $2.00

---

[32] The Rev. Calvin S. Kingsley was the first principal of the Portland Academy started by the Methodists in 1851. Surrounded by high trees, the school was quite a way out of the little village. A cow path led downtown. Mrs. C. M. Cartwright, "Early Days in Oregon," *Oregon Hist. Qtly.*, IV, no. 1 (March, 1903), pp. 66-67.

[33] Thomas Jefferson and Nancy Dryer. He was founding editor of the Portland *Oregonian* newspaper. He served several terms in the State Legislature and was a member of the Oregon State Constitutional Convention in 1857. Howard M. Corning, *Dictionary of Oregon History* (Portland, 1956), p. 77.

[34] Albert Alonzo and Marianda White Durham were founders of Oswego, Oregon (now Lake Oswego). It was named for a county in their native state, New York. He was a pioneer lumberman, ran a saw mill. They had traveled to Oregon in 1847. Leslie Scott, *History of the Oregon Country*, II, (Cambridge, Mass., 1924), p. 271.

7th Friday Every thing pleasant in school Mother is sick and has been since she has been here. Took calomel to day Aunt Elizabeth has the ague. Gustavus spent $2.00 shopping. I went to uncle Harvey's. Saw uncle G's family for the first time. Uncle G house. I can do better teaching at Oswego. Attended singing school in the evening. Mr. Shipley teacher Pleasant. [unreadable] Julia.

8th Saturday No school to day I went to uncle Harvey's & opened our boxes which have been out a day or two Every thing comes out right Nothing damaged. Went down town for the first time. Was surprised at the business aspect of the place [unreadable] returned to Oswego

[October] 9th Sunday Attended church AM. Much pleased with the looks of the congregation Did not attend in the evening on account of rain. Mother a little better Messers Marsh & Walter came to see us

10th Monday Uncle H's people went to Oswego Rather rainy this morning Gustavus splitting wood here

11th Tuesday Commenced raining a little before noon.

EPILOGUE

There was another family who accompanied the Hines' 1853 wagon train: the Judsons, Holdon A. and his wife Phoebe Goodell Judson. About 72 years later in 1925, Phoebe Judson's reminiscences of her life was published in Bellingham, Washingon. Part of the work described in intimate detail the overland experience. The book was called *A Pioneer's Search for an Ideal Home*. We have republished below selections from the Judson book that add to the knowledge of Celinda Hines' experience of the journey:

It is the oft repeated inquiry of my friends as to what induced me to bury myself more than fifty years ago on this far-off corner of the world, that has determined me to take my pen in hand at this late day.

Did I come around the Horn, cross the Isthmus, or come across the plains? Was I not afraid of the Indians, and much more they ask. So I have decided to answer them all and singly by writing a short history of our pioneer life, and to affectionately dedicate my book to the memory of the late Holden A. Judson, my dear husband, who journeyed with me for half a century in the wilderness.

This will be but a condensed narrative of events which I shall endeavor to recall out of the mists of the past, written with no attempt at literary display, containing no fiction, but simply a record of the homely, everyday incidents of a plain woman, who has now exceeded her three score years and ten, and who has roughed it in the early fifties on the extreme northwestern frontier... [p. 7]

Our pioneer story begins where love stories (more is the pity) frequently terminate, for Holden Allen Judson and Phoebe Newton Goodell had been joined in the holy bonds of matrimony three years before we decided to emigrate to the vast and uncultivated wilderness of Puget Sound, which at that time was a part of Oregon.

Little did I realize how much it meant when I promised the solemn, but kindly faced, minister in the presence of a large assembly of friends, to obey, as well as to love, the one whom I had chosen for a partner through life, for the thought of becoming a pioneer's wife of only seventeen summers, romantically inclined, should have chosen from among her suitors one possessing a spirit of adventure.

Mr. Judson was five years my senior. Seldom were two more congenially mated to travel the rough voyage of life. Both were endowed with vigorous health, fired with ambition and a love of nature.

Our childhood days were spent together in the little town of Vermillion, Ohio, located midway between Cleveland and Sandusky, on the shores of Lake Erie, on whose beaches we strolled, and on whose blue waters we sailed in company, little dreaming our future lives were destined to be passed together on the far away shore of Puget Sound... [pp. 7-8.]

My parents had already found a home on the banks of the Willamette, in Oregon.

The parting with my husband's parents and only sister was very affecting, as he was their only son and brother, and our little two-year-old Annie their idol... [pp. 9-10.]

Gustavus Hines was elected captain; we could not have made a better choice. As a leader, he was qualified by experience, and his personal appearance and manners commanded our admiration and respect, inspiring our little band with hope and courage. When leading the train, mounted on a magnificent gray horse, I looked upon him more as a general than a captain — often mentally comparing him to General Winfield Scott. On him devolved the duty of selecting our camping places. On Saturday he was particularly careful to select a suitable situation for our Sabbath encampment, which would afford water and grass for our cattle, these being of the first importance... [p. 11]

We reached La Bonta [LaBonte] Creek on Saturday, a little before sundown, and made our encampment on its banks, among the cottonwood trees, one of the most charming spots of the whole route, where we found good water, grass and wood — which was greatly appreciated.

The Sabbath dawned most serenely upon us, a bright, lovely morning, the twenty-sixth of June. I am certain of the date, for the day was made memorable to me by the birth of a son.

Monday morning our party were so considerate of my welfare, and that of the "new emigrant," that they proposed remaining in camp for a day or two. I assured them that we were both very comfortable, and, though reluctant to leave this most beautiful spot (the romantic birthplace of our baby boy) I urged them to proceed with the journey.

The next morning we found the name of Platte La Bonta inscribed on our wagon cover. The name was suggested by the captain in commemoration of the birthplace on La Bonta Creek, in the Platte valley.

The name did not exactly suit me, so we compromised by adopting half of it, adding his grandfather's name, Charles! so the little fellow took his place in the ranks of life under the name of Charles La Bonta Judson... [p. 39.]

The captain decreed that our wagon should lead the train (although it was not our turn), saying if "our wagon was obliged to halt the rest would also."

It proved the roughest day's journey through the Black Hills. The wind blew a perfect gale, and while going down some of the rough sidling hills it seemed that the wagon would capsize; but I had little to fear, for Mr. Judson had become an expert in handling his team. Some of the ladies remarked that "he drove over the stones as carefully as though they were eggs."

When we halted for our noon lunch the ladies hurried to our wagon with anxious inquiries. Are you alive? etc. I quieted their fears by informing them that little "Bonta" and I were doing finely — that Annie held on to her little brother with both hands while going down the steepest hills, for fear that he would roll out of bed among the pots and kettles. Mr. Judson had buttoned and tied the wagon covers down so closely that I could not get a peep out, and I suffered but little inconvenience from the wind and dust... [pp. 40-41.]

I was able to sit in the little rocking chair my kind husband had thoughtfully purchased for my comfort the last thing before starting on our journey... [p. 42.]

The oldest couple were good Jedediah Hines (who was called "Diah" for short), and his devoted wife, who was always by his side while he drove the team. When he got into the wagon to rest, she did also, but not before. The influence of these loving spirits was felt as a benediction by all in our little band.

Usually on the Sabbath Captain [Gustavus] Hines or his youngest brother, Harvey Hines, preached us a short discourse, of a nature to cheer our drooping spirits. The three brothers took turns in leading our daily devotional exercises of the camp. This family altar in the solitude of the wilderness was very impressive ... [pp. 58-59.]

When we reached Fort Boise we found that our wagons must be ferried over the Snake river at the exorbitant price of eight dollars per wagon. The families were safely ferried over, and we

made hasty preparations to have dinner ready by the time the
swimming of the stock should be accomplished. Having replen-
ished our stock of provisions at the fort, we were enabled to
provide a better bill of fare than usual; and as this was the last
crossing of this dreaded river we were all in the best of spirits,
hoping soon to be out of the Snake river region.

Dinners were ready, and had been waiting for some time, when
Mrs. Diah and Harvey Hines, becoming uneasy at the delay, and
fearful that some accident had happened, started to go to the river
and were met by a messenger with the shocking intelligence that
one of our number was drowned.

From a fearful premonition, or spiritual perception, Mrs. Diah
Hines cried, "Oh, it is my husband, I know it is Diah." Yes, her
husband was drowned in the treacherous stream. His horse had
thrown him, while helping to swim the stock, and he probably was
hurt, as he did not come to the surface.

It was with much difficulty that the loving wife who was so
suddenly overwhelmed with anguish was kept from throwing
herself into the river. As I again recall this pathetic incident of our
journey, I find myself again weeping in sympathy with the
stricken ones.

Each felt his loss a personal loss, for he was not only a loving
husband, affectionate father and brother, but possessed as social
and genial a nature as ever animated the human form.

There was no food here for our stock, and, though our
sorrowful hearts longed to linger a while near the watery resting
place of our beloved friend, we were obliged to proceed on our
journey, meditating on the mysteries of death, of which we only
see the dark side. Could the veil, or shadow, of material nature be
lifted we would witness the transition, and what appears so fearful
would then be as glorious to us as to the angels in heaven. . . [pp.
62-63.]

SARAH PERKINS
Used with the permission of the Pioneer Museum, Tillamook, Oregon.

The Jottings of ⚹ Sarah (Sally) Perkins

INTRODUCTION

"Artless" is the key word for the daily jottings of Sarah Perkins. She was a woman of thirty-three years with a bare minimum of education, trying to summarize in a few words or phrases what must have seemed important during the journey over the Oregon Trail. There are no flights of fancy or romantic interludes. The spelling is particularly inventive.

The journal begins on April 20, 1853, near Wassonville, (now Wellman), in the northwest corner of Washington County, Iowa. They arrived at the "masury river" on May 15 and crossed it on the 17th. They traveled by "ft Carney," along the "plate river," crossed "ash holler," "cottonwood crick," saw "Larmy peak" and numerous other misspelled places. The death of a little child by falling into a kettle of scalding water is summarized with the words, "George lost his child." No name is given for this child of George and Harriet Perkins, her husband's brother and his wife. Her journal ends on September 10, 1853, when they "nooned at John Days river."

Sarah J. Jones [Perkins] was born in Genesee, New York, on March 17, 1820. The family moved to Lafayette, Tippecanoe County, Indiana, when she was a child. We know nothing of the succeeding years until she and William Hull Perkins, a farmer, were married by a justice of the peace on August 4, 1837. The official record lists her as "Sally J. Jones." She was seventeen and had consent of her mother, Hannah Jones, "expressed by Norman L. Jones her brother."

Over the years six children were born to the couple. Only two of them survived to maturity: Maryette and Myron, both born in the mid-1850's.

During the 1840's and 1850's there was a mass movement of Perkins family members to Oregon. William's parents, Eli and

Sarah, and his brothers, John and Joel, went overland in 1844. William also made a journey to scout out the land. He is listed as living in Lafayette, Yamhill County, Oregon, in the 1850 census. The town was named by his brother Joel for Lafayette, Indiana, the hometown. William returned east soon after the census, and plans were made for another overland journey in 1853. This was the journey documented by Sally. William's brother, George, and his wife, Harriet, were also part of the wagon train.

William and Sally lived in Yamhill County for several years, then in 1861 made one more move to Tillamook Bay on the Oregon Coast. No place in the world could be more different from their former Indiana homeland. The town of Tillamook was just aborning with a total population, according to the census of 1860, of 117. There was no post office until 1866. How the Perkins arrived in Tillamook is unknown. The best route would have been by ship from Portland. The overland way was most difficult with dense Douglas fir forests and rushing streams. However, the lure of lush farmland, today the dairy capital of Oregon, was a strong magnet. The Tillamook County Deed Book indicates that they purchased a farm in February and March 1861, and added to it in 1866 and 1869. They lived out their lives on their farm east of Tillamook. Perkins Hill is still so designated.

Both lived until a ripe age. William died on March 14, 1893; Sarah lived on to November 20, 1912, when she died at "91 years, 8 months, and 3 days old." The same November 21 issue of the Tillamook *Headlight* newspaper from which the above is quoted, also indicated that she left two children, "14 grandchildren, several great grandchildren and six great great grandchildren." In their later years William and Sarah were known as Uncle Billy and Aunt Sally Perkins.

The original journal is part of the collection of the County Museum at Tillamook, and we are grateful to Director Wayne Jensen for permission to publish it. The museum also has a letter written on Feb. 11, 1951, by Mrs. A.F. Kerremans, granddaughter of Aunt Sally. We conclude our introduction with her description of life in early Tillamook:

The early settlers relied altogether on boats to bring in supplies &
they came irregularly leaving the people without such necessities
as sugar, flour, kerosene & other commodities. My grandmother
Aunt Sally Perkins made her own candles from tallow and soap
from lye from ashes & tallow. Baked her Salt Rising Bread in a
Reflector before the fireplace. Delicious too. Also baked potatoes
& squash in a Dutch Oven heated with coals from the Fireplace,
and what a fireplace it was, burning 4 ft wood.

THE JOTTINGS OF SARAH PERKINS

April 20. Wednesday. first day out   Wass[onville][1] snowey
& rained   all got wet
April 21. Wassonville 10 mile   got in Ramsy co[mpany][2]
April 22. 16 miles   very mudy   traded oxen   Cost 1.25
April 23. laid by   rained   Cost 1.25
April 24. Sunday. 8 miles   snowed & rained   4.40   hurt
my thum hurts   its out
April 25. 12 miles   roling preraris   crossed coal
crick   awful mudy   doubled teams   cost $3.20
April 26. laid by & made a bridge across ceder cr   cost $6.70
April 27. hurt my thum   out   12 miles   crossed scunk
river north fork   awful mudy   seen blue island company[3]

---

[1] Wassonville, Iowa, in the northwest corner of Washington Co., is not shown on
modern maps. It was established in 1849. The name was changed to Daytonville in 1875
and then to Wellman in 1879. Guy Reed Ramsey, *Postmarked Iowa, A List of
Discontinued and Renamed Post Offices* (Crete, Neb., 1976), p. 449.

[2] There were Ramseys who were neighbors of the Perkins both in Tippecanoe Co.,
Indiana, and in Yamhill Co., Oregon. Most of the 1853 Ramseys seem to have settled in
present-day Lane Co. (the Eugene area). Thomas L. Ramsey's land claim indicates that
he arrived in Oregon on September 25, 1853. *Genealogical Material in Oregon Donation
Land Claims* (Portland, 1962), III, #2078, p. 150. The Ramsey neighbors in Lafayette,
Yamhill Co., were relatives of David and Susan, listed in the 1860 federal census as
being from Indiana.

[3] Blue Island, Ill. Wagon companies were sometimes designated by the name of the
locality from which they came.

April 28. laid by till night. crossed the south scunk   great
times   cost 3.50

April 29. 18 miles   very mudy roads   Oskaloosa   Cost
5.13

April 30. 18 miles   verry mudy fields   cost 2.50

May 1. 25 miles   good roads   struck north road   cost
2.50

May 2   8 miles   good roads   crost desmoin fork & racoon river   racoon fork   cost $3.90

May 3. 18 miles   good roads   preary   cost 2.00

May 4. 20 miles   verry good roads   Traveled with
Randles[4]   heard of Wells[5]

May 5. laid by   rained all day   0.80

May 6. 16 miles   muddy   camped on middle river   shot
at a deer in pilot grove

May 7. 16 miles   verry good roads   good times, went
poson hunting

May 8   15 miles   verry good times

May 9. 15 miles, good times. indian took raizer   a mill

May 10. 12 miles   verry good roads   verry cold   good
times

May 11. 15 miles, verry good time   verry cold

May 12. 15 miles, verry good times   crossed Isheny botony
[Nishnabotna]   cost $5.00

May 13. laid by on Ishny botony & washed   mudy stream

---

4 U. Randall and his wife, Elizabeth, are listed in the 1860 federal census as neighbors
of the Perkins and the Ramseys in Lafayette, Yamhill Co. He was a "master saddler."
Nellie C. Hiday, *U. S. Census, 1860 and 1870, Yamhill County, Oregon* (Salem, n.d.), p.
37.

5 This was the larger family of Giles and Elizabeth Wells, who indicated on their
application for a land claim that they had arrived in Oregon on August 30, 1853, and
settled on land in Jackson Co. in southern Oregon on "15/20 Sept." They also listed at
that time eight children. *Genealogical Material, op. cit.,* #73, p. 6. *See also* many
references to the Giles Wells party in Edward B. Ham, ed., "Journay Into Southern
Oregon: Diary of a Pennsylvania Dutchman," *Oregon Historical Quarterly*, LX, Sept.
1959, pp. 375-407. The writer of this 1853 diary was Nathaniel Myer.

May 14. came to sidney & done our trading   bought flour   lead 12 miles   cost $40.—

May 15. 7 miles to Tomsons ferry on masury river   camped all night   killed a deer

May 16. Ferried part

May 17. Finished crossing   cost 11—75 cents

May 18. Traveled 12 miles, very cold weather   good roads

May 19. Come 20 miles   good roads except some deep gulfs to cross   bridges gone   past 7 graves   buried in [18]50

May 20. come 10 miles & camped to make a raft on a crick ["Salt crick" scratched out.]

May 21. made a raft   come 10 miles

May 22. crossed   good luck   heard of W.C. Stives

May 23. 23 miles   good time

May 24. 20 miles   good times   had to pick weeds to make a fire

May 25. 20 miles   crossed clear crick   good times

May 26. 20 miles   camped at Indian Town   all well   met a company going back

May 27. 20 miles   killed an antelope

May 28. come 20 miles   Sandy bottom   no timber

May 29. 20 miles   no timber, rainy and cool   past a new grave

May 30. 20 miles   bad roads   passed ft Carney [Kearny] gathered weeds for fire   rained all nite

May 31. 20 miles   good roads   grass short   swam the crick for wood   swaped horses   past a new grave

June 1. Wednesday. 12 miles   good times   to a crick called plum crick   camped

June 2. laid by & washed   cilled an antelope & a black tailed deer

June 3. 18 miles   better roads   good times   plenty of alcaly water

June 4. killed a antelope   20 miles   bad roads   raining at nite   went 5 miles for wood and men packed it on mule   new grave

June 5. laid up & shod the cattle   very windy & cool

June 6. 20 miles   wood   poison water

June 7. 20 miles   dog town   struck the ford on plate [Platte]

June 8. crossed over   came 5 miles   good luck   warm pleasant

June 9. 18 miles   Killed 2 buffalow   good grass and water warm

June 10. 20 miles   killed a buffalo and deer   warm

June 11. 18 miles   warm   good luck

June 12. 15 miles   ash holler, verry hilly   wood & water   hailed ice as big as walnut

June 13. 15 miles   heavy sand   rain hail and wind crossed elm crick   good ford   I was sick

June 14. 11 miles   Heavy roads   good feed   rain at nite

June 15. 23 miles   good roads, nooned opisite court house rock   Stoped within 6 m of Chimney rock

June 16. 28   Warm day   stoped at Scots Blufs   wood and water   parted train

June 17. 20 miles   Verry hot   seen lots of Indians   ruff roads

June 18. 18 mils, good roads   very hot   rain hail and wind toards nite   wood and water

June 19. 10 miles   come to the fery

June 20. crossed   come 15 miles

June 21. 16 miles   camped on cottonwood crick   good roads wood and water

June 22. 18 miles   ruff roads   camped on [unreadable word] passed Larmy peak   snowed hailed & rained

June 23. Struck the river   road very hilly   camped on red

bank crick   Had all the overcoats & blankets on & then
frose

June 24. Some better roads   poor grass   good waters
warm & pleasant

June 25. Shod the cattle   Come 15 miles   prety good
roads   good water   grass short   camped on big deer crick

June 26. laid by and set the tyre on deer crick

June 27. very cold and windy and dusty   camped on mudy

June 28. some warmer   crossed north plat   6 dollars a
wagon

June 29. rather cool   camped on Sulpher Spring

June 30. 15   cool and good roads   camped on fish run

July 1. Friday. 18 miles, good roads   Cold winds   nooned
at independence rock   camped at develgate

July 2. laid by   the boys went after snow & did not get eney

July 3. laid by   DeLongs overtook us

July 4. laid by and washed on Sweet water   quite warm,
snow in 10 miles

July 5. traveled 14 miles   Sandy roads   warm days   cool
nites

July 6. 12 miles   good feed   crossed Sweet water 3
times   had to block up the boxes

July 7. 17 miles   Sandy roads   good grass   rained at
night   lots of snow in site   water scearce

July 8. 20 miles   rough roads   water plenty   had snow to
eat   good grass on the Larmy Crick   snow 4 feet deep in
drifts   Strawberrys in bloom   rain at nite

July 9. 24 miles   good roads   got over the summit of the
rocky mountain   poor feed   cool nites   water plenty

July 10. 23 miles   good roads   water plenty   poor
feed   camped on big Sandy   Sage plenty for wood

July 11. 20 miles   good roads   15 miles to water   no
grass   camped again on big sandy   a little rain

July 12. 20 miles   gravely road   struck green river   poor feed   good water and plenty of wood

July 13. crossed over   6$ a wagon   12 miles   camped on a creek   killed some sage hens   musquetoes plenty   good feed

July 14. 18 miles   rough roads   camped on a spring grass scarce   sage wood   cold nite

July 15. rough roads   hard hills   camped at a spring good feed and water

July 16. Struck bear river valy   hard roads   good feed and water

July 17. laid by   good grass and water   traviled ½ day and laid up

July 18. laid by to rest the team   good feed and water

July 19. traviled ½ day   camped on hams fork of bear river   good feed and water

July 20. laid by   caught some fish

July 21. 18 miles   very hilly   crossed bear river mountains   good grass

July 22. good roads   fine grass   good water

July 23. level roads &c   bad water on the ground but good springs past soda springs   wood plenty

July 24. pleasant roads   good water   the best of grass willows   wood   camped   partner [Portneuf] crick

July 25. very rough road   good water   plenty of grass   camped on ross crick   George lost his child[6]

July 26. laid by   buried it & washed

July 27. 18 miles   good level roads   good grass and water   crossed ross c   crossed and camped on port neff [Portneuf] river

---

[6] The child who died was the son of George and Harriet Perkins. A less matter-of-fact writer of George Perkins' biography in 1893 described the loss in this way: "While they were on the plains their little two-year-old boy accidentally fell into a kettle and was scalded, dying soon afterward." Nowhere is the child named. H.K. Hines, *An Illustrated History of the State of Oregon* (Chicago, 1893), p. 1097.

July 28. 20 m good roads feed and water sage Crossed Bannac river musquetoes by the bushel

July 29. 18 m hot day struck Snake r at american falls deep sand & steep hills good grass water sage wood camped on falls

July 30. 8 miles very dusty & hot crost raft river good grass and water sage wood

July 31. 16 miles no feed or water till goose crick stoney road camped on the crick sage

August 1. Monday. 35 m level but stoney roads nooned on goose river good grass no more feed till dry run 20 m camped at 12 oclock at nite

August 2. laid by to rest the teem and washed hear the Indians are very bad willows wood good water

August 3. 20 m level roads some places stony water once in 8 miles called dry run sage wood

August 4. 26 miles no grass camped on Snake at 6 oclock

August 5. Started at day light come 10 m camped found grass 1½ m on the hills at sammon falls

August 6. 18 miles very hot & dusty water at Snake grass on the hills

August 7. 16 miles heavy sand and hilly no grass till we came to the three islands swam the stock into it and staid till wednesday.

August 10. Wednesday. very rough roads 23 m camped on snake good grass

August 11. 16 miles better roads camped on catherines creek good feed

August 12. laid by

August 13. 16 miles camped on a small stream good feed

August 14. 15 miles camped on the plains no water Some buntch grass lost an ox sage

August 15. 15 miles   camped on the south of a little crick on Snake   good grass   sage   very hot

August 16. laid by and washed   hot day, Sage wood

August 17. level & dusty roads   camped on Snake river   short grass

August 18. very dusty and hot   camped on Snake   good grass river water   willow wood   lost a cow

August 19. very hot and dusty   camped on cold spring creek   good grass

August 20. laid by   cold nite

August 21. 16 miles   cool   good traveling   good roads   camped on furtunate creek   good grass   sage

August 22. 25 miles   good roads   camped on Burch C   poor feed   good water

August 23. 15 m   rough stony roads   camped on burnt river   good grass & water

August 24. 20 miles   level dusty roads   camped on burnt river   good grass & water   Sulpher Springs

August 25. 16 miles   hilly roads   camped on br fork   good grass   Spring water

August 26. 23 miles   hilly   camped on powder river   willows good grass   lost 3 cattle

August 27. laid by

August 28. 12 miles   camped at the foot of blew mountan   good feed and water

August 29. 10 miles   hilly and stoney   camped in grand round   good feed   no wood

August 30. Laid by

August 31. 12 miles   heavy hills and very stoney   camped on grand round river   rained all day   very cold   pine timber

September 1. laid by and caught some fish and a coon   cold nite   pleasant day

September 2. cool day   laid by   rained all nite

September 3. 20 miles   rough and hilly   rained all day and nite   very cold

September 4. cool day   18 miles   better roads   got over the blue mountains   camped on umatily river   Bunch grass & water

September 5. 18 m   good roads   camped on umatily bunch grass   pleasant day   wood plenty

September 6. 15 m   good sandy roads   passed Indian Agency   camped on butter Cr   wood and water   bunch grass   good weather

September 7. 18   good roads   good feed   sage

September 8. 12 m   willow creek   willow wood   poor feed   creek water

September 9. 20   good roads   good feed   creek water   sage wood

September 10. 18 miles   nooned at John Days river heavy hills camped in the prarie   good grass   no water or wood unless carried[7]

---

[7] Here the diary ends. They are traveling along the south bank of the Columbia River, essentially the route of modern-day freeway #84. Today there are bridges crossing all of the tributaries that flow into the Columbia.

Overland Trip Across the Plains

§ Rachel Taylor

INTRODUCTION

The following diary was written by a teenage girl: Rachel Taylor, age 15. She was a perceptive, alert young woman who would become a school teacher after arrival in the Oregon Country.

The Rachel Taylor diary was brought to our attention by Mrs. Nevah Clifford, a descendant, of Eagle Point, Oregon, in response to a notice of this publishing project in the Medford, Oregon, *Mail-Tribune*. In her letter, dated June 18, 1980, Mrs. Clifford said, speaking of the 1853 wagon train:

> In this group were my great grand parents, Stephen Phelps Taylor and wife, Abigail Clark Taylor and several of their children including my grand parents, Stephen Clark Taylor and wife, Mary Ann Prescott Taylor. These families with several other wagons came on into Oregon, settling near Roxy Ann Mountains south side, taking up land near the hills as they were farmers and wanted to be near the hills for grazing for cattle.

Mrs. Clifford has been most helpful in conversations on the telephone and correspondence since the first letter. She told us of Mrs. Jeanette G. Person of Nevada City, California, who has also been helpful in supplying names and data of family members. We learned of Mr. & Mrs. Arthur Person of Sacramento, California, who have the original diary and kindly sent us a photocopy of it.

Rachel Taylor was born on July 22, 1838, in Pecatonica, Illinois. There is a family tradition that she was the first white baby born in Winnebago County. We have not been able to verify this. Rachel celebrated her fifteenth birthday on the Oregon Trail by exploring the Devil's Gate near Independence Rock, but she did not mention her birthday.

This diary is distinctive in that it describes a journey over the Oregon Trail, but they departed from that route to take the California Trail along the Humboldt River in present Nevada to enter Oregon from the southeast. They settled in the Rogue River Valley in Jackson County in southern Oregon.

Rachel arrived in an Oregon with a great superfluity of men. Naturally a single woman — no matter what age — received a great deal of attention. Her sister-in-law, Mary Ann Taylor, wrote east to her own family on August 1, 1854, "Rachel is the same, only grown considerable. She is going to make a nice woman if she holds out." Rachel held out for nearly two months. She and John Court Wheeler, a farmer from New York State, were married in Phoenix, Oregon, on October 12, 1854. John Wheeler had come to Oregon in 1850. The couple became the parents of three children before the father's death on October 16, 1868. Rachel married for a second time, this time to Benjamin Mensch, another farmer, on June 23, 1870, at Grants Pass, Oregon. There were two children by this marriage. Rachel, herself, died on March 30, 1880.

She was a schoolteacher off and on for many of her adult years. In the same letter, quoted above, Mary Ann Taylor wrote: "Rachel gets along well with her school, likes it much and they all like her in return. She shows a good deal of sense for all she is so young."

One aspect of Rachel Taylor's diary is that it tells of the overland journey of the oft-mentioned but little documented "preachers' wagon train" to southern Oregon in 1853.

Rachel's uncle, Sylvester Taylor, wrote a letter from Council Bluffs to the Waterton, Wisconsin, *Chronicle*, in which he said, "We go out in a company of about 20 effective men — three of them Methodist preachers — 13 wagons and about 200 head of cattle." The three preachers were the Rev. William Royal, his wife, Barbara, and their minister sons, Thomas Fletcher Royal and James H. B. Royal, and their wives. The Royal family became influential leaders of the Methodist Church in the Pacific Northwest.

Rachel's diary often tells of her close friendship with Mary Elizabeth Royal, the twenty-year-old daughter of the William Royals. They became lifelong friends over the following years. Mary Royal in 1856 became the wife of Rev. John Flinn, a much-beloved Methodist leader.

One issue that came up over and over with the Royal-Taylor-Burt wagon trains was whether or not to travel on the Sabbath. An illustration of this is found in Rachel's entry for August 21st: "Did not have but one service as it took so much time to drive the cattle two miles to water and back again. Some proposed hitching up the teams and moving our encampment. Thinking it preferable to driving the stock so far twice a day, but Father [William] Royal says he will not put a yoke on one of his oxen on Sunday."

Some of the younger men itched to move on faster and threatened to go over to another train. Some did go. As a matter of fact, those who rested on the Sabbath often caught up with the others, for the oxen had to be given lots of rest whether it was on Sunday or on other days.

SOURCES FOR THE TAYLOR AND ROYAL FAMILIES:

The Taylor Family papers are in the Oregon Collection of the University of Oregon Library in Eugene. We appreciate the use of Mary Elizabeth Taylor's letter from this collection. There are Royal papers in the Willamette University Methodist Archives, Hatfield Library, Salem, and also in the Southern Oregon Historical Society, Jacksonville, Oregon. Somewhat helpful is Thomas D. Yarnes, *A History of Oregon Methodism* (Portland, 1957).

TAYLOR FAMILY MEMBERS IN THE
WAGON TRAIN OF 1853

Stephen P. Taylor Family
Stephen Phelps Taylor (June 7, 1801-May 3, 1866), 52-years-old at time of the crossing.
Abigail Clark Taylor (Nov. 1, 1801-May 5, 1892), 52 in 1853.

Abigail Irene Taylor (Apr. 1, 1826-Feb. 11, 1860), oldest child, unmarried.

Stephen Clark Taylor (Sept. 17, 1828-1891), m. Mary Ann Prescott. He was referred to as "Clark."

David Hobart Taylor (Sept. 4, 1831-Oct. 3, 1882), m. Jennie Fitts Greenman, 1871. He was referred to as "Hobart."

Rachel Merriam Taylor (July 22, 1838-March 30, 1880), the writer of the diary, m. John Court Wheeler, Oct. 12, 1854. He died on Oct. 16, 1868. She married Benjamin Mensch, June 23, 1870.

Sylvester H. Taylor Family

Sylvester H. Taylor, brother of Stephen P. Taylor (1827-winter, 1861).

Clarissa Taylor, wife of Sylvester Taylor (b. 1825).

Nellie (or Helen) Taylor, b. 1843.

Clara, b. 1844.

Harriet, b. 1849.

Florence or Flora, b. 1851.

THE DIARY

Apr 6th 1853. [Pecatonica, Illinois] After weeks of preparation we are at last ready to take our departure for the Pacific Coast, to find a new home far away, to form new ties and other acquaintances amid far different scenes.

We know not the dangers we may meet, the difficulties that will have to be overcome on this long and perilous journey.

We could not start early in the day, on account of a multitude of things to be done, but about three o clock in the afternoon, the last articles was packed, and stowed away in the covered wagons, the last "Good byes" spoken, and we started on our way. We ascended the hill in wagon drawn by slow-paced oxen, and looked our last on the old home and its surroundings — We traveled about four miles, and stopped at the house of our friends, Mr. Hinman Browns, where we spent the night.

Apr 7th   We bade our friends a long farewell, and are now fairly started on our way. Besides our own family, we are accompanied by my Uncle Sylvester H. Taylor of Watertown, Wisconsin, his wife and four children,[1] a hired man by the name of Noble,[2] another Uncle by the name of Kennedy[3] who leaves a family in Indiana, and two young men who go with us to assist in driving cattle or any thing else necessary to be done, and answer respectively to the names of Augustus Blake[4] and Philip Goodman.[5]

Night found us at Rydott about four miles from Twelve Mile Grove.

Apr 8th   Started early in the morning and met with nothing worthy of mention.

Father left us to day to go to Rush Creek to attend to some business, expecting to be gone two days. Staid all night at Mt Morris.

Apr 9th   This is a pleasant country through which we are now passing. Crossed several beautiful streams, one with pine trees growing along its banks.

The day was too cold and windy for horseback riding. At

---

[1] See "Letters of S.H. Taylor to the Watertown [Wisconsin] Chronicle," Mar. 16, 1853-Mar. 29, 1854, *Oregon Historical Quarterly*, XXII, No. 2 (June, 1921), pp. 117-160. One letter was written by the wife, Clarissa E. Taylor, Aug. 10, 1853, pp. 136-138, from Fort Laramie.

[2] Orrin Noble, age 35, and his wife, Eliza (Brimley) Noble, age 33, traveled from Indiana to Fall Creek, Lane Co., Oreg., in 1853, with the Royal party. He was a farmer. *Pacific Christian Advocate*, Sept. 27, 1888.

[3] Unidentified.

[4] Augustus Blake, age 28 at time of journey, was still living with the Taylors in 1854. "Census of Oregon, 1854," Oreg. Archives, Salem.

[5] There are several Goodmans in early Oreg. records, none with the given name, Philip.

night we stopped at Buffalo Grove, at the house of Mr Webster.

Apr 10th   Our present stopping place proves to be a very good one, the family being pious members of the Presbyterian Church. We spent the Sabbath here and late in the afternoon Father came up with us.

Apr 11th   Two of our loose horses were hitched behind our wagon, and after traveling awhile, they evidently concluded to go the other way, and commenced pulling backwards. The result of this strategem was the pulling in two of the wagon cover. This was soon mended and we were again upon our way. We staid at Genesee. It was very rainy both out and in doors.

Apr 12th   So rainy this morning that we did not get started until almost noon, then we were hindered by one of the cattle being missing and which they failed to find.

Our stopping place for the night was Union Grove. Still raining hard.

Apr 13th   We found the roads very bad. Uncle Sylvesters team, being heavily loaded, became fast in the mud, — which is extremely plenty here — and was extricated by means of "double teams."

Crossed a deep stream, but forded without difficulty. On account of the bad roads, and wearied teams, we came to a halt early in the afternoon.

Apr 14th   We are now at Fulton City, the crossing place of the Mississippi River, and waiting to be ferried over. This accomplished, we proceeded on our way, and stopped for the night at the house of Mr Burkhead.

Apr 15th   Roads extremely bad and Uncles team had to be pulled out of the mud five times. Of course this does not increase our speed, and after going about ten miles we came to De Witt, where we stopped. This is a little town set down in a desperately muddy place.

Apr 16th   Roads still worse. Uncles team and wagon fast in the mud eight times. At night we put up at Buena Vista, where we pitched our tent for the first time.

Apr 17th   The Sabbath has again rolled around, and we do not move to day. After considerable inquiry, a meeting was heard of at a short distance away, and Father and Abigail attended.

Apr 18th   Crossed the Ferry on the Wapsipinicon River, and were much relieved to find the roads considerably improved. In the afternoon it rained quite hard, and we stopped early, taking possession of an empty house, which afforded us protection from the drenching rain.

Apr 19th   Still raining this morning, and we started late. Stopped for the night at Tipton. Camped out as before.

Apr 20th   Started in good season, and had very good roads. We were overtaken by Mr Long, one of our old neighbors, from Illinois. They are also bound for Oregon, but they are "rushing" and we are not, so let them go ahead. Crossed the Cedar River Ferry and went five miles beyond.

Apr 21st   The wind blew so hard in the night as to blow the tent down and we received quite a soaking from the rain. Tried to raise the tent again, but could not, as the wind was still blowing, so we went into a house.

We dried our clothes as well as we could, and started. Passed through Iowa City, crossed the Iowa river and put up for the night.

Apr 22   Had our breakfast early, and all looked propitious for an early start   But Mr Long took it upon himself to

drive of[f] two of our cows, and this hindered us, as they had
to be followed and brought back. Roads very bad, and we
traveled slowly.

Stopped at Mr Dantons, and encamped. Looks quite
rainy.

Apr 23rd   Very early in the morning we were awakened by
the water coming in upon us. It was raining and the tent
leaking. We could do nothing but sit down patiently in as
dry a place as we could find and wait for fair weather. Instead
of this the tent blew down, and we betook ourselves to the
house, wet and sleepy.

Apr 24th   The storm continued, and the waters were so
high, that we did not think best to leave our present stopping
place. After a while the rain changed to snow, making it still
more unpleasant. Towards night it cleared away.

Apr 25th   A lovely day, clear bright blue sky overhead, but
the roads are wretchedly muddy   The heavy rains have
been no advantage to travellers   After going about six
miles, we came to a deep stream with steep banks, but by
raising the wagon boxes with ropes and chains, we landed
safely on the other side. Encamped for the night near a surly
old Irishmans.

Apr 26th   Started in good season and found the roads
much improved. Crossed English River which was very
much swollen by the late rains and encamped early.

April 27th   Roads very good. Two of our cattle are about to
fail, but by going slowly made out to get them to our
stopping place, where they were sold. We are now at the
residence of Mr Parker, very pleasant friendly people.

Apr 28th   Did not move our encampment, as it rained
some and was otherwise unpleasant.

Apr 29th   Found good roads and made very good progress. Night found us at Montasuma [Montezuma], rather an imposing name for a few houses set down in the mud. But it is likely that the good people here have never "traveled," and think this the garden of Iowa, if not of creation.

Apr 30th   Encamped early as we were told that beyond that certain place, there was no grass to be found.

May 1st   Sunday. Did not travel but staid and attended preaching.

May 2nd   Still another day we tarry here, for the benefit of the cattle, and improve the opportunity to do some washing.

May 3rd   Were hindered in the morning by the cattle scattering, but finally got them together, and started. Encamped near a low marshy place, where our cattle found good feed.

May 4th   A very rainy day and no travelling.

May 5th   Started early, but traveled slowly on account of bad roads. Found one stream with an unsafe bridge, and were hindered some time in getting the wagons across. The cattle and loose horses had to swim. Crossed the Skunk River Ferry just at night and encamped.

May 6th   Bought a yoke of oxen and sold a feather bed. After travelling about 4 miles we came to Pella, a settlement composed almost entirely of Holland Dutch, there being, as we were told, only thirteen American families in the place. They look comical enough, stumping about with their wooden shoes.

The roads are so extremely bad that it is difficult to travel at all. Encamped near a small stream where wood was convenient and grass plenty for our weary cattle.

May 7th   Were hindered some time, by the cattle straying, but finally they were collected together again.

Crossed the Des Moines River at Red Rock, and for about a mile, the roads were in desperate state. But after getting onto the bluffs, we found them much improved. Staid over night at Round Gap Grove.

May 8th   No travelling to day.   Wrote letters to the friends we left behind us.

May 9th   Roads very good the most of the way. Found one place where the horse wagon became fast in the mud and had to call on the oxen for assistance. Travelled until very late trying to reach the timber, but failed, and had to encamp upon the prairie.

May 10th   Our cattle were scattered and could not be found until late in the afternoon. After travelling two miles we came to a stream, difficult to ford on account of its muddy banks. Encamped as soon as safely over

May 11th   Were delayed in the morning, as a new ox yoke had to be constructed to take the place of the broken one. Roads in good condition, and we traveled along nimbly. It was quite late before we found a suitable stopping place.

May 12th   About noon we passed Oceola, a town consisting of one store, three taverns, and about half a dozen dwelling houses. Encamped about four miles from the city just named, where our cattle had excellent grass.

May 13th   After travelling awhile we came to the old Mormon road which is much traveled and very good. It is to be hoped that mud will be rather more of a scarcity after this. Passed the Mormon town of Pisgah, now left with only one family to inhabit it. Shortly after we came to Grand River, which we had to ford. This being accomplished safely, we traveled about a mile farther and encamped.

May 14th   This night finds us at Twelve Mile Creek, where we were told that it was 15 miles to any more water, and 27 miles before any more fuel could be obtained.

May 15th   Did not rest as we usually do on the Sabbath, because we are at a great distance from any house, water poor and grass scarce. We found water at convenient intervals all day, but no wood except at some distance from the road. Encamped near a slough where there was plenty of good grass and water.

May 16th   Came across another company bound for Oregon and traveled with them all day. In the night there came up a terrific storm of wind and rain — our tent blew down and we were as completely soaked as "drowned rats."

May 17th   Roads very muddy and water high. Bridges are swept away in many places, and delays are frequent.

   Stopped at noon and built a bridge and had just time to cross and encamp before dark.

May 18th   Traveled another half day, and again had to stop and go to bridge building. Did not get it completed and are fast here for the night.

May 19th   Finished the bridge in good season and crossed. Had good roads and traveled along lively. Came to some river — name unknown and had to ferry.

May 20th   Crossed another ferry, found good roads and met with no adventure worth relating. Stopped near a small grove and stream where we had plenty of water and wood and the cattle good feed.

May 21st   Crossed the "Nishna Botena" [Nishnabotna] River but were hindered so in crossing, that we did not travel far. Encamped near a spring but the grass is not good.

May 22nd   After travelling some distance we fell in with

some people from Illinois by the name of Royal[6] and encamped with them.

May 23d   We are stopping here for a few days to lay in our supply of provisions to last us across the plains as we are now in the vicinity of Kanesville, the "Jumping-off-place"

May 24th   Still tarrying here waiting for matters to get arranged.

May 25th   Started late and went to Kanesville. Were hindered some time in the city, and after starting out were furthered hindered by the breaking of a wagon. The men of the company here commenced standing guard.

May 26th   Did not start until late as the broken wagon had to be repaired. Found the roads hilly and bad traveling. At noon we stopped and waited for the rest of the company. We encamped on the bottom land where grass was good, but water very poor. The Royal family consist of one old gentleman and his wife, three sons and one daughter. The oldest son is married, and the rest are single. They are accompanied by two nephews, William Sells[7] and George Ebey,[8] also a Swede by the name of Laurence Johnstone.[9]

27th   Went to the Ferry, on the Missouri River, but found such a crowd of wagons and cattle that we could not cross till afternoon.

Went about two miles beyond the ferry and encamped.

May 28th   Were hindered by some of the company branding their cattle. Encamped near a small stream, where we found a spring and wood sufficient for camp fires.

---

[6] See introduction to this diary for discussion of Royal family.

[7] On Dec. 27, 1854, William M. Sells settled on claim #6228 in Jackson Co., having arrived in Oreg. on Oct. 28, 1853. He was born in Franklin Co., Ohio, on June 5, 1828. Genealogical Forum, Portland, *Genealogical Material in Oregon Donation Land Claims*, IV (Portland, 1967), p. 104.

[8] George Ebey was the younger brother of Mrs. Barbara Royal, wife of William Royal. He was born in 1811 in Ohio and died July 13, 1889, in Illinois. *Pacific Christian Advocate*, Oct. 30, 1889.   [9] Unidentified.

May 29th   Sunday.

Had preaching in one of the tents. I think that I did not say that Father Royal and two of his sons are preachers. During the day 27 teams came to the stream, but could not cross on account of high water.

May 30th   After traveling about 8 miles over a smooth and pleasant road, we came to a brush bridge — not the best kind surely. A little farther on we came to the Elkhorn River where there was a ferry. This was speedily crossed, then came a long slough, after we reached the end of that we encamped.

May 31st   Roads very muddy all day. Encamped on the prarie and it rained so hard in the night that the men on guard left the cattle to themselves and came into camp.

June 1st   Two of our horses are missing and Father started in pursuit. After a while he came back without them and Clark started. Soon after three others started with their loaded guns not doubting that the Indians were at the bottom of the affair. Soon however they all came back with the horses not having fired a gun. The horses had become frightened by the heavy thunder of the preceding night and had strayed away. This adventure hindered us some time, and we did not get very far on our journey. We came at night to a bridge constructed of rough logs and nearly under water. We made all haste to cross it, fearing that it might float off and leave us. Went about half a mile and encamped.

June 2nd   Traveled all the fore noon in a slough, after the roads were much improved. Took a horse back ride with Mary Royal and had a very pleasant time. We tried to reach the timber but could not — However we found very good water and excellent grass.

June 3rd   Started very early to get the ferry on Loupe Fork in advance of a large drove that was encamped near us.

When we had traveled about four miles we heard that we could not cross on account of high water. So we turned off from the main roads and camped where grass and water were plenty.

June 4th   Water still high and no crossing. Reports are continually reaching us of Indian depredations.

Mary Royal[10] and I took a walk up onto the bluff, and after rambling around for a while, we looked over to another ridge and saw some living moving objects which we thought could be nothing but an Indian. After looking at it awhile, and seeing it raise up and then stoop down quickly out of sight, we ran into camp and told the news. Away went the men with their guns to the top of the hill, and saw not a hostile Indian but one of our men, who had been dipping water from a spring with a dipper. We came in for a good share of jokes and there is no end to the fun at our expense.

Poor Phil! what a dangerous situation was his — exposed to the murderous fire of their empty guns.

June 5th   Sunday. Had preaching at our tent in the forenoon, and at Mr Colburns[11] in the afternoon. Both meetings were well attended. Two Indians were seen skulking around the camp.

June 6th   Went to the ferry in the morning, but could not cross on account of high winds. The river is so full of sand bars that it is difficult to cross even in a fair day.

June 7th   Succeeded in getting across the river finally but so late in the day that we could only travel a short distance.

June 8th   Followed along the Loupe Fork nearly all day. Just as we encamped we saw some objects on the north side of the river, which we thought were buffalo, but they turned out to be Santa Fe traders

---

[10] *See* introduction above.
[11] Unidentified.

June 9th   Saw some elk this morning, as we were traveling along but too great a distance from us to observe them distinctly.

June 10th   Roads were very sandy and hilly and hard travelling. Passed several small lakes some of them very deep. Encamped near one of them which was filled with dead cottonwood, and served a very good purpose for fuel. Very high wind in the night but no rain.

June 11th   All day we found very poor roads, muddy, sloughy, hilly, rough and every thing else bad that could be mentioned. Crossed two streams with steep bad banks, and traveled on until nearly sundown   We were in a region of grass, but no wood or water. Nothing could be but to stop and let the cattle rest graze awhile and then go on. Accordingly, the weary oxen were unyoked and turned loose. After a while we started and traveled until 11 oclock before we found a suitable stopping place. We were all hungry, tired and sleepy, and thankful that at last we had come to a halt.

June 12th   A very pleasant day — but rather windy   A great many people had come to the creek crossed and encamped, and as their number exceeded the number on our side, preaching was held over there.

June 13th   Crossed this creek which is called in the Guide Book, Wood River and made better progress than usual, as the roads were smooth and level. Near our encampment was a little colony of prairie dogs.

June 14th   Night found us near a stream where water was plenty but not very good. Plenty of prairie dogs, and large gray wolves in this vicinity.

June 15th   In the forenoon crossed Elm Creek, and later in the day Buffalo Creek. Encamped in a bend of the last named stream. There is no timber in this place, but "buffalo chips" are abundant.

June 16th   Nothing worthy of mention occurred. Encamped near a small spring of very good water, at least good in comparison with that which we have been having.

June 17th   Traveled near the Platte all day and encamped near it at night. This is a turbid river, no trees of any size to be seen. We make out to use the water by sprinkling in a little corn meal   This makes it a little cleaner.

June 18th   About noon we came to a large spring of pure cold waters, and here we pitch our tents   Employed the remaining part of the day in washing and such other work as could not be done in the wagon as we travel along.

June 19th   The men took two tents and put them together in such a way as to make a large awning and quite an audience gathered under it to hear preaching. Several companies of emigrants are camped at a short distance from here, and all came out to meeting.

June 20th   Hobart and George Ebey started out on a buffalo hunt, and did not overtake the train until late in the day. Their only game was a large white wolf. Encamped as usual near the muddy Platte

June 21st   As the tired teams are taking their noon day rest, we went to fish near by but did not have a "nibble"

June 22nd   Streams of pure water are abundant in this region, and at our stopping place for the night we found a good spring

June 23   As usual Father was out early this morning to see about the horses and found that one of them had become twisted up in the *Lariet* ropes, and had broken his leg.

There was no chance for him to get well, and Blake took the gun and shot him. This threw a damper upon our feelings to think of our favorite thus coming to an untimely end and some tears were shed as we left him on the *plains.*

June 24th   Saw a company of emigrants and a large drove of cattle on the opposite side of the river.

Prickly Pear is abundant here, and white wolves, antelopes and prarie dogs were often seen. These latter animals are very small lively little fellows and in some respects resemble the squirrel.

June 25th   Clark, Phil and George went hunting   We traveled until camping time, then stopped and but there was no appearance of hunters. After dark we began to be very uneasy, as they still came not   Bright lights were made that could be seen some distance, that in case they were lost they might find their way in. Sleep was effectually banished from our eyes, as we watched and waited. But not until after midnight did they reach camp, tired enough. As the fruit of their labor they brought in an antelope.

June 26th   Preaching this forenoon, and prayer meeting in the afternoon.

June 27th   Traveled a short distance and then stopped to rest our foot-sore cattle. Our present home is on Shoal Creek.

June 28th   Cool and windy but otherwise pleasant. On the opposite side of the river, we can see very plainly "Court House Rock" Far in the distance looms up Chimney Rock.

June 29th   Roads very sandy and hard for teams   One of our wagons has lost a tire and will have to be left. Several of our cattle are getting *lame* and we will have to rest again for their benefit.

June 30th   A heavy thunder shower came up and drenched us nicely. Encamped at a distance from the river and as there is no wood to be had, we will have to subsist on what is already cooked until we reach some more favorable locality.

July 1st   Visited an Indian wigwam, where there was four children, several men, and a squaw. Encamped near a small stream, where we found good grass, for our tired animals. In this days march, we passed a magnificent pile of rocks called in the Guide Book Scotts Bluffs.

July 2nd   Some of the hands in the company are getting dissatisfied. One of our men — Blake and one of Mr Royals nephews talk of leaving the Train. There will not be many tears shed even if such should be the case.

July 3d   The Sabbath has at last rolled around and as usual we do not break up camp, but tarry here and spend a part of the time in religious services. Two ladies came to meeting from a neighboring encampment.

Blake and Will Sells have gone to find a place more suitable to their minds. William came back at night but no Augustus.

July 4th   We hoisted a flag belonging to some of the company, and as we saw the stars and stripes floating in the breeze we felt quite patriotic. After finding an excellent camping place we stopped and pitched our tents. Wrote two letters to far off friends.

July 5th   One of Uncles oxen "came up missing" and hindered us some time. In the afternoon we met a company of Californians returning to the states, and sent some letters by them to be mailed when they reach a post office. One of the men proved to be an acquaintance of Uncles, and of course were mutually pleased at the meeting. Saw several Indian wigwams scattered along the road. Our present stopping place is about opposite Fort Laramie, and distant two miles. Blake has picked up his "duds" bid us all a kind farewell and taken his departure to join the train of Brierly and Dillon.[12] William will remain where he is, at least for the present.

---

[12] M.M. Brierley's train went to California, where they lived for many years. In 1885

July 6th   The boys all crossed the river and went over to the fort to see what could be seen. One of the soldiers came over to our side and made us a visit. Our road in the afternoon was quite hilly and we traveled slowly.

July 7th   Very hilly roads.

Mary and I undertook to climb one of the highest and steepest mountains that we could see. This we finally achieved and as we looked at the teams and wagons, as they wound along the road far below us, they looked very diminutive and "beneath our notice." The hillside is covered with evergreens intermingled with flowers of different kinds. A beautiful place, and we would love to stay longer but the advancing train reminds us that we must be hurrying forward. Stopped for the noon day rest at a beautiful clear spring and were sorry when the time came to leave. We visited some more Indians Wigwams, where there were some squaws. They shewed us some of their ornamental work, and seemed very friendly. Encamped at a distance where there was neither grass or water for our poor animals.

July 8th   In going down a steep sideling place one of our wagons upset, but no damage done. We have another hand in the place of Blake, a boy by the name of William Williams.[13] Visited a traders house. The old squaw — his wife, had just lost a brother killed by the Pawnee Indians and had her hair cut short as is their custom when mourning.

July 9th   Had good roads & no accidents. Hubert and George moved by a spirit of adventure and curiosity went onto the mountains with their guns. Saw several mountain sheep, and sage hens but did not kill anything. Camped near the river to spend the Sabbath. Had a large congregation at

---

he and his wife, Barbara, went north to vast Harney Co., Oreg., and settled near Burns. They engaged in sheep raising. There was one more move to Grant Co. where they settled near Monument in the John Day River valley. *An Illustrated History of Baker, Grant, Malheur and Harney Counties* (n. p., 1902) pp. 478-9. Dillon is thus far unidentified.

[13] Unidentified.

our tent in the forenoon and at Smiths and Strattons[14] in the afternoon. We practice singing together nearly every Sabbath.

July 11th   Started quite early, and found good roads.

July 12th   Mr Burts[15] company are now traveling with us. We did not get an early start as there was several lame cattle to be attended to. This region abounds in curiosities and we find many on our frequent rambles.

July 13th   Grass near the road is getting scarce, and frequently the cattle have to be driven some distance from the road before they can get any thing to eat.

July 14th   Quite an excitement was raised among the masculines by seeing a buffalo. All hands gave instant chase, wounded him badly, but did not succeed in taking him. Passed a place where a dead Indian warrior was placed on a scaffold, their way of burying. A bunch of feathers had fallen down and we took each of us one in memory of the departed *brave.* Grass and water scarce, but sage brush abundant. When dry this makes excellent fuel.

July 15th   Started rather earlier than usual, but did not travel far. As soon as grass could be reached, our weary oxen were unyoked and turned loose. A company near us have just killed a buffalo and kindly gave us some of the meat. Fletcher Royals man Laurence Johnstone has become

---

[14] Smith unidentified. Curtis P. Stratton, however, with wife, Lavinia, and family settled in Douglas Co. They became best known by the prominence of their children: Riley E. Stratton, Chief Justice of Oreg.; Carroll C., President of the Univ. of the Pacific, Stockton, California; Julius A., Superintendent of the Oreg. State Penitentiary. H.O. Lang, *History of the Willamette Valley* (Portland, 1885), p. 821.

[15] There is a manuscript diary written by Ellen Burt, a 13-year-old girl, who traveled west to Oregon in the same wagon train as Rachel Taylor. The Burts became pioneer settlers of Glide, in southern Oregon. A descendant of Ellen Burt, Marsha Melvin, now Mrs. Marsha Ruhn, gave the Western Oregon State College a photocopy of the original manuscript diary when she was a student at the college in 1978. The original is kept in a bank vault in Glide.

dissatisfied. Several times lately he has been reproved and scolded in such a way that his sensitive feelings were wounded, and before they knew any thing about it, he had his clothes all packed up ready to leave. He had made arrangements to go with Mr Burns,[16] a company traveling near us, but Mr Royal persuaded him not to leave our company, and so he has taken up quietly with us. He is a Swede talks quite broken, but is an good young man.

July 16th   We encamp to night for the last time near the "river of silver" and it seems like leaving an old friend. Several companies of emigrants are encamped near us, intending to keep the Sabbath here. Feed is very poor on this side but by driving the[m] onto an island they can get enough to eat. This route is now very pleasant, as there is no way to cross except by swimming, either for man or beast. They will have to be guarded while there as Indians are plenty. Several of the young men swam over, and then with long ropes pulled a couple of wash tubs over containing dry clothes and other articles of comfort and convenience.

July 17th   Had two meetings both well attended. Other spare time was devoted to singing.

July 18th   The boys are calling loudly from their side for breakfast and tobacco. The horses caused them a great deal of trouble as they were unwilling to be caught, and after being caught were unwilling to swim. George Ebey and Hobart, being the best swimmers had to bear the greatest share of the labor. George came over in the morning and got some breakfast, but Hobart had to stay there until all the stock had crossed, and was so exhausted that he could scarcely swim over.

All this took until nearly noon, consequently we did not

---

[16] There were several Burns families in Jackson Co. in the 1850's, but this one is unidentified.

travel far and we encamp again near our old friend Platte. A rainy and unpleasant evening

July 19th   Another day of traveling towards the setting sun, and we encamp near a small clear stream, where there is a spring of comparitively good water. One of our faithful oxen had to be abandoned on account of lameness.

July 20th   Were hindered this morning by missing cattle. After starting found good roads, most of the way. Our light wagon had the misfortune to get one of its hubs broken, but Father brought a good share of Yankee wisdom to bear upon it, and it was soon all right. Encamped in a very pleasant place where water is convenient and plenty of sage brush for fuel.

July 21st   Started in good season and about noon reached the Sweetwater, a swift clear stream. Later in the day passed Independence Rock. We forded the river here and were somewhat hindered. Encamped near the river where grass is abundant. We have here a frightful as well as romantic situation. Just back of us Independence Rock stands out in bold relief, and in front of us yawns the Devils Gate.

July 22nd   To day a party of us go to explore the Gate, and find the place as wild and rugged as could be imagined.

Passed a trading post and saw the first house that we have seen since leaving Kanesville. A smart shower came up in the afternoon and those of us who were walking in advance of the train got a nice soaking.

July 23d   Started rather early and traveled steady all day   Our road ran for the most part near the river, and was rather rough. We had to go some distance from the road to find grass.

July 24th   Had preaching but our prayer meeting was omitted on account of the rain. Mary is quite unwell to day, but better towards evening and able to walk around. Again the peace of our company has been disturbed by family troubles. George Ebey and Will Sells have become dissatisfied by either real or fancied ill usage, and threaten strongly of leaving on account of some circumstances of a peculiar nature   Mr Royal and his wife wish them to leave the company entirely, but this is not their intention, they like the company, and only want to find some other place in it. Phil too — who every day gives some evidence of his weak mind, thinks he will leave if they do. We know no cause for this resolution.

July 25th   The boys — George and Will — concluded to put their oxen onto Mr Burts wagon, bestow their share of the provisions therein and thus proceed. But after their things out of Mr Royals wagon, and having a general overhauling of all the bad deeds of which they had been guilty, and some besides, they made a treaty of peace, and concluded for the present at least to remain where they were. All this delayed us somewhat, but we traveled steadily all day to atone for it.

July 26th   Another quarrel among our neighbors and one which will not be so easily settled. It seems that Will sold his Uncle a yoke of cattle and now refuses to give them up. He used abusive language to his Uncle and aunt and finally went to Burts. We started on in the morning and left them and they did not overtake us until after dark.

July 27th   Forded the river early, and with the exception of a few hills found the roads very good. Father went to hunt a camping place towards night and when our usual time for camping came he was still missing. We kept on and traveled over hills, mountains, brooks, rivers and valleys until ten oclock at night.

We then began to be afraid that he was still behind us, and

came to a halt. Hobart took a horse and went to see what was ahead, but came back reporting no feed and no encampments. Still Father came not.

July 28th   Soon after starting we met Father back. He had taken another road from ours and came in ahead of us. He found in his travelings a Methodist preacher with whom he spent the night. This man whose name is Grey[17] wishes to join our company.

July 29th   There are plenty of Indians in this vicinity and they are rather more friendly then we desire. We overtook the company that Mr Gray is in and I supoose that they will travel with us. There are several families in the company.

July 30th   Heard from Stearns Company[18] to day. They are five days ahead of us, and anxious for us to overtake them.

Taking the advice of some traders we went several miles from the road to encamp, and were rewarded by finding excellent grass. There are 32 wagons here including our own company intending to remain over the Sabbath.

July 31st   There was a large congregation assembled for Divine service, and the Sacrament of the Lords Supper was administered probably for the first time between the Missouri River and the settlements of Oregon.

Aug. 1st   Found very good roads and traveled fast. Uncle has bought a new wagon, and by this dividing his load will

---

[17] The Rev. John Grey (Gray) was "a superanuate preacher... of the Methodist Episcopal Church," who, with his wife, Flora, took up a claim (#153) in Jackson Co. *Gen. Mat.*, III, p. 11. *See also* typescript in the Methodist Archives at Willamette Univ., Salem, "A Half Century and More Ago in Southern Oregon," no author. They became founders of Phoenix, Oreg.

[18] David and Fidelia Stearns were founders of Phoenix, Oreg. Marjorie Neill Helms, *Early Days in Phoenix, Oregon* (Grants Pass, 1954), p. 6 and *passim. See also* Joseph Gaston, *Centennial History of Oregon* (Chicago, 1912), III, pp. 568-9, for much information about the Stearns family, farmers and stockmen.

improve affairs   Did not encamp until after dark and then found no grass.

Aug 2nd   Started very early and traveled until we found good feed. Philips conduct gives us a great deal of trouble. He is both profane and bad tempered. We have treated him just as well as we know how, but he has his seasons of anger without any cause.

Aug. 3d   Found excellent roads all day. Started onto a desert directly after noon, but as we were not aware of the fact we did not take any water with us. Encamped where grass was abundant.

Aug 4th   Started early and found good roads. Reached Green River about 1 oclock   The cattle were extremely thirsty, and one of our cows drank so much that she died immediately. Crossed the Ferry and paid at the rate of five dollars per wagon. Traveled only a short distance and encamped.

Aug 5th   One of our wagons will have to be mended again. Found the roads in some places very hilly, but met with no accident. Found good grass and water at camping time.

Aug 6th   The roads were for the most part of the day mountainous. Encamped by a good spring, but the cattle have to be driven some distance from the road to find grass.

Aug 7th   Preaching as usual but a very small congregation.

Aug 8th   Roads all day very bad. Crossed a great number of small streams. At night we forded a branch of Green River and encamped near it.

Aug 9th   We had to ascend a very long steep hill, but after reaching the summit, we had good roads for several miles. Our course lay through lovely glades, and beautiful groves of fir, and then again more mountains. Thus we proceeded until a late hour of night and then had to encamp without suitable feed for our jaded teams.

Aug 10th   Roads very much improved, and at noon we reached a place where feed was excellent and abundant. So we pitched our tents and gave our animals a chance to rest. Dr Owen[19] and several other men, a large drove of cattle and sheep, are now traveling with us. Went fishing with our usual success, that is none at all.

Aug 11th   Forded the river   had good roads and went on our way rejoicing. Encamped again where there was the best of grass, and wood and water in plenty.

Aug 12   Again had very mountainous road   I feel almost too weary to night to write having walked several miles.

Aug 13th   Father was very unwell for a while to day caused by a rush of blood to the head, but after a few hours he was well again. Crossed a great many creeks of good water. Encamped in a pleasant valley where we have every convenience that way faring people can expect. Thus another Sabbath we are well provided for.

Aug 14th   This morning one of our best oxen was found dead, supposed to have eaten something poison. Preaching as usual

Aug 15th   Roads good and nothing occurred worthy of record.

Aug 16th   Visited the celebrated Soda and Steamboat Springs. Several of us walked a mile from the road to see an extinct volcano, but did not feel paid for our trouble.

---

[19] John Owen (Owens) was an old-timer in the Oreg. Country. He crossed the plains in 1843 from Missouri, helped Jesse and Lindsey Applegate survey the southern trail to Oregon in 1846. He settled on claim #92 in Jackson Co. in Dec. 1853. He later abandoned it to become an Indian Agent. How he got the apellation, "Dr." no one knows. Lindsey Applegate, "The South Road Expedition," *Oregon Historical Quarterly*, XXII, No. 1 (Mar., 1921), pp. 12-45.

Encamped without water but plenty of grass and sage brush for fuel.

Aug 17th   Crossed a beautiful clear stream. Water almost as cold as ice. In the afternoon the roads were very bad. One place particularly was so sideling that they tied ropes to the sides of the wagons and held with all their power to keep the wagons from rolling over. Encamped on Bannack River. Some of the company went fishing and caught a fine mess of trout, the first that we have had.

Aug 18th   Had very good roads the most of the way. There came up a terrific storm of hail and rain, accompanied by a strong wind but there was nothing injured.

Aug 19th   Nothing worthy of note occurred, and we encamped where the sage brush grew to the dignity of small trees.

Aug 20th   Had very bad roads, and the ladies will have another opportunity for exercise.

Encamped near to the mountains where there was a small stream of water but not sufficient for so much stock.

Aug 21st   Did not have but one service as it took so much time to drive the cattle two miles to water and back again. Some proposed hitching up the teams and moving our encampment. Thinking it preferable to driving the stock so far twice a day, but Father Royal says he will not put a yoke on one of his oxen on Sunday.

Aug 22nd   Roads tolerably good. Encamped near a good cold spring, but the cattle had to be driven to the mountains for grass.

Aug 23d   Found water at every turn of the road almost all day. We followed up a beautiful clear stream, crossed it four times and encamped upon it.

Aug 24th   Started earlier than usual and with the exception of one small hill, the roads were very good. One of our horses is getting lame and will have to be turned loose. To night we make our home on a branch of Raft River.

Aug 25th   Good roads, abundant pure water and a lovely spot for our encampment.

Aug 26th   Rode on back in the morning in company with Maria Ducker.[20] Passed through Pyramid Circle. The Pyramids resemble more than anything else petrified hay stacks. Broke the wagon tongue and we will have to walk, but we are accustomed to that

Aug 27th   Had the worst roads that I ever saw. Up and down all day long, Sometimes on the top of a high mountain, and then again in the valley   Sometimes crossing creeks and then wandering through mazes of luxuriant sage brush. Encamped on Goose Creek where there was plenty of grass, although at some distance from the road.

Aug 28th   The winds blew and the rains fell, and as our cloth house was founded upon the sand of course it fell. Phil and I were standing in the door of the tent and did not have time to escape, but shared in the general overthrow and were rolled some distance enveloped in the folds of the tent before we could regain our footing

Aug 29th   Nothing occurred to disturb our usual peace and quiet and we encamped again on Goose Creek

Aug 30th   Had very good roads and traveled until very late before we could find water. There is scarcely a spear of grass, and the poor animals will have to suffer the consequences.

---

[20] Maria Ducker was the daughter of William and Sarah Ducker, settlers in Jackson Co. *Gen Mat.*, IV, p. 79. Maria has been lost track of and has not been found in the records, probably because she married and changed names. This is one of the problems associated with research on women's history.

Aug 31st   Started early in the morning and traveled until we found grass. Mr Royals Gray and Burt with their teams stopped before we did. After baiting our teams we started again and traveled until nearly dark before we could find water.

Sep 1st   Traveled about half a day and encamped and were overtaken by the rest of the company.

Sep 2nd   Started late, had fine roads, and encamped early.

Sep 3d   Only traveled about five miles, and then let the cattle rest and graze.

Sep 4th   We spend the Sabbath in this lovely spot. One service as usual.

Sep 5th   Mr Fletcher Royals upset his wagon with the family in it but no one was injured.

Sep 6th   Very hilly roads in the forenoon, but in the afternoon they were greatly improved.

Sep 7th   Reached the Humboldt River and forded   *A bad bank* to go down, and one of the wagons was upset, but no damage sustained. After camping the stock was driven across the river where grass was good. Were visited by a lot of Digger Indians. They are a filthy thieving race, and would not scruple to take a persons life if could be done without risking their own.

Sep 8th   Made a short drive and encamped. Again tried the fishing business but found it very dull

Sep 9th   No occurences worthy of mention. We now travel about half a day and rest the other half to let the cattle recruit.

Sep 10th   Several of our family are quite unwell at this time. It is surprising that in so large a company as this there should be so little sickness.

Sep 11th   Mother is quite unwell to day. A digger came to see us and came into the tent. Omar Burt happened to be in and made signs to him   Mother had the small pox whereupon our dusky guest separated and was seen no more

Several of our company went to visit a boiling spring, and report it a great curiosity.

Sep 12th   Had very bad roads, and did not encamp until after dark.

Sep 13th   Traveled only a short distance and then stopped for the benefit of the cattle.

Sep 14th   Had very rocky hilly roads, and traveled until late.

Sep 15th   In the morning the roads were rather bad, but after a time became more level. The dust is very oppressive in some places being half way up to the wagon hubs.

The nights are becoming so cool as to be uncomfortable.

Sep 16th   One of our cows was left behind, and Father went back after her on horseback. As he was returning to the company again, a Digger came out of the Willows and wanted to talk with him. One sight of his revolver however was sufficient to clear the road.

Sep 17th   Very windy and cold. Nothing occurred worthy of mention. About 20 Indians came to our encampment, but we have very little to do with them.

Sep 18th   Preaching as usual.
Sep 19th   Fine weather, good health and excellent roads.
Sep 20th   Roads sandy but otherwise good. Only travelled half a day.

Sep 21st   Came to a very bad slough, but crossed without much trouble   Encamped near the river.
Sep 22nd   Traveled very slowly on account of sandy roads. Grass is very scarce.

Sep 23d   Nothing special occurred, and we encamp where there is excellent feed

Sep 24th   We are going to stop here one day and cut hay to do the cattle in crossing the desert. We have not arrived at the Big Meadows yet, but as grass is good here we wish to make sure of it.

Sep 25th   There are in the company several that are almost entirely out of provisions, and we think best to travel every day that we can. This is agreed to by all except Mr Royals.

Sep 26th   Came to the Junction of the California and Oregon roads and are now fairly out upon the desert. Came to water at night but it was not good and the cattle would not drink it. Started on again and traveled until night and encamped.

Sep 27th   Started very early and traveled until noon when we came to Rabbit Hole Springs. Water plenty but poor. Went from here a few miles then stopped and got supper started again and traveled until about 10 oclock and encamped.

Sep 28th   Started long before daylight and traveled until we came to Black Rock Springs. Here we stopped and got breakfast. The water in the spring is boiling hot, but below some distance it gets cool enough for cattle to drink. Started again & came to very good grass and more hot springs.

Sep 29th   Started before sun rise and in the gray light of the early morning & counted the smokes from 22 hot springs all within the distance of half a mile. At night we found good grass and water.

Sep 30th   Traveled about 4 miles and stopped for the day. Excellent water and good grass.

Oct 1st   Roads very sandy and hard on teams. Encamped in a very good place

Oct 2nd   Roads very hilly and rocky, consequently traveled slowly. Encamped just as we entered Big Rock Canon   A good spring some distance above us on the side of the mountain.

Oct 3d   The Canon proved to be very long and it was late before we got through. Our light horse wagon has broken down completely and will have to be abandoned.

Oct 4th   Two men John Owens, and a Frenchman named Batis[21] have gone forward to get provisions and bring to those who are without. Another Canon short but very bad. To avoid it we went around over the mountains. The grass here is dry but abundant and water good.

Oct 5th   No water at our present encampment

Oct 6th   Mrs Fletcher Royal has a fine boy,[22] so we learn from the Doctor who went back to their encampment.

Oct 7th   Very bad hilly roads. Encamped near a hot spring.

Oct 8th   Traveled all day through excellent grass and found in like region at night.

Oct 9th   Traveled half a day and encamped.

oct 10th   Several of us started in advance of the teams and went over the Sierra Nevada Mountains. It was very cold and the boys built a fire under a large cedar, and we staid there until the wagons came up.

Oct 11th   Roads very rocky, making unpleasant either to

[21]"Batis" was probably a former Hudson's Bay Co. French trapper, who, with John Owen, had long been in the Oreg. Country. The surname "Jean Baptiste" was ubiquitous among the French Canadians. An interesting note in the land records shows a "Baptist Zegus" (?) listed as a witness for John Owen's abandonment of his Jackson Co. claim. American officials had a hard time with French names. *Gen. Mat.*, IV, p. 100.

[22]This baby was Miller G. Royal. He grew up to become an educator, served as principal of So. Oreg. College (now a state college), for a period. His wife of many years was Tirzah H. (Bigelow) Royal. A.G. Walling, *History of Southern Oregon* (Portland, 1884), p. 506.

walk or ride. Wild plums are abundant here but so hard and sour that they are not very good. To night we have a beautiful camping place, among the stately pine trees.

Oct 12th   It is snowing quite hard this morning which makes it uncomfortable for those who are thinly clad, and several of Dr Owens hands are in that condition. Good roads and no accidents.

Oct 13th   This morning the unwelcome discovery was made that the Indians had stolen all our horses, five in number, also two of Mr Hoffmans[23] and made good their escape. We met a party of soldiers and told them about Mr Royals people and they hurried back to find them.

Oct 14th   Roads rocky enough to break every wagon to pieces   Encamped about noon and waited for Mr Royals to overtake us, which they did soon after dark. Several of the women joined together and got as good a supper for them as possible and had it ready for them on their arrival.

Oct 15th   Road continue[s] to be very rocky, and besides are very mountainous

Oct 16th   Mrs Royal is unable to travel, and a portion of the soldiers stay with them. We go on to the Natural Bridge on Lost River, where we expect to be hindered by the sheep.

Oct 17th   Roads sometimes rocky and sometimes good Encamped near Clear Lake.

Oct 18th   Started in good season, and after some high mountains we found the roads level. Traveled until after dark before we encamped.

Oct 19th   Crossed the Bridge on Lost River without

---

[23] William and Caroline B. Hoffman settled in Jackson Co. on Claim #50. In the So. Oreg. Hist. Museum in Jacksonville are the Hoffman Family Papers, including several diaries. *Gen. Mat.*, III (Portland, 1962), p. 4. He was listed as an insurance agent in the 1880 Jackson Co. census.

accident. It is a natural bridge of rocks, and is under water. Several of us felt some fears about riding over this place, and walked across on a little natural foot bridge, where the water was about six inches deep. Feed very poor at our present encampment

Oct 20th Had a mountainous road nearly all day, and encamped without water, but found excellent grass.

Oct 21st Good roads most of the day. Found good feed for our faithful oxen.

Oct 22nd Traveled half a day. Crossed Klamath River and encamped. The sheep are very troublesome about crossing.

Oct 23d Got the sheep over to day, some in wagons and some by swimming.

Oct 24th Horrid roads all day, and traveled until late. Mr Hoffmans wagons and one of Mr Burts did not succeed in getting over the mountains.

Oct 25th With the exception of a long bad hill to go down, we had very good roads. Encamped early in a good place. Mr Royals people are encamped near us.

Oct. 26th Rained all day, enough to make the roads very slippery. A tedious days journey, but we are at last over the mountains, where we have good water and excellent bunch grass.

Oct 27th We are now in the white settlements, and through our long tedious trip, safe and sound.

"My Journal"
❦ Hannah Tapfield King

INTRODUCTION

The Hannah Tapfield King journal is that of a cultured English lady whose writing is introspective, questioning, philosophical. She had spent most of her life in that world center of learning, Cambridge, England. She could make reference to English poets, the Anglican *Book of Common Prayer*,[1] and the *Bible*. Her journal was not some special creation begun to record a journey, but a lifelong practice. She asked questions of herself, probed the motives and practices of other persons, and recorded her answers and conclusions about such probings. In her later years she reminisced about her home in England:

> The university town of Cambridge, England, I am proud to say, is the place of my nativity. I was reared among its classic shades and bowers. For the last thirty years America has been my adopted country, and I love her with a loyal and devoted appreciation, but the home and haunts of childhood and youth, leave on every mind indelible impressions and when brought to focus upon the past as at the present moment, "The distant spires and antique towers rise up before me in all their vividness by the power of that most wonderful faculty, Memory."[2]

Hannah Dorcas Tapfield was born on March 16, 1808, to Mary Lawson and Peter Tapfield in Sawston, Cambridgeshire. The Tapfields were devoted members of the Church of England. Her grandfather had been a rector of that church. Her father was a businessman who traveled a great deal. She related years later how, at her father's suggestion, she wrote him many letters when

[1] See her entry for July 10.

[2] This quote and others below, also much information, came from "My Story — Hannah T. King," *Treasures of Pioneer History*, III (Salt Lake City, 1954), pp. 43-45.

he was away from home. Those letters were her first effort at
written expression. Her parents also encouraged her to keep a
journal and "a book for choice extracts." She branched out in her
writing, sending short pieces to local papers, where they were
often published. After some years of married life she wrote *The
Toilet* and *Three Eras*, "one for my girls and the other for the
boys." These books, she reminisced later, "were patronized by
the aristocracy of England." She also wrote some poetry.

Hannah Tapfield and a young farmer named Thomas Owen
King were married on April 6, 1824. In the years that followed
Hannah bore ten children, only four of whom lived to adulthood.[3]
As the years went by, Thomas King became more successful as a
farmer. The English census of 1851 listed him as the cultivator of
350 acres and the "employer of 14 labourers." Their homestead
was called Dernford Farm or Dernford Dale, near Sawston, seven
miles south of Cambridge.

In 1849, a young woman who worked in the King house as a
seamstress, Ann Newling,[4] age 22, asked if she could talk to
Hannah about her newly-espoused religion, The Church of Jesus
Christ of Latter-Day Saints. The upshot of this and other private
talks was that Hannah King and her 18-year-old daughter,
Georgiana, were baptized by Joseph W. Johnson into the
Mormon faith on November 4, 1850. Thomas King did not
become a Mormon, but he did not discourage his wife.

On January 24, 1853, the entire family left England for the
long journey to Utah. They crossed the Atlantic from Liverpool
to New Orleans in the sailing ship, *Golconda*. The next leg of
their journey took them by river boat up the Mississippi to
Keokuk, a jumping-off point for the Mormon trail across Iowa.
There, with the help of emissaries of the church, Horace
Eldredge and Hector C. Haight,[5] they put together teams and
wagons, took in needed supplies, and departed for the promised

---

[3] Third and Fourth Generation Family Archive Records, Genealogical Society of
Utah, S.L.C.

[4] Her name appears with the names of the Thomas Owen King family in the 1851
census of England, Cambridgeshire.

[5] See "Dramatic Personae" which follows, p. 88.

HANNAH TAPFIELD KING

Taken from a pioneer photo by C.R. Savage, and used with the permission of The
Daughters of Utah Pioneers, Salt Lake City, Utah.

land. They traveled to Council Bluffs, where they crossed the Missouri, and followed the traditional Platte River route across Nebraska, and arrived in Salt Lake City on September 19.

In the following years, Thomas King began farming again, while Hannah became deeply involved in the life of the pioneer Mormon community. She made friends with other woman leaders such as Eliza R. Snow and Martha Spence Heywood.[6] She participated in the Polysophical Society,[7] an intellectual Mormon discussion group open to both men and women. She wrote both prose and poetry for the *Woman's Exponent.* Two of her books were published: *The Women of the Scriptures* in 1878 (published by Dernford House, Salt Lake City); and, in 1879, *Songs of the Heart,* a book of poetry.

Now a word about her family:

The oldest daughter was Georgiana, age 22, who had also become a Mormon in 1850. Georgiana was married April 2, 1852, to the leader of the traveling group, Claudius Victor Spencer, a pioneer Mormon out of Massachusetts, who had been active as a missionary in England. Spencer is mentioned time after time in Hannah's journal, sometimes in a friendly, sometimes in a suspicious way. Georgiana died tragically on September 26, 1853,[8] soon after the family arrived in Salt Lake City.

A second daughter, Louisa, age 20, also traveled with the party. She would be married to Claudius V. Spencer less than a month after her sister's death, on October 9, 1853.[9]

Bertha Mary King, age 19, was mentioned a number of times in Hannah's journal.[10] Hannah speculated as to whether Claudius Spencer was trying to develop a serious relationship with Bertha,

---

[6] Maureen Ursenbach (Beecher), "Three Women and the Life of the Mind," *Utah Hist. Quarterly,* XLIII, No. 1 (Winter, 1975), pp. 26-40; Juanita Brooks, Edit., *Not by Bread Alone, The Journal of Martha Spence Heywood, 1850-56* (Salt Lake City, 1978).

[7] Joseph Heinerman, "Early Utah Pioneer Cultural Societies," *Utah Hist. Quarterly,* XLVII, No. 1 (Winter, 1979), pp. 76, 78-79.

[8] Hannah King's Journal entry for Monday, September 26, 1853.

[9] Third and Fourth Generation Family Archive Records, *op. cit.;* also *Deseret News,* January 26, 1912, p. 5.

[10] *Ibid.*

and/or whether Bertha was in turn responding to his approaches. There are several passages in the journal about this situation which someone has crossed out. We have sought to reconstruct them through a comparison with a typescript.

Thomas Owen King, Jr.,[11] a 13-year-old boy on the journey, received a great deal of Hannah's attention. He continually suffered from impaired health. In her introspective way Hannah expressed her thoughts about the precarious condition of this bright young boy. In the long run his health was restored, and he lived a long life in his new homeland. He and Dorcas Debenham were married on May 22, 1868. She, too, was English-born from Norfolk. They lived in Salt Lake City until the late 1870's, when they moved to Almo, Cassia County, Idaho, where they lived out their lives as the parents of eight children. The *Deseret News* of December 24, 1921, announced the death of Thomas Owen King, Jr., in Almo, Idaho, on November 16. The *News* emphasized his experiences as a pony express rider.

Hannah King lived to old age. Her husband, Thomas, died on November 16, 1875. Hannah died in Salt Lake City at the home of daughter Louisa Spencer on September 25, 1886. News of her death received broad coverage in the press. The *Woman's Exponent*, for which she had written for many years, gave her nearly one page of coverage in a story about her death in its October 1 edition, and another page in an October 15 report of the funeral.

In the October 1 issue, an unsigned article by a friend quoted Hannah as saying not long before her death, "I write as a bird sings, free as the air and untrammeled; I care not who blames or praises, I sing for love of singing."

The Historical Department of the Church of Jesus Christ of Latter-Day Saints in Salt Lake City has been most cooperative in granting permission to use Hannah King's journal. We thank them for their aid. We are also grateful to Mrs. Addie Dyal of Salem, Oregon, who, while on a journey herself to Salt Lake City,

---

[11] *Deseret News*, December 24, 1921, p. 10; "Thomas Owen King," in *History of Idaho, The Gem of the Mountains*, II, (Chicago, 1920), pp. 943-4.

used her expert knowledge of genealogy to locate primary documents of the first order about Hannah Tapfield King and others associated with her.

DRAMATIS PERSONAE

As in the cases of other diarists in previous volumes of *Covered Wagon Women*, Hannah King mentions numerous individuals who were her fellow-travelers on the wagon train, and those whom they met along the way. Usually these descriptions are quite brief, such as Mr. So-and-so in the case of non-Mormons, or Br. So-and-so in the case of Mormons. She mentions visiting Sister Jones, yet there is no way of identifying Sister Jones, as is true of a number of other references. In the following list we have tried to identify as many of those references as possible.

The principal sources are Andrew Jensen, *Latter Day Saint Biographical Encyclopedia* (Salt Lake City, 1920); Davis Bitton, *Guide to Mormon Diaries and Autobiographies* (Provo, Utah, 1977); and Third and Fourth Generation Family Archive Records on microfilm from the Genealogical Society of Utah. These records are available in Church of Jesus Christ of Latter-Day Saints stake libraries. In this case we used the library of the South Stake in Salem, Oregon. Other references accompany the item they identify.

"Br. Arthur" could have been either Chrisopher Abel Arthur or his son, Christopher Jones Arthur. They traveled from Liverpool to New Orleans, up the Mississippi by riverboat, and by covered wagons to Salt Lake City in 1853. They were Welshmen from Abersychan, Monmouthshire. The older Arthur was a shopkeeper and baker. He was wealthy enough to pay for the emigration fare for forty persons. His wife died in 1852.

Reynolds Cahoon and his first wife, Thirza Stiles, arrived in Utah in 1848 with several Ohio-born children, four of whom were "stalwart sons." A second wife, Lucinda Roberts, bore three more children. Any two of the older boys could have given aid to the new arrivals. Stella Cahoon Shurtleff and Brent F. Cahoon, *Reynolds Cahoon and His Stalwart Sons* (S. L. C., 1960), *passim*.

Sister Clarissa and William Chambers from Gloucestershire, England, were on the same trek as the Kings. They had three children and settled in Cache Valley, Utah.

Samuel and Mary Ann Crawley were British Mormons from Bedfordshire. They settled in Kaysville, Utah.

Sister Dye was Harriet Coman Dye, who, with her husband Robert, a master bootmaker, migrated from Wymondham, Norfolk, England, in 1853. They had two children: Harriet, age 11, and Elizabeth, age 5. Harriet gave birth to a baby boy somewhere along the banks of the Platte. They settled in Salt Lake City.

Elders Horace Sunderlin Eldredge and Hector C. Haight were stationed in Keokuk in order to aid immigrants on the way to Salt Lake City. They were authorized to purchase supplies for the travelers as well as give advice and encouragement. A. M. Taylor, *Expeditions Westward: The Mormons and the Emigation of Their British Converts in the 19th Century* (Edinburgh, 1965), p. 125.

Hector C. Haight. *See* above.

John Joseph Hayes was a 25-year-old Irishman from Clonakilty, Cork. He and Rachel Eleanor Wagstaff of Bedfordshire met on board the ship *Elvira Owens* and married "between England and the U. S. A." on February 23, 1853. They settled in Pleasant Grove, Utah.

Joseph W. Johnson was the missionary in England of whom Hannah King had written in her journal on November 4, 1850: "I formally changed my religion and was baptized by Elder Joseph W. Johnson... my dear Georgiana at the same time..." Hannah King, "Journals," entry for November 4, 1850.

Eijah and Sarah Parfey Larkin had been friends of the King family in Cambridgeshire. They were baptized on Novmeber 3, 1845, and were married in April, 1847. They lived in the village of Chesterton. The Larkins had two children, George William, age 5, and Joseph Smith, age 2. Elijah was a policeman in England. They sailed for America ten years after the King family, arriving in Utah in the fall of 1863. Elijah became what we presently call a "security guard" in Salt Lake City.

William Warner Major was an active missionary in England. He traveled from Salt Lake City and met the Spencer wagon train enroute. Br. Major gave Hannah several letters and in turn took some of hers to England. He was a native of Bristol and became a Mormon while in London in 1842. He died on the English Mission on Oct. 2, 1864.

Philemon C. Merrill was one of the Mormon leaders who was met by the Claudius Spencer wagon train. The party was headed east on their way to carry out missions. "Captain" Merrill was a New Yorker who had become a Mormon in 1839. He was a major figure during the early years of the new faith.

Samuel Francis Neslen's name or initials (S. N.) are often mentioned in Hannah King's journal. The two became fast friends on the westward journey. He was a single man, age 22, from Suffolk Co. in England. He was traveling with his parents. The Neslens were co-travelers with the Kings from Liverpool, on the *Golconda*, up the Mississippi from New Orleans, and across the plains. Samuel and his brother, Robert, returned to England on a brief mission. Samuel became quite ill in England, nearly collapsing one day on London Bridge. He and Robert sailed for New York on Jan. 21, 1858. Samuel died on May 13, 1858, in Williamsburg, Va.

Daniel Spencer was the 58-year-old father of Claudius. The King family spent their first days in Salt Lake City at his home. They had known Daniel in England, where he had stayed behind on a mission, that lasted from 1852 to 1856.

Henry and Ann Preece Walker emigrated from Bullingham, Herefordshire, in 1853 as members of the Claudius V. Spencer ox company. They settled in Salt Lake City.

George B. Wallace was one of the missionaries in England who had been instrumental in influencing Hannah King to Mormonism. They were friends for many years, and Wallace was the main speaker at her funeral on September 28, 1886. *Woman's Exponent*, Oct. 1, 1886. He said he had met many noble women, but he never met but one Hannah T. King.

"MY JOURNAL"

[May] 20th [Iowa]   Lovely morning — Oh! this is a sweet spot — the same party breakfasted with us — at Eleven I made them Eggs beaten up with wine and Brandy — They dined with us — I then went & sat in my carriage as usual   Br Eldredge came & Talked with us — In the course of our talk, it came out he had 2 wives! He was the

first man that ever confessed that to me   I exclaimed Oh!
Br Eldredge! he is a good man — I liked him as soon as I saw
him   There is a chaste look about him —

Saturday 21st   Lovely day   In the Evening I went for a
walk alone — I shall long remember this lovely location — I
do so much enjoy it — Saturday night & Sunday morning
Violent thunder storm and poured with rain which
continued until Sunday 22   I had my break fast & dinner in
my carriage   We all felt triste — Had it been fine we should
have had much company. Went to bed early — in the night
was awoke by some one touching the Carriage. looked out of
the window & saw S.N. sitting over a fire he was on watch —
felt rather poetical about it but have not yet Embodied my
thoughts —

May 25   left our late Locality and went up the Hill   Here
we have been till this morning

May 27th   My first daughter's birthday[1] — She would
have been 24 or 5 — but she has gone to her Father in
Heaven   Walked alone in the Evening down to our late
Location   enjoyed it — a meeting in the Evening to
organize the company — Mrs Neslen complained to me and
seemed in a bad spirit — 27th   Left again & came into our
present Location — a lovely spot! Oh! how I enjoy these
Exquisite places — They are my delight! and I feel I have
nothing to regret   "The lines have fallen to me in pleasant
places" literally and I Bless God for all things   would that
all were as happy as I am — S.N. is often my companion —
always my friend & confident

28   Left Sugar Creek at 8 A M and journied to the prarie a

---

[1] The "first daughter" had been Margaret, born May 27, 1827, in Sawston,
Cambridgeshire. She died in July, 1828. There had been a stillborn son in 1825. A
second daughter, Charlotte, was born on Jan. 2, 1829, and died the following April 29.
Third and Fourth Generation Family Records, Genealogical Society of Utah.

distance of about 15 miles where we camped — We passed
thro' Farmington and over the Mississippi [Des Moines],
Just before we reached our destination we had nearly had a
serious accident — Going down a steep short hill with a
muddy place at the foot of it our Horses sank in up to the
middle & could not extricate themselves or the Carriage —
They got them out and then Br Arthur brought his horses &
fastened them to the back of the Carriage and drew it out —
The brethren pushing at the wheels   One of our Horses in
the morning had been very gay and had broken the whipple
tree — which we had stopped to get mended. had he been in
it might have been serious affair — but every thing proves
daily — hourly to me that "Whatever is — is right" when
applied to the people of God! I feel thro' all things, to rejoice
and to Thank Him always, for indeed He has been very good
to me from the beginning of my life even to the present
moment — and I daily experience "Not more than others I
deserve — yet God hath given me more" —

Sunday May 29th   Had a good night and awoke refreshed
— being very tired last night   I wish Mr Shores could have
come again to take me out for a drive once more — he
certainly was very kind, and kindness in a foreign Land is
doubly valuable — how it calls out the heart with it's noblest
and best affections —

Monday arose early, and started. had to pass a terrible place
— but Claudius went forward & they laid down trees &
bushes & we got over pretty well — had nearly had an
accident with the carriage, but our Guardian Angels were
around us, & it all passed off with a little fright! — Camped
soon after we passed "Dog Town —" walked at the back of
the Camp in the Evening, & fell in with a Scotchman — he
had been in America some Years — Mr King bought a Yoke
of Oxen of him — he brought them up next morning and

drove me over a bridge & places that I was afraid to pass —
we talked much during the Time, and he seemed pleased —
and said he hoped we should meet again — also a friend of
his a nice man who had been in England — I drove over
some horrid places, which made me very nervous for long
after — Often when coming to a dangerous place I have
stopped the Horses & prayed the Lord to give His Angels
charge of us — I ve got over — Sometimes I would call Anne
when no man could be got & she would head the Horses or
perhaps drive them thro' — At last we camped near String
Town — a thunder storm came on us as soon as the Tent was
put up — I had not felt well for some days & this Evening I
feared was going to have an attack of erysiplas — I had worn
my English bonnet this day and the Sun scorched my face —
it felt on fire — Mr Shores took particular pains to caution
us against getting our complexions spoilt — even Anne he
talked to about covering her arms — he said he hated to see a
Woman's fine skin burned up — Mr Shores! Thou wert a
Man!! Went to bed Early & had a tolerable night — Was
awake with the men greasing my carriage wheels wherein I
was sleeping   I found my face & eyes swollen lips parched
& tongue white — I have been excited by driving over these
awful places — however I eat 2 or 3 mouthfuls & mounted
my post i e to drive the Horses — They are pets [unreadable
word] — but plenty of spirit and such frightful places! I feel
sure few women (English) dare drive over where I have gone
— and it has shaken my nerves into a muddle — at ½ past 2
a Thunder storm came on — Could do nothing but sit still
and *wait* — it poured down in torrents   At last we got some
tea — I did not get out of the Carriage — Anne brought it to
me and I enjoyed it as well or better than I ever did in my
drawing room — I then made part of the bosom of a shirt for
Tom Owen — and made up my Journal so far — Thank

God for all things — I rejoice ever more and am grateful that I feel well to night — Bertha not very well — The rest quite well —

Wednesday 8th, June Anniversary of Margaret's wedding day, 20 years ago! It is some days since I journalized — Much has transpired of small matters but which at this time seem all importance — True it is that "trifles make the sum of human things"

[Here she writes an entry dated June 1, which tells of personal problems with Bertha. Some one has crossed these lines out (Bertha?), but we have ferreted them out with the help of the typescript.]

The 1st of June   Bertha has taken poorly & has continued up till the present time — I believe it is the Lords plan to punish her for a complaining disobedient Spirit to which she has forever given way to and had not been produced by this Journey or anything attendant on it — it seems inherant in her   had she only given way to it I should have thought the present circumstances were too trying for her but such is not the case   For when surrounded by all that mortal Girl could wish she was discontented as at the present time and that complaining — unhappy spirit has attended her every step of our voyage & journey — & my heart tells me it is necessary that she should be afflicted that she may be brought to know herself — I have prayed much a bout her, and give her entirely into the hands of the Lord to do as He pleases with her for I have long felt she was more than I could manage! —

June 6th   a baby died — Oh! by the bye on Sunday we camped on a beautiful hill & had afternoon service and all seemed to enjoy it much. The sacrament was administered — a few strangers were present who expressed themselves much pleased & Edified   Friday morning we came down the steepest & most frightful hill I ever saw — Tho' we had passed thro' a splendid Country before we came to it — Monday Sister How's baby died & was buried the next morning before we started — we then travelled on thro' the new Town of Chariton [Iowa] —

June 7th   Went to a Store and bought a few things that we needed and we then came on to our camping place this morning —

June 8th   We started at 8 oc but it came on rain and we were obliged to Camp at 12 oc — All very wet. I brought Bertha in the carriage — but she complained of cramped limbs & fatigue so she might as well have been in the wagon — here we are all wet & uncomfortable externally but with a tolerable degree of peace and equanimity   for myself I feel happy all the day, and only wish that all surrounding spirits were as happy & peaceful as my own — I have been blest with good health except sea sickness & debility in consequence ever since I left England — and I am a marvel to myself, for truly I have had many trials — but then God has blest me every day — and raised up friends that have been kind & good to me even in a foreign land — I have ever found friends or at any rate one friend go where I might that has stuck closer to me than a brother! —

Saturday June 12th   started at ¼ to nine in the morning   reached Pisgah about 4 — and our Camping place about 5 oc   Had tea & went to bed soon — Anne washed some things for us —

[Once again several lines are crossed out. We have again used the typewritten copy to aid in seeking the exact words.] Bertha still ill and very trouble some — she is a strange unaccountable girl! I feel she did not enter this Church with the right spirit of the Church — & has not progressed in it   Yet *she came in of her own will & pleasure*

Here I take a breathing pause. — it seems hardly worth while to write every days journal for they consist all the time of thunder storms — mud holes making bridges — getting wet thro' beds and all   I note down some of these, and then add how I enjoy my Carriage bed & how thankful I am for my many blessings &c &c

June 24th — 53. Yesterday morning very busy packing in the waggons — re-arranging the things — luggage &c &c   In the afternoon Mr King Saml Neslen and I went to the Bluff City [Council Bluffs] to see Sister Merrill — She was quite overjoyed at seeing us — She had letters for me from Br Johnson, Wallace, and Larkin as also one from Mr Barber — but Oh! That ugly little word — They were in a box that had not yet arrived — and indeed she almost feared was lost!!! Heighho! how trying are such things   But 'tis vain to repine — disappointment in such matters appears to be my lot — or rather I seem in my present dearth to be unable to lose any thing — The Bluff City is most beautifully situated   it is a spot marvelous for its beauty — but the Houses are poor — and the people look queer and uncultivated — S. N. and I richly enjoyed ourselves — We had some delicious coffee with Sister Crawley — where Sister Merrill is staying   We also called on Sister Bray — then came home rather late — Mr King being very nervous on acc of the bad road — However at last we got into Camp safely and to bed — Claudius sent me a glass of port wine, enjoyed it much. — S. N. came to bid me good night. I anticipate that "Good night God Bless You" as the Ultimatum of the good things I experience thro' the day — He has been ever kind — gentle and respectful to me — and in the dearth and the wild of this Journey such are to be blessings that I cannot over look   I acknowledge the kindness of the Lord in sending him to me — in my present

circumstances for whom can I make a friend of? — I dare not
tell Mr King much that has troubled me and does still — he
came out for the love of his family and for the cause of God &
the love I bare him   I wish to make his path as smooth as I
can — My son is a child — I cannot tell him & Claudius I
have not full confidence in — and he holds me aloof and is
often unkind to me — and inconsiderate of my feelings but
Samuel is *wise* & kind, & withal my friend and I can *trust
him with my life* if need be — and all that is dear to me —
Oh! my Father! give Thine angels charge concerning them
— for in my present dearth all things are Valuable! that is, of
love & kindness   Mr King and Claudius gone off to buy a
waggon and cattle — Mr K. to give him 43 — 10S and he
will buy them and bring on our Luggage but the waggon &
cattle are to be *his* all the time! I don't understand this logic!
Well I am in a school, and if I receive the lessons aright, I
shall be improved by them   if not, they will do me harm —
Oh! my Father! hold me and bless me or how shall I proceed?
Last day of peace — encamped on the banks of the Missouri
River — I feel weary today and my Spirit flags — drove
thro' the water up to the axel of the carriage — few women
would have cared to have done it — I went behind Claudius
— Met two brethren in the water — One turned and walked
by my Carriage till I was out of the "deep waters"   it was
very kind of him & I will not forget it   I must learn his
name! I know his face well   I wish I could get my letters —
but it is a satisfaction to know they have written — Bless the
Lord for the kind friends that I have — it is in answer to B
Larkins' prayers & his words   Certainly no woman had
ever had more disinterested Love & Kindness offered to her
than I have ever had bestowed on me! & thank God, for it is
better to me than Gold or Silver — Here follow a few petty
disagreeables — Tho' not petty at the time to those who

were made to feel them — but I will not write them down —
let them go! — A few weeks more and I shall enter that
renowned place, "The Valley" I feel I cannot analyze my
feelings at the present time — They are so complicated —
and I see thro a glass very darkly. There is a strong Vein of
pleasure and happiness and then there are uncertainties —
but my Father, Thou Knowest — I have given all my affairs
into Thy Keeping — & I know in whom I have trusted —
This night a dreadful thunderstorm & other annoyances —
here follow some more remarks which I throw into my
Oblivious Reservoir — and I finish by blessing the Lord for
his goodness!

July 3rd — Sunday. — Lovely morning — No prayers   I
feel starved spiritually — but soon we will hear the prophets
voice — S. N., Lizzie & I walked to the top of one of the
beautiful hills that surround this spot — Sat on the top,
Lizzie gathered some "fat hen"[2] for dinner — descended &
returned home — put my Carriage in order read in the Bible
& wrote — The sun is now setting on those beautiful hills —
The Cattle are feeding as tho' they knew it was their supper
time — and all around looking beautiful   The girls are in
the Tent talking — Anne washing the supper things — Mr
King sitting at the side of the Tent & Claudius with him —
talking! S. N. walking around our circle — he ever appears
to be happy to be near us — & I feel he is my friend & does
me good — How I wish I could hear from my dear
parents   it would comfort me and be a delight — Here
follow a pouring out of sorrowful feelings — always winding
up with Thankfulness for my great blessings — seven oc
same day — Claudius gave me a glass of port wine being the
4th of July!! and asked me for a Toast for my adopted

---

[2] *Chenopodium alban*, a succulent or fleshy-leaved plant also called "shepherd's
purse." W. K. Martin, *Concise British Flora in Colour* (London, 1965), plate 71.

Country! This filled up my heart which was full before — I got out of the Tent and walked to the top of one of these beautiful Hills — where I sat down & prayed & thought. Then returned; — Georgey came & sat in my carriage also Br Robert — Then he went and Sam came   The fire flies are beautiful here   They are like diamond dust over every thing at night.

7th   Better this morning — Anne brought me, with her accustomed attention, some tea & toast, enjoyed it much. felt better — at 7 oc started on our way — [unreadable word.] have felt better to day as S. N. said I should last night — Got safe into camp & to bed. Anne has been very attentive to me and her duties generally and this is something on the plains   Started at 7 oc — nice morning — a flat road — high grass   road not very good — camped for an hour to water the cattle — We also got some Refreshments Started again & got to our Camping place about 4 oc — a tolerable nice place — had tea &c — felt better as S. N. said I should   he came & sat with me a short time at luncheon hour — mosquitoes troublesome — but all things considered all is well   My heart rejoices that every day we are approaching nearer the Valley. I long for my letters — dreamt last night that Louie & Mr Barber were married in secret   saw him very plainly — I know all about it

9th   Started at 4 oc in the morning — got to a camping place at 9 — had breakfast — On again — crossed the Platte River — last night we had a syllabub.[3] S. and R. Neslen with us — A tempest in the night — Alarm from the Watch at 3 oc that the Cattle were gone astray? false report — made partly a sun bonnet to day — Went to bed — slept nicely —

10th   Rose at ½6 — got ready to start at 7 — Went 10

[3] A *syllabub* or *sillabub* was a concoction of sweetened milk or cream to which wine or cider was added and whipped up into a frothy dessert.

miles to Loup Fork Ferry   ferried over by 5 oc PM   set the wagon & tent — washed & had tea   I wrote this much of my Journal and here I feel to thank Thee Oh My Father for Thy Great and boundless Goodness to me & mine and to the Camp generally for His Great Kindness to us on this long Journey — truly His Hand has been displayed almost palpably to us His frail & erring people! — This is the 7th Sunday after Trinity[4]   I recall how often we have sung that beautiful collect and its no less beautiful accompaniment — and a 1000 recollections crowd upon me — S. & R. Neslen came into our Tent in the evening — We sang — a beautiful moonlight night — soon all went to bed   S. N. & I walked thro' the Camp last thing — then bade good night at the Carriage door —

11th   Woke in the morning with the cry that the Cattle were all gone astray!! All the men called up! false alarm!! — at 6 oc S. N. put two lovely Tiger Lillies thro' the curtains of my Carriage — The offering pleasd me — every kind act however small seems a blessing in the dearth of the present time — He is ever kind to me — God sent him to me! — We went off to a pretty Camping place late — but a regular mosquitoe bottom —

12th   Wet morning   set off — went on till the Evening   Camped again — S. N. not well — came and sat in the Carriage with me — had some nice conversation — as we always do when we talk at all   bid him "Good night" and to bed — at 9 or before.

13th   Slept feverish and awoke unrefreshed — Thundered in the night — off at 9 — not good roads — slight mud holes

---

[4] She was referring to the 1839 edition of the *Book of Common Prayer* of the Anglican Church. The Collect for the Seventh Sunday after Trinity read as follows in that edition: "Lord of all power and might, who art the author and giver of all good things; Graft in our hearts the love of thy Name, increase in us true religion, nourish us with all goodness, and of thy great mercy keep us in the same; through Jesus Christ our Lord. *Amen."*

— & no good water — got to a place at 4 oc where there was some tolerable good water long grass & hosts of snakes! which destroy my happiness — Got into the Carriage and finished my sunbonnet for Georgey   Carried it into the Tent when I went to tea — had nice tea & toast bacon — pudding & rice — enjoyed it much   Felt grateful for all things & happy — Mr King was in a grumbling spirit which marred it as he often does — finding fault with every thing — This is his way at times — he would do it were he surrounded with all he wished — so I do not feel so bad over it — I detest a grumbling spirit — I had washed him and brushed his hair & did what I could for him — S. N. a little better — This morning before starting I gave him a glass of new Milk with some brandy in it — I love to do good — & he says I always do him good   I have not much Scope now — but I do all I can and that the Lord will accept —

14th   A long day's travel   all weary and worn — I felt used up — All things looked dark — The dark things darker — and the bright things clouded — much that I have suffered crowds upon my mind — the harshness I have suffered the *changes* — the privations — all — all crowded upon me and steeped my soul in the waters of Marah![5] — Oh! how I wept! for I felt how changed were all things around me — & what was far more trying to me how changed were those who were so lately *all* to me! but there has been an influence at work, ever since I have been on this Journey trying to withdraw *my* influence from those dear to me — Can this be right? — I cannot think it is! — felt low and nervous — but slept tolerably —

15th   St Swithen — did not rise till 7 oc   got some breakfast — felt shaken and *triste* — Set off to walk — having declared I would not drive the Horses again — as I

[5] Exodus 15:23. "And when they came to Marah, they could not drink of the waters of Marah, for they were bitter. . ."

had been *made* to do — Having had an accident yesterday
— poor Tom having run his waggon against the carriage as
we were waiting at a horrible mud hole — I have often been
spoken to severely when an accident has happened — so I
came to the decision — I would drive them no more — and
poor Tom — a mere child — has been made to drive a
waggon — when of course he knows nothing about ox
teaming — Proposed Mr Spencer to drive it — But Mr
King would not hear of any thing but that I must drive it as
before, — So I walked on leaving them to settle it: Anne was
started off with it and overtook me — I soon rode, still
feeling queer — On we went Louie looking gloomy, I have
done what I could to cheer and comfort her on this Journey
— I think also that I have done much to keep up faith and
good feeling & love — but I have failed in most cases —
however, I feel to leave all tho' my heart often suffers — Oh!
for the Valley — Last night I had a few words with
Claudius   he has taken a curious Course with us, & me in
particular — he does not seem to me to have the element of
happiness within him self & therefore he cannot confer
happiness. We crossed "Prarie Creek"a wicked creek as C.
calls it. They threw in grass and brush — wood & earth & so
filled it up enough for the waggons to cross — all are by this
time nearly over — Sam & Robt. Neslen came & chatted
with us — these young men cause ennui often to disappear
from my Orbit — They are always on hand to do us good
where they can —

Sunday July 17th   We again crossed this wicked Creek
twice — and then went on to Wood River which was a bad
place to cross, but all got over safely — Camped by the side
of it — In the Evening about 11 oc a dreadful Tempest —
yea, awful — I think I never in England witnessed such a
one — I thought it would have blown the Carriage over — I
prayed earnestly & felt my prayers were heard — Mr King

dead asleep the whole time   at last after about an hour it abated — The Watch were indefatigable & the Cattle were all safe — our bed got very wet — at last got some sleep — dreamed I got my letters — but I thought they had been opened & were briefer than usual — This I do not believe would be the case — at any rate I wish I had the trial — In the morning felt tired and prostrated as I often do after a tempest — Walked some of the way with Bertha & Br Samuel — sang two hymns with Anne & him — then came into my Carriage & wrote this much of my Journal   I feel happy & cheerful but by no means elated — had meeting in the afternoon. Br Hayes, Neslen, Walker, and Spencer spoke — A Baby blest by the name of Samuel, My Brother's & Grandfather's name — May all the blessings spoken over it be ratified in the Courts above   Some Californian Emigrants passed while we were in meeting —

Monday 18th   felt tolerably — Sister Dye confined last night with a son — These Mormon Women   I think I should have been left in my grave in similar case — but truly God fits the back to the burden — This we realize daily and I think in nothing more than in such cases — She went on with the Train and reported "all right" at night   "Going on well"   "Beautiful boy" &c &c   Long drive to day got in late — had a deal of trouble to find a Camping place — at last Br Spencer selected a spot in the midst of the wild Prairie   Our carriage was set close by a g[rea]t hole, which we all thought was a grave! Had the Carriage & waggons moved on a little — Went to bed at dark — after I got in smell a very unpleasant smell. Thought it came from the old grave! The thought of it made me feel ill — and I could not sleep — at last fell asleep — soon awoke feeling ill — all next day felt unwell — Was it fancy? — it was not fancy that I felt ill, but the cause I leave in doubt   the idea was enough

Tuesday 19th   Drove to wood river. crossed a deep ravine

and then on 2 miles — Camped close by some Californians with a large flock of sheep. — Slept well —

Wednesday 20   Started early — Claudius drove the Horses attached to the Carriage. Georgey I and Lizzie rode with him — also Louie — Had some agreable & edifying talk upon plurity — the first wife being head or Queen   Lizzie said she would be first wife or never be married and Br Spencer tried to convince her it was a mistaken idea — but it seems to be in corporated in her system   the idea of *being* great according to *her* notions of greatness — perhaps she'll learn better in time — we are all more or less biased by such feelings — Crossd several creeks & above all Elm Creek, where Br Spencer was driving the horses over. it was an awful bridge where few but "Mormons" would think of crossing   a large piece of wood stuck up at which the brown mare shied & Lo! she pushed over the other Horse right into the water! — but by dint of real presence of mind & management we saved the Carriage from being dragged in — The Californians came to our assistance, & we got the horses landed without a buckle being broken! — After this wonderful feat (Br Spencer jumped into the water to his Knees) He helped over the 48 waggons! One of the Californians killed a buffalo — We had a large portion of it   Had some fried for dinner — got into camp late — had tea & to bed — did not sleep the first watch! S. N. on watch till 12 oc — saw them thro' the window of the Carriage — Then composed myself & went to sleep — dreamed an uncomfortable dream about my Mother —

21st   Rose early — breakfast & then off we were. Claudius drove us — Louie & Georgey & Lizzie rode with us — had more talk upon plurality — but it never seems a happy theme — arrived at Buffalo Creek. — Found a letter stuck in a stick from Br Atchinson saying they were all well, i e his company and had left some Buffalo meat for us   I had the tongue to pickle — Got safe over the creek. as Sister Chambers came up her Son told us his Father was dead! — He had been ill a long time   They asked me to go & look at him which I did   He looked like a statue so thin & wasted — Death is ever aweful! and it made me feel low & triste   at last they all came up & got safely over — we then went to Sister C. and asked her if we could do any thing for her — she gave me some domestic to make a shroud or wrapper for the corpse — which I did. Then sent her some wine — for herself and the women who laid him out — dined & Br Spencer decided he would not go on till to morrow so we prepared to wash some clothing — at ¼ to 3 the grave was completed & Br Spencer told us he wished us to attend the funeral of Br Chambers to the grave — We did so — it was a nice dug grave   They laid leaves at the bottom & then lowered the Corpse into it   some boughs over him & then was filled up   Br Samuel assisted all thro'   Br Neslen made a head board — on which was "Joseph Chambers — Native of England aged 53 — Anno — 53 — We can only say "Resquiescat"

22nd — Last night a very heavy tempest — Br Spencer says *the* heaviest we have yet had — And we have had many — Our bed was very wet indeed — we got but little sleep — had breakfast and started at 10 A M — passed thro' a very wet road — saw many Buffaloes & a Rattle Snake — at 1 oc arrived at deep creek — water too deep for us to cross — Obliged to Camp   got our Biscuit wet — had some fried for dinner and Bacon & boiled beef — fine day and a nice healthy Air — Claudius — Georgey — Louie & Lizzie rode in the Carriage — wrote a few of my Thoughts to S. N. not being able to have a word with him and wanting to do so —

Oh! how I long to be in the Valley! to behold the Servant of the Lord! and those that have been so good & kind to me in past days — & whose society I have so much Enjoyed in England — I feel when I attempt to realize it it will be almost Happiness too much — and that I shall almost feel like Israel of old "Let me die since I have seen thy face" — it is Enough —

26th of July — Days have passed & I have not Journalized   Today rose early and started on our Journey — after Camping near the Platte river — had a good night   Walked on — after a time got into the Carriage alone with Claudius — We got into an agreable chat — He asked me who Susanna was engaged to?!! — as I had told him I Knew — I at once said, "May I speak plain?"   he said Yes — I said to you!!!   This led to an excitable conversation — for certainly I did not think he had treated well very often — and we then got up to the Girls & feeling quite unfit for conversation or Company — I got out walked alone — and at last rode in the waggon   Staid & had some refreshments at 1 oc — in the afternoon rode again with Georgey — Louie & Lizzie — at last I suggested we staid, as I was afraid of Indians — C. said there was but one Lady to take — being Miss Stayner — as I and G. were married & Louie engaged! — Louie started and said — It was more than she knew! — The conversation then went on in a diamond cut diamond fashion — strain between C. & me — at last he said I should either do an immense deal of *good* — or an immense deal of Evil!!! I felt this to be a most cutting remark — God knows how I desire to do right — and as I told Him I will have no other faith than that I shall do an immense deal of Good — In my past life I have had the power to do so & I believe that *God* will love and nurture that which He alone has sown & fostered — I will believe that the past will be a guarantee for the future but I thought it unkind & unmanly to attack me in that rude manner, for we can not but Know how great are my trials & how I *do* try to be brave.

27th. Claudius brought me a note this morning in answer to one I wrote him last evening after his cutting remarks. It was good, but somehow he does not comfort my heart — is the fault in me? not all certainly — I think we lack that confidence in each other which makes advice acceptable — I drove the Horses a good part of the day — C. being with his team — staid in midday nearly one hour — Saw a company of people upon the hills opposite — Set off again   A tempest gathering — Got to the camping place at 5 oc — a sharpish tempest   Sat all the evening in my Carriage — Read Brigham's Sermon & other things in Deseret News   S. N. came for a few moments but no talk — It appears we can seldom talk now — it seems there is an influence at work trying destroy our friendship or at any rate the Life & beauty of it — went to bed at 8 oc —

Sunday July 25th, 1853   MCIII   Set off in the morning having been detained a day on acct of the Creek being so swollen   Got over safe — Br Walker taken ill and died almost instantly — On we went — came in sight of a company & found it was *the Elders* that we expected — and Oh! Joy! As soon as I got [to the] creek, Br Spencer being first with Georgey Louie Miss Staynes & Lizzie with Mr King — Louie held up a letter   found it was one from Br Johnson sent to me by the Elders — This was an unexpected pleasure and I Enjoyed it much — tho' it was a brief affair — but all's right — it was *a* letter! and thats some thing as times go — In the afternoon we had a meeting   Several spoke — among them Bros Ross & Major   Br M. brought my Letters, and I gave him some to carry to England — and

½ a Sovereign for a present   Gave Captain Merril a Sovereign for the Company   Mr King gave him one also, ditto — ditto   A party of them took supper in our Tent — and we did what we could for them. Baked some cakes for them & gave them sugar & tea &c — They stood on the opposite side of the creek & prayed & blest us as a company, and said we *should be blest*   We then bid farewell & on we went on our Respective Journeys.

July 28. Had a good night   wind very high — feared the Carriage would be capsized — started in the morning at 7 — soon reached a mudhole — flies & mosquitoes very troublesome   it was a horrid place — Claudius drove me over — the girls went in the waggons   Some wheels were broken — had to wait for them to be mended — 'tis very troublesome but words are Vain in such a case — Deeds, not words is indeed the motto of this Journey — if not of the Church itself. — I feel weakened & my Spirit Caged by stopping —

Last of July   Sunday — Rose — breakfasted & started at 8 oc — Lovely morning. — drove over mudholes — creeks — &c till we arrived at an immense bluff, which we ascended & found ourselves on a high Eminence — soon Camped, at 3 oc — Poor water — but otherwise pleasant   We had some wood with us & found Buffalo chips   I have no Sunday feelings while travelling on Sunday   Yet I desire to go forward — Yesterday we had a long day's travel & camped near the Platte River   S. N. came for a few minutes   Said he felt sad — we had a little talk — but said nothing tho' both inferred that something made us feel triste — we seemed truly to understand each other —

[July 29] Friday Evening — he drank tea with us but there did not seem to be a happy spirit with in the Tent — The fact is C. V. feels — towards tho' I Know for what reason — we all parted and said good night. Louie & Lizzie stood by their waggons for a moment, & I stood by my Carriage when some one came behind me — it was S. N. came to bid me good night   Valley fashion! he is ever good & kind to me & in this dearth I can but love him — may God bless him for his goodness

August 1st   Another day nearer the Valley — We have come about 19 miles today, — good road a few creeks & no mudholes and no accident. I hear S. N. singing — I am glad for he has seemed low of late — We all feel tired and somewhat used up but we shall be immortal till our work is done   Oh! my Father my heart is full but I do not feel to make it all palpable but to *Thee*   Work for me and by the whisperings of Thy Spirit, lead me right — remove far from me those that stand in my path to Salvation!

2nd   Lovely morning. This day 20 years ago — Mr King Sen[ior] died — We started at 8 oc — we went on very cherily — at last met an Indian on horseback   He told us 300 were a head   He seemed very friendly — rode by the side shaking hands, &c, Br Spencer made a few arrangements — and soon we met the whole body of them — a party of Horsemen came forward to meet us — Br Spencer advanced with his gun — & made a sort of Military Salute or pass — which they responded to very gracefully — descending from their Horses & kneeling or rather squatting in their not ungraceful Indian fashion   Br S. then went up & shook hands with the Chief who presented a paper recommending them to white men they might meet — The name of the Chief was "Shell" — He came forward to the Carriage with Br S. who introduced him to us & to Georgey as his Squaw!!   he shook hands with all of us — Br S. gave

him some whiskey & water which he seemed to Enjoy after
he had tasted it — but he seemed to fear to taste it till Br
Spencer had done so. We i e the Camp all contributed some
sugar, coffee — biscuit &c &c for them and we then bid them
adieu — they drawing off on one side to allow our train to
pass on — did not camp till 2 oc — by accident I got a long
way off — but still in sight — Enjoyed my silent position as
I ever do enjoy solitude   at last gathered the Cattle and off
we went — had not gone far when a thunder storm came —
had to "put up" — When it ceased on we went and are now
Encamped 2 miles from Crab Creek. —

3rd   Rose & breakfasted & started   passed Crab Creek —
Camped at 1 oc after passing the Bluff ruins — They are
very beautiful — I should like to have an explanation about
them — but I suppose none know their history — They
stand out in bold relief with a silent eloquence that speaks
trumpet-tongued to every thinking mind — There they are
looking eternally silent — walked as I often do after dinner
or rather Supper   The Mosquitoes dreadful! Had a talk
with Sister Smith of Northampton   She said she quite
enjoyed it   We have had the Platte river by us for the past
week   it is very pretty — full of little islands — Oh! I can
write no more   the mosquitoes drive me mad! Oh for an end
to this Journey! truly we pass over "The bridge of sighs" to
the Valley of the Free!

August 5th   A long day's travel! this day these Sublime
Bluffs in view all day! — They plainly speak a designer —
tho' ages must have rolled along since that design was carried
out — I felt extremely ill & prostrated last night & this
morning I revived again — on we went without water all day
till 8 oc in the Evening when we camped — I went to bed at
once and Anne brought me my tea in bed   S. N. came to bid

me good night — Br Spencer also came and we had a long talk in the Carriage — enjoyed both!!

August 6th   Arose & set off at 8 oc   got into Camp at 3 oc — Cleaned out the Carriage & other jobs — got tea —

Sunday, 7th   Fine morning — Got into Camp about 3 oc — Just as tea was ready two indians came & put us about a little & frightened us some   a strong Guard was put on at night. I dreamed several things, among other things that I returned to England and to D. D! and all looked so changed & I felt so wretched that I had been so foolish as to return, I will not go into particulars — suffice that when I awoke & found it to be a dream, I did not Know how to feel Thankful enough — and I feel sure such would exactly be my feeling — All is well.

Monday   Louie very poorly — nervous and weakened. Claudius laid hands upon her — & advised her going into *his wagon with Georgey.* — so she went all day & they seemed very happy & to enjoy themselves right well — I have had some conversation lately with C. & G. They told me their minds a little — but I do not feel to write — Yea, I don't feel to analize my own feelings — but somehow they do not feel happy and comfortable when I think about it — Whether my feelings are right I do not Know — but I wish to do right, & to be right — I must leave it where I leave all I possess — in the Hands of Him who is my Father as He is the Father of All! Some American Gentlemen came from the Fort & talked with us — One is going on to the Salt Lake & offers to take letters for me — I sent one to Br Johnson by him

August 9th — Tom Owen not very well to day

11th   Dull weather this morning — rose & drest — had breakfast in the Carriage — then got out and arranged my bed &c — and then went into the Tent   a Gentleman soon came, who staid nearly all the morning   had quite a chat — I then went to the Carriage & found S. N. sitting there — he remained a bout an hour reading to me — but there is no rest — They came to grease the Carriage! Soon Tom came feeling ill — wanted me to wash him — I did so and he felt better —

12th   Finer day — Louie's birthday   We had a plum pudding — some Gentlemen came & dined with us — Mr. MacDonald — Fleming Stewart & Haight   had a meeting in the afternoon   enjoyed it pretty well — but I feel saddened — All seems changed & somehow against me! —

13th   Left our encampment near Fort Laramie   Journeyed on to a place near a Creek — where we found Brs Haight & Stewart already camped — felt low — mournful & worn down — I see the determined attention Claudius keeps to Louie, and it takes away my Soul — drinks up my Spirit. I feel too that it affects Georgey! Surely he might wait till he gets to The Valley. — it seems to me that such a girl as Georgey ought to content a man for a proper time at any rate — I cannot reconcile myself to this new doctrine coming in such a form — I feel that it works upon Georgey's feelings also — Oh! my Father — help me & give me not up to my own dark thoughts — Tom Owen very unwell — Went to bed unhappy and dejected

14th   Tom awoke us this morning about 2 oc — having got up in a delireum. Came to our Carriage calling to us that some of the Carriages were gone ahead   We took him into our Carriage bed for an hour to soothe & comfort him — & then Mr King took him back to his own bed   He rose again early — we had breakfast & started at 7 oc — T. O. in the Carriage with me — he was drowsy & quite delirious all day

— Oh! how unhappy I have felt this day! Claudius is so very odd & unkind to me — God Knows I desire to do right — & to please him as far as is consistent   but it appears I have not the power. —

15th   T. O. very ill — which makes all look dark with me — Br Neslen & Claudius administered to him at noon as he lay in the Carriage — I felt wretched but hope at the bottom of all — Claudius asked him before he laid his hands upon him — if he knew what he must do to get well — he said, have faith in God! He then clasped his hands & went off into a beautiful little prayer which startled us all — Claudius thought it was one he had learned — but not so   it was sponteneous   it broke up the deep fountains of my heart & all seem affected — They then laid hands upon him and we all felt he had received a blessing   The disease Mountain fever seemed arrested from that time — tho' he still continued very ill — Claudius slept with him that night

16th   T. O. still very ill — delirious — travelled all night till 1 oc "under the moon" my thoughts were "Legion" & have been for some days past — but when is it they are not? — Thought with me is a Kingdom — Got into Camp & had some tea & went to bed at day break. — Tom slept with me in the Carriage   Rose Early —

17th   Rose & washed him all over with Saleratus Water — got him into the Tent and soon again into the Carriage which was set in a shady place — Sat with him all day — he was calmer   seemed Exhausted — S. N. came & sat with me in the afternoon —

18th   T. O. still very ill — had him administered to by Br Arthur & Claudius he being all unconscious   Yet I felt more happy and hopeful.

19th   Set off at 8 a m   T. O. no worse — a beautiful

morning lovely air — Got into Camp at 1 oc   John Tom
ran against one of our other waggons & smashed the wheel!
Consequently we could not go on — Sat in the Carriage all
the aftenoon with T. O. he no worse — I hope better — S.
N. went on "Doctor" to our Late Camping place to find one
of their Lost Oxen   Slept in the Carriage with T. O. —

20th   Lovely   morning — beautiful   pure   air   quite
ambrosial! I hope Tom is better — but still nothing very
decided about him — I washed him all over in vinegar and
water — changed his bed & put him on all clean Linen — he
looked comfortable and comforted my poor wounded heart.
— I feel still hopeful — I cannot think the Lord will take
him from me — in this embryo stage of his temporal &
spiritual Existence! Surely He will remember mercy seeing
the integrity of my heart all my life Long   for 'tho
conscious of my imperfections — Yet thro' all one strong
pervading bias has run thro' all I did & said, i e the Love of
my God & the desire to do *His Will* — I have also sacrificed
as few women have the strength to sacrifice — I stepped out
of my beautiful happy Home & from all I held dear for the
Gospel's Sake — *His* Gospel — & will He forget all this?
And is not this dear boy one who promises well to be good &
useful — & have I not already buried 4! — and have I not
again & again dedicated him to the Lord? and if he will
restore him I will religiously carry out my determination and
my Vow! — He will be faithful to His promise that those
who trust in Him shall not be confounded and I believe &
therefore will I speak — therefore will I hope — therefore
will I contend asking all only and entirely in the name of
Jesus Xt — Amen. —

[Aug. 21] 4 oc   P M Sunday   We are now camped at
Deer Creek, a beautiful place for such wild surroundings
Trees & water and a patch of green grass make it an

Arcadian Paradise after our weary toil for so long over such
an arid soil — After we got in T. O. appeared worse — he
had a paraoxysm that quite alarmed me — it appeared anger
when I at tempted to wash him — he is now calm & lies
peacefully   Oh! My Father! Grant that the destroyer may
have no power over him — forgive me if I have done any
thing to bring this up on myself for God Knows I value his
life & would not for the world lose him   Oh! set a watch up
on my mouth & Keep the door of my lips — Oh! spare this
child to me Oh! God my Father   4 weeks more & we shall
be in the Valley or very near it, if we have good fortune — is
it possible that this Long Looked for and anticipated —
much sought after — much talked of — prayed for —
worked for and suffered for Event — This Consumation,
devoutly wished for is really so near at hand!!! I cannot
realize it — Am I to realize also Thy afflictive Hand? —
Oh! spare me my Father this one more dreaded event   I ask
it only in the name of Jesus Xt —

Monday 22 nd   I have been too much engaged & my mind
too feeble & full & too unhappy to journalize — T. O. has
been very ill — I feel nothing but faith has saved him   But
today he is decidedly better — and my heart rejoices — Yes
I am right Thankful to my Heavenly Father, to His
Servants and to my beloved friends for the blessing of his
restoration — I ever felt our faith & prayers & exertions
would Keep his life on the Earth — Bless the Lord Oh! my
Soul, & forget not all His benefits for indeed he has been
gracious to me   He raised up Bertha who was nearly as sick
as T. O. — yet I never saw *Death* around her but I did
around him every day — but she is healed & I feel he is *saved*
& for all this my heart swells with gratitude — We are now
about 380 miles from the Valley — Can it be possible? Oh!
how sad it seemed to me travelling all night last Thursday &

he delirious all the time — but his voice was weak & pretty of 5 or 6 & he talked innocently but not outrageously — Once he called out "Mama — Grandfather has been here & Eddie!" — Oh! how Kind is my Father in Heaven!! how *gently* He chastises me, & warns me of the frail tenure of all Earthly possessions! Oh! may these Gentle Lessons be never forgotten by me but may I apply them to the bettering of my Nature — for I desire to *be* right & to do right — The scene around is wild & dreary   Oh! for the beautiful Valley — where my heart has long been — Upper Platte River —

28th August — Sunday — I have not journalized for some days — Much has transpired & I have intended every day to write — but something has always prevented me or we have been late in Camp. — Thought as usual has been busy with me & I have felt weary & worn both in body & mind — Tom O. has been exceedingly ill — but faith has saved him — and he is better Thank God! — I have many thoughts about many things but God is all-sufficient & I will leave all my affairs in His Hands — Who knows what is best for me — Oh! may His will be revealed to me — and may I be obedient to it — We have been for some days passing the "Rocky Mountains" they are rather more wonderful than beautiful — yet they are certainly Sublime — it seems something marvellous & mysterious that our Cavalcade should pass along breaking the Eternal Silence of these wild places — my feelings are undefinable but there is a degree of awe & sadness about them to me   Yesterday we passed "The Devil's Gate" but I did not see it — Louie went & Lizzie — and others went but I staid in the Carriage with the invalid — S. N. rode a little while in the Carriage with me — We are now only 300 and a few miles from the Valley   Marvellous! wonderful! I rejoice & yet I dread I hardly Know why Either

— Lord Charles Fitzwilliam[6] came by invitation from
Claudius into our Tent and took wine & some refreshment
with us — he seemed to Enjoy it — he spent a few hours
with us   he is returning from California — he was Entirely
clothed in *buckskin* from head & feet — like a Mountaineer
— I told him I should like to see him walk into some of the
splendid drawing rooms of London — how the ladies would
stare — Memo, first saw a Splendid bearded Comet[7] on the
22nd of August — 1853 — A death in Camp —
Vincent   T. O. very poorly — I in low spirits — thinking
him worse — This death makes me feel gloomy — All were
to be off as soon as a wheel was mended   The funeral had
taken place   We set off — T. O. improved as we went
along, and before Evening I saw a decided change for the
better   Sister Neslen brought him some broth which did
him good — All were Kind   he has lost his Voice & cannot
articulate a word — thro' excessive talking while delirious
— Bertha lost her hearing in her attack — both mountain
fever — To day we passed the splendid Rocky
Mountains   Truly, they are "the everlasting hills" — they
are immensely high & look as if piled up by Giants and some
huge stones thrown down — We passed Green River 3
times & saw several Indians — an Indian Village and a
multitude of Horses — One of the sisters strayed off & lost
her way & fell in with them   They took her money &

---

[6] Charles William Wentworth, son of Earl Fitzwilliam, galavanted over the western
trails from 1851 to 1854 with an entourage of ten men. The Kansas City, MO, *Public
Ledger* reported on Aug. 8, 1851, that this party had arrived from New Orleans on the
Saranak. Over the following years Fitzwilliam met many of the mountain men, visited
most of what became the western states, traveled with wagon trains, and dressed in
western trappers' clothes. He became notorious among the overlanders in those years.
He and Hannah King, both from Cambridgeshire, must have enjoyed comparing notes
about their experiences. Louise Barry, *Beginning of the West* (Topeka, 1972), pp. 1033-
4, 1106, 1194.

[7] This was comet "1853 III." *See* introduction to Celinda Hines' journal, p. 77 above.

looked for earrings & jewels — but when the Chief heard of
it he whipped them, and made them restore all they had
taken & then saw her home himself to our Camp! — Good
for him — had a duck for dinner at 6 oc or later — chatted
around the Camp fire then to bed — but my rest was
troubled — heard the wolves howling close to us — had a
watch to guard. —

30th   Rose & got off Early   T. O. mending Thank God!
Sandy road saw some graves — S. N. came & drove for me a
little while — he is ever kind   Claudius & I by no means
happy together — why I hardly Know — but I do not feel
that he fills the place of *one* Son to me yet & he desired too —
to which I am not yet reconciled — Oh! may the Lord reveal
His will to me — Mr King is better — he is Kind & Good in
many ways — tho' no Mormon — How often I think of my
own dear Parents — and their Love for me!!

31st   Rose after a good night which is something as times
go — Felt happy & refreshed — Temperance in all things
sweetens Life! — set off on our daily trip — the wind
blowing a perfect hurricane   Crossed Green River 3 times
before 12 oc!! What a serpentine affair it is! — Camped — I
hope not for the night — One of the Sisters is ill so we wait
for her — how foolish of women to be in that way on *Such* a
Journey as this! but some people consider nothing but their
own appetites Bah!! T. O better Thank God! Most heartily
do I thank Him — Saw several graves this morning.

1st Sept. Thomas Robinson's birthday   I wish he was here
with all my heart — he would be a great Comfort to us all —
This has been a long day's travel to us — camped at Sweet
Water Creek — in a perfect basin — Got in late — and then
off to bed feeling cold & the carriage not placed nicely or
comfortably — but these things are trifles — Which by the
bye "Make the Sum of human-things" — Came over

mountains high & ridgey — They are truly named "Rocky Mountains" for they were nothing but rocks piled up   T. O. mending but still slowly — very weak. The Saints are all Kind — The Children i e the girls assemble round my carriage every morning Just before I start to ask how he is — and to bring him flowers &c — Kind little things! Only 240 miles from the Valley!! 'Tis wonderful! I seem I cannot realize it —

Sept. 2nd   Rose after a tolerable night — T. O. somewhat better — The Cattle all tired out — Set off in the morning & come on 7 miles & here we are camped at Willow Creek. — We wait to day   Yesterday Sister Jones was confined with a daughter amid Thunder & Lightening — I should think something of it were it my case — We often get wild ducks & hares & other game which I like very much but I pine for the Valley —

Sept 7th   Lovely morning — We are Camped in a nice place. — We are just going off — I have not Journalized for some days — perhaps it's as well — for my mind has been shook up into a muddle by what I see going on around me, but I hope all will be well — & that the Lord will reveal His *Will* to me, & then I shall be able to obey   We have seen such a number of dead oxen it makes me sad   We have lost one thro' carelessness   perhaps before we get to the Valley we shall be taught the folly of such neglect

Sept 8th   Just going to start this morning when came that Sister Sutton was shot in the arm accidently of course — Br Spencer went to administer to her & Sister Neslen to bind up the wound — We travelled late & met Br Decker with the Mail from the Valley — Claudius gave them some wine *coming to ask me for it*   nearly a week has passed & I have not bidden S. N. good night! I suppose it could not be — but I miss his kind "bless you" which ever does me good — The

road pretty good the last few days   prospect wild   were it
not for the Lovely Skies and pure atmosphere it would be
bleak indeed but they are something Heavenly! — different
to any thing we ever saw in England — Reminds me of
Byron's exclamation, "So cloudless clear, & purely
beautiful, that God alone was to be seen in Heaven"![8] T. O.
mending fast tho' he cannot yet speak! he has been very very
ill! — I had a dream this morning that I was pulling out one
of his teeth that was horribly decayed — Which I don't
like —

Sept 10th   Yesterday we travelled till quite late & passed
some splendid bluffs ruins — These Bluffs are something I
cannot describe   They are Sublime & Mysterious —
There is beauty & order in them — and it requires no very
fanciful stretch of imagination to form Baronial buildings —
"Keeps" — gateways, &c &c — & Georgey even made
"The Porter" looking over the Gate!! They are very high —
I should like to hear a philosophical discription of them —
They please and interest me more than I have language to
express — There is much design in them — yet they say
they are solely the work of Nature — Well I must leave
them like all mysterious things — T. O. mending up to last
night when he had an attack of diarhea   Could my dream
portend this? — I trust he will do well yet — but he is very
delicate tho' he has an immense appetite for Eating — Last
evening S. F. N. came & had a nice chat with me which I
enjoyed much — This morning we started at 9 oc & went
only 2 miles — Camped to feed the Oxen here being some
food & water — Black's Fork being the name — We now
are going on for Fort Bridger — We saw the smoke from it

---

[8] These lines are from Lord Byron's poem, "The Dream," and read in the original as
follows: "So cloudless, clear, and purely beautiful,
                    That God alone was to be seen in Heaven."

last night — The air here is so pure and rarified and the sky lovely —

[The following paragraph has been crossed out and is very hard to read. It is, however, of such interest that we reproduce it here.] Louie not very well — I expect her mind is bothered about what she shall do and I expect C. V. is always after her either by a "dumb expression" or otherwise and she "halts between two opinions" — Well I shall leave it but as I now feel I shall never give her to him — if it must be it will only be to Georgey that I can ever give her — & she is a gem of the first water, and she is worthy of all I can do for her, or her husband either — I only hope he appreciates her! — he ought to — here is another Saturday [September 10] — how fast time flies!

Sept 17th   I have not had a moment to Journalize the past week — I would fain recall a few things   We have passed beautiful & sublime scenery, Echo Canyon especially — that surpasses every thing I have yet seen before — and some spots yesterday I felt I could live and die in! but here we have truly "no continuing city"

[The following was entered here evidently as one of the "few things" she would "fain recall."]
Sept 15th   Last Thursday was a day of days! The iron belonging to the whipple tree of the Carriage broke — I called to Anthony to come and assist me & Mr King went on — Br Spencer then detained him to help mend the road — Soon Claudius & I went on — When we soon saw one of our waggons overturned! The very one T. O. was in on acct of his enfeebled health   Oh! the agony I suffered till we got up to it & found he was safe & well — Darling Georgey, with her ever prompt kindness came towards the Carriage leading him gently along to let me see he was safe   blessed children!!

how dear they were to my poor heart! — even then the
Excess of Joy was as hard to bear — but suffice 'twas a
moment of agony that I shall long remember   We soon got
the waggon over & all right again and we camped close by —
S. N. came back as they were sent forward in the Evening!
— he ever does me good by his Manly comfort — days
passed over after this — beautiful Bluffs — beautiful
Kanyons & some things that were any thing *but* beautiful —
sorrows & troubles & tears! &c &c were mixed up with the
beauties of nature   Our Carriage Horses gave out —
perfectly worn down   We had oxen put to our Carriage —
but on Sunday the two Brs Cahoon met us & put to our
Carriage their horses & at last on Monday 19th of Sept 1853
we entered the Valley of the Great Salt Lake!!! the goal for
which we had so long panted — and were set down at Br
Daniel Spencer's — found her pleasant and kind — she
provided for us a delicious supper and was very hospitable
— felt tired — worn & exhausted — Dear Georgey has been
ill some days very ill to day   The company did not come in
with us   Lost therefore our kind friends & fellow travellers,
the Neslens — and I ever miss kind friends — They are
scarce!

The Diaries, Letters, and Commentaries

§ 1854 ℞

Council Bluffs to California, 1854

⚭ Mary Burrell

INTRODUCTION

On May 31, 1854, Mary Burrell of Plainfield, Illinois, wrote in her diary, "My Birth day, aged 19." She continued her entry for that day by writing about the scenery along the Platte River, "See some spots in the hill side occasionally which are as red as brick, sometimes rocky & red   Beautiful scenery, *splendiferous.*" This was a teenage writer for whom one day was dull and the next extra splendid — "*splendiferous.*" Her last entry, made on September 1st in the Green Valley of Sonoma County in California, read that they had ended a journey "which for care, fatigue, tediousness, perplexities and dangers of various kinds can not be excelled."

Her sense of humor appears now and then. Here is part of her entry for June 2: "Some Indians came in our camp & one asked me if I was going to have a pappose. Ha! ha! ha! Much lightning & heavy thunder & large hail! tremendous time getting supper. Wet beds. 'Tis sublime, sublime."

After they had been traveling along the Humboldt River[1] through the deserts of present-day Nevada, she wrote, on August 5th, "I am Humbolted pretty badly these 2 or 3 days past."

Her most unforgetable line was penned on August 15, "Would feel pretty well myself if I had not eaten so many beans. They make me feel so w----y." 'Nuf said.

Lucy Foster Sexton, who was but a toddler during the journey, wrote a description of her friend, Mary Burrell, many years later:

> Mary Burrell, the younger, was a lively, rosy-cheeked, good-looking girl who found a great deal to enjoy during the trip. She was quite accomplished as a musician. Like many others she kept

[1] For a perceptive treatment of this river *see* Dale L. Morgan, in "The Rivers of America" series, *The Humboldt, Highroad of the West* (New York, 1943).

a diary which was preserved by members of her family. Her engagement to Wesley Tonner was announced before they started westward. The neighbors wagged their heads wisely, and declared no engagement would stand the strain of so much hard work and worry under disillusioning circumstances. But they were mistaken; the young people were more deeply in love at the end of the journey than they were at the beginning, and the wedding followed their arrival in California. Unfortunately Mary Burrell Tonner died while still a young woman in her thirties.[2]

Mary was still alive on June 22, 1860, however, when the census-taker came by their home and recorded the following:

Wesley Tonner   30 m.   b. Pa.
    School Teacher b. Real Estate 1500 Personal   500
Mary Tonner   25 f.   b. N.Y.
Carrie Tonner   4 f.   b. Cal.
Mary Tonner   1 f.   b. Cal.
Jennie Tonner   1/12 f.   b. Cal.
Mary Burrell   62   b. Eng.
(The last-named person was Mary Tonner's mother.)

The original manuscript of Mary Burrell's diary is located in the Beinecke Rare Book and Manuscripts Library, of the Yale University Library. They kindly supplied us with a microfilm of the diary and have given us permission to publish it here.

Accompanying the diary in the Yale collection is a letter written on September 10, 1854, ten days after Mary's last diary entry. This letter written by Wesley Tonner tells the story of the same journey from a different perspective. It adds something special to the record of the same historical happenings. It is published by the permission of the Yale University Library.

PERSONNEL OF THE BURRELL GROUP OF THE PLAINFIELD WAGON TRAIN

Mrs. Mary Burrell, widow of George Burrell, an Englishman, who was

---

[2] Lucy Foster Sexton, *The Foster Family, California Pioneers,* (Santa Barbara, 1925), p. 180.

listed in the 1850 Federal Census as 55 years old, a farmer, in Will County, Illinois, near the town of Plainfield. He had died sometime between 1850 and 1854, leaving her a widow. Mrs. Burrell was 54 years old at the time of the overland journey. In 1860, according to the census of that year, she was age 62 and living with her daughter, Mary Tonner and family in San Jose, Santa Clara County, California.

Edward Burrell was the brother of the younger Mary. His wife was Louisa (Hannibal) Burrell. The census of 1850 indicates that Louisa was not yet married, so the wedding must have taken place sometime between 1850 and 1854. She was 20 years old, born in England.

Wesley Tonner was Mary Burrell's "affianced." He was listed as a schoolteacher in the 1860 census of Santa Clara County, San Jose township, age 30 years. His future wife often referred to him while on the overland journey as "Wes."

Isaac G. Foster was one of the leaders of the exodus from Plainfield, Illinois, to the Pacific in 1854. He had been over the trail in 1852. *See* the introduction to the diary of Marriett Foster Cummings, Volume IV of this set, pp. 117-119.

Grace Foster, wife of Isaac Foster, was born in Connecticut.

Eugene P. Foster was the 6-year-old son of Isaac and Grace Foster.

Lucy Foster was in her own words "barely able to toddle about" at the time of the journey. It was 71 years later that she wrote *The Foster Family, California Pioneers* (Santa Barbara, 1925), which has been an indispensible resource in learning about the Burrell and Tonner families.

Fred Foster was the baby born on the journey to Grace Foster.

William and Mary Hannibal were the parents of Louisa Burrell, the wife of Edward Burrell. According to the 1850 census of Plainfield, Illinois, William was a miller, age 40 in that year. Mary Hannibal was 37 at that time. They were both born in England.

Putnam ("Put") Robson, was a nephew of Mrs. Mary Burrell. According to Lucy Sexton in *The Foster Family* book, p. 177, he "afterwards figured prominently in the social, political and business life of San Francisco."

Isaac Harter was listed in the 1850 Plainfield census as a hired hand in the house of one I. C. Andrew, 17 years old, born in Ohio. Lucy Sexton wrote that he also became an active citizen of San Francisco *(Ibid)*.

Silas and Oscar Wightman were brothers. They were the children of
    Mr. and Mrs. Josiah Wightman of Plainfield, Illinois.
"Old Holmes" and Mrs. Holmes are so-far unidentified.
"The boys," none of whose surnames have been identified, were Elijah,
    Alexander, Frank and Stucky. (*Foster Family*, p. 180 and "Roster.")

THE DIARY

April 27th   One month since we left Plainfield [Illinois].
Arrived here at Council Bluffs the 16th, have been here since
that time & are now making ready to cross the Missouri river
tomorrow   have spent the day in packing &c   Wrote to
Betsy, two sheets & a half

28th   Had a fine ride on horse back on the new side saddle
up on the bluffs. shall not get ready to cross the river today.
Fine weather, beautiful country. Had music from the ship'
last evening. All in good spirits   Elijah slept

29th Sunday. wrote to Margaret. had a fracus with the
Indians. The emigrants killed 2. Wes[1] got stabbed in the leg
a little but not very seriously. got well frightened and left our
old camp at dark & moved up to town. All slept in the tent, 8
of us.

30   Fine weather: anticipate some difficulty with the
Indians on account of the disturbance which occurred
yesterday. No Indians to be seen today. Stewed apples, fried
cakes, baked cakes & bread. After dinner started for St.
Mary's; arrived there & encamped near the Missouri river
12 miles from Council Bluffs. Boys kept guard.

[May] 1st   removed from the Bluffs to St. Marys

May 2   Crossed the river on the ferry which cost $9.10.

---

[1] This fracas is described in much more detail by Wesley Tonner in his letter of
September 10, 1854, which follows the diary.

Good-bye to the states   Saw old Sarpee[2] & several Indians.
About a mile from the ferry is the Belvieu mission & trading
post. 7 log houses, a beautiful situation & delightful scenery,
rolling prairie, with scattering groves. good roads fine
weather, & good spirits if we are in Nebraska. Camped at
noon near a little creek. got dinner, noon where there had
been an Indian village   Hitched up & within a few miles
the Elk horn near a creek called the little Papea
[Papillon]   the Indians tried to make us pay toll at a little
bridge, but we showed pistols & they let us pass. Mother
gave the old squaw a silk tab off of a stock; she seemed very
much pleased.

3   Passed many teams; fine farming country. As we neared
the Elk Horn on a large plain & was a beautiful sight. Could
see the Platte river 12 miles distant seemingly on the top of a
plain   it glistened & looked delightful to the beholder.
plenty of timber & side hills, ravines &c.   camped the east
side of the Elk Horn ready to cross in the morning. Fine
stream & bordered with timber

4. Crossed the Ferry about noon after Put [Putnam] had
found the old cow about 12 miles back. Washed, baked
ginger snaps. Shook hands with several Pawnee Indians, &
Bid them Good Bye. Very dusty & sandy. Camped near the
Platte in sight of 35 waggons & several hundred cattle.[3] Saw
an Indian village at the left & 20 or 30 Indians

---

[2] This was Peter A. Sarpy, a 50-year-old man of the American Fur Company. He had
been in charge of the post at Bellevue, the oldest town in Nebraska. Anticipating that
Nebraska would soon become a territory of the United States he had set up a post office
in 1850. His hat was the mailbox. Dorothy Weyer Creigh, *Nebraska, A Bicentennial
History* (New York, 1977), p. 51; Lilian L. Fitzpatrick, *Nebraska Place names* (Lincoln,
1967), p. 124; John E. Wickman, "Peter A. Sarpy," LeRoy R. Hafen, Edit., *The
Mountain Men and the Fur Trade*, IV (Glendale, CA, 1966), p. 283--96.

[3] The Missouri Valley newspapers reported over and over again during the spring of
1854 that thousands of head of livestock were being driven over the plains that year.
There were cattle, sheep, horses and mules in vast numbers. Louise Barry, *The
Beginning of the West* (Topeka, 1972), pp. 1200-01.

5   Fine morning, little frost last night, sweet sleep. Left the
Platte in the morning   travelled about 17 miles

6   Fine day; passed many hundred cattle   plenty of dust
& sand, made some nut cakes in the morning & baked.
Encamped near the River Platte or Elk Horn, I know not
which. Washed after dark some things & took a refreshing
wash before going to bed. Always sleep sound no matter how
much noise is going on among the boys. No one sick

May 7. Very dusty, tremendous wind   got blown over
while eating my dinner. Victuals full of sand. Came up with
Isaac Foster & wish to join his company on account of
getting clear of watching quite so often. Although it is
Sunday still we are traveling. We see but little regard paid to
the Sabbath in this part of the world. One would not know
when the Sabbath came from appearances and conduct of our
neighboring emigrants. Dont have any trouble with the
Indians. Saw Mrs Holmes   Put & I stood guard till 1
o'clock. Saw a wolf but did not shoot him for fear of awaking
the company thinking it was Indians. Windy.

May 8   Still very windy & cool. Saw 2 Antelopes across the
creek but was not in shooting distance; cream colored looked
like Deer   About noon we thought our time had come. We
came to a small creek which was bridged, but very narrow &
sideling. Ed crossed safe & drove up on the hill. Alexander
came next with 4 horses & covered waggon, but did not come
down on the bridge square & the horses got frightened. The
wagon fell over into the drink but lodged on a fallen tree,
which drew the horses all in also Ed had come back for a
drink & was there to witness the catasrophe. Frank Wes &
Ed were at work immediately. Alexander had been through
out beyond all the horses & with considerable difficulty
swam ashore. Water was 8 or 10 feet deep, besides the mud at
the bottom. Ed seized the ax & cut the tongue off which

assisted the horses some. They came to the surface. Kept
their heads out, but got entangled in the harness. That was
soon cut loose. Plunging & splashing was kept up. Ropes
were procured & fastened round their heads. Wes & Ed
were in the water up to their waists & In great danger of
being drawn in by the kicking of the horses. One poor horse
was so much encumbered with the harness & so far gone that
before assistance could be rendered he had breathed his last.
Blood rushed out of his mouth; he looked for help but it was
impossible to relieve him, & assist 3 others which were in the
mud & water as much as he was. The others were saved after
a few moments, but they were very helpless & bruised & cut.
Mother & Mrs Hannibal were running & shouting for the
cow drivers to come back, but they did not see or hear for
some time & when they were made to understand that we
were in trouble, they thought it that Indians had attacked us.
It was a very lucky move that mother got out of the wagon
before they went down the hill or she would have been
thrown in the water also & drowned before assistence could
have been rendered. We felt like returning thanks to God for
her narrow escape & that it was no more than it was, or might
have been. The wagon was soon unloaded, & got out. No
damage done, except the tongue & one bow broken, & dash-
board split. One carpet was wet which had Isaac's [Harter]
clothing in. All this time Louisa was over the hill in the first
wagon asleep, & tired of worrying for Ed to come back with a
cup of water untill the fracus was nearly over with. The boys
which were driving the cows got there after the horses were
all out. Got straightened round & encamped over the hill;
mended up the harness & tongue, washed off the horses, &
tended to greasing their bruises. Very windy. Isaac Foster
passed us but crossed the same creek at a ford without any
difficulty   We washed & made 2 fruit cakes; had mush &
milk for supper, good grass — We passed some old ruins

which had been burnt down   Nothing remained but chips & burnt logs; there had been a fence of logs driven down close together all round the houses built of logs, also where there had been some corn fields & fences. Nothing remained which would indicate that there had been any improvements, though, at this day, but Ed saw them there when he passed before. We are nearing the place where Mathus dwelt once & buried Marcellus.[4] Still see no Indians.

9   Windy & cool, not quite ready to start yet, but will get away about noon, I think. Traveled 17 miles; awful windy. I expect we passed near the place where Mathus lived & where Marcellus was buried, but not having any loose horse, we could not search it out. Saw where the village had been & sod fences. Crossed some very fine prairie & deep ravines or hollows. Camped near the Loup Fork   Saw a grave on the top of a mound down on the river bottom. Mr. Roe of Wisconsin buried in 1849 the day before Ed got there. Was shot by the Indians   Passed a piece of country which looked very much like a burying ground; as many as 2 or 3 hundred graves visible. It must have been a Battle Field, I think   some remains of a village & in the river bottom were some sod fences thrown up. (Had a Prairie hen for supper).

10.   Fine day; crossed the Loup Fork about noon. Spent the forenoon in shoeing cows   Very bad river to cross. thought we should be drowned in crossing. The sand kept changing & sometimes we would go down 2 or 3 feet & then up again. 6 horses on a wagon & a tight match at that. Could not find

---

[4] Here she is writing on the site of the Grand Pawnee Village that had been destroyed by the Sioux not long previous. In her reference to Mathus and Marcellus we are reminded that in reading and interpreting any 19th century educated person, one had better keep handy Smith's *Smaller Classical Dictionary*, for classical studies made up a major part of education in those days. Here Mary Burrell is evidently referring to M. Claudius Marcellus, who in 40 B.C. was murdered by his own close attendant, P. Magius Chilo. She seems to be comparing the killing of Indians by their Indian brothers.

grass or water. Camped near a well, good water but little of it. In company with Foster.

11   Sandy road. no water until we camped at noon near a small creek called Prairie creek near a grave. Had to cross the creek again. Very bad hole, got stuck. Was pulled out with oxen. Deep mud, & camped about 2 miles beyond it

12   Rained & very cold. Camped about 2 o'clock on Wood River or Prairie Creek. I do not know which, & washed, baked & wrote to Betsy. Still raining

13   Got to Wood River.[5] Crossed the toll bridge price .50 for wagon & .01 cts for cows. Grocery here & things to sell to emigrants, trade stock &c. Dr Clarke hospital here   Very cold in the morning. Lost ½ a day in trading, &c. Sold the old corn wagon for $5.00 & the lame cow for $7.50. Saw many cattle & horses. As many as 100 wagons passed here. Put the letters in the office but the office is nothing but a tent.

14   Fine day. Heavy dew last night. We all eat hearty & feel well & in good spirits. Going to Cal is not as hard after all the talk. See Fosters company every day & Zumwalts company — Sam Gilson also — Sunday again but it is less like Sunday than ever. I rode horse back all the afternoon & drove cows. Camped late & had heavy thunder & shock lightning, right smart sprinkle of rain. I reckon, near the river.

---

[5] This trading post would eventually become the pioneer town of Wood River, but not until 1869. Lilian L. Fitzpatrick, *Nebraska Place Names* (Lincoln, 1960), p. 70. The "Dr Clarke" mentioned here as running a hospital was probably George W. Clarke, an Indian agent, who would be placed in charge of the Pottawatomie Agency in present Kansas. Louise Barry, *The Beginning of the West: Annals of the Kansas Gateway to the American West, 1840-1854* (Topeka, 1972), pp. 1191 and 1201. Elizabeth Myrick also mentions "Dr. Clark the United States Indian Agent" in her entry for May 25.

[6] There were several pioneering Zumwalt and Gilson families in early California. We have not been able to sort these out. Colusa County became the locale for several Zumwalt families. Willis S. Green, *History of Colusa County* (San Francisco, 1880), p. 175.

15. Louisa wont elevate in time for breakfast. The boys saw some antelopes & wolves, & one white wolf. Shot at one but did not hit it. Camped on Buffalo Creek. Had a heavy thunder shower, sharp lightning. Towards 2 o'clock it commenced blowing & raised the tent.

16. Still raining & very cold. Started about noon. Hailed a little & blew tremendously at times. Camped near a creek   Good feed & slough water

17. Clear weather, but cold. Camped near the Platte. Did not watch the stock. Childs grave 11 months   Rode horse back all the after noon. Feel stiff & lame

18. passed the Pawnee Swamps   Good feed at noon. Sand hills. Did not watch.

19. Awful muddy roads. Got sloughed twice   we had to wade through in the fore noon. No wood or water scarcely; used slough water & Buffalo chips & willow sprouts to cook dinner. Rode horse back in the afternoon on old David without a bridle. Jumped a hole. Killed a skunk which madé Isaac [Harter] sick. Encamped at the foot of the bluffs. Good feed & water, no wood; burn dry grass & chips.

20. Warm. Saw 4 antelopes, Lizards, blue snake, beautiful flowers, purple peas like sweet peas, pleasant smell, & a kind of Dock or sorrell with a blossom in the shape of a pie plant seed but great deal larger & reddish seed within it like the Pie Plant. Ascended the bluff which is very sandy.

21   Started, & soon found a sulphur spring; smelt of sulphur some. Looked up the stream a little & saw 7 others boiling up out of a bed of white sand. Very sick. water cool, but smelt of sulphur   took a chase after 2 antelopes but it amounted to nothing   Sunday today — Camped for the rest of the day at noon & laid over to rest on Rattle Snake Creek. Killed one & a blow snake, besides 3 others of a

different kind. Had a thunder shower. The Platte is ¼ of a mile south west of us & is lined with high bluffs on the other side which are scattered with cedar or pine

22nd   Clear & pleasant in the morning. Killed a Prairie Dog as large as a good sized Gopher   Very warm in the afternoon. Crossed the bluffs which were very sandy. We still follow along the foot of the bluffs near the Platte

23. Saw plenty of Prairie Dogs & snakes; very warm. Trading Post the south side of the Platte. First the gnats or musketoes troubled the boys much, poisened stings which raised up in lumps whereever they were bit — Very painful in deed. They have see Prickley Pears, many flowers [unreadable] as of old but more pink shade. Woman encamped near us with 7 or 8 children going to Cal

24. Very warm. Gnats as thick as ever. Crossed more sand hills — beautiful scenery, flowers   Came in sight of Chimney rock, but I missed seeing it not knowing which was it until it was too late. We are now at ancient Bluff ruins. Went up on one hill which looks to be about ¼ of a mile from our camp, but before I got to it it was a mile & a half, I should guess. On the top is a plat of grass & moss of different kinds, beautiful. Prickly pears & at the out edge a few feet it is paved with beautiful stones & flat rock nearly as smooth as a floor. An Indian tent is near us, trading   The boys have bought some moccasins.

25   Did not travel in the forenoon but spent the time in rambling among the ruins, rocks, prickly pears, &c. Isaac, Wesley, Frank, Ed & wife & myself all on horse back; rode around the mountains nearly all the forenoon. Some timber, red cedar growing in the rocks. The trees are very much twisted. Swallows in abundance living in the rocks; owls & hawks. (& an hour come gone so I guess) Traveled nearly 21 miles.

26. See Chimney rock at a distance & bluff. Had the sick head ache in the afternoon very bad

27. Saw Scotts Bluff — west of Chimney Rock. Tried to draw it off on paper. See teams & cattle for 4 or 5 miles in length. This world is all a cattle show, sure enough. Passed many. Rode horse back & got caught in a shower. Had to lope to the wagons in short order. Baked till 12 o'clock at night

28. Raining Sunday. See Laramie Peak. The clouds could be seen mid-way on the Peak. Encamped in a beautiful little grove of cottonwood — most delightful.

29   Wrote to Betsy. Got to Ft Laramie. Two-story house made of Adobe. Wigwams in abundance. 5 Indian squaws came & begged for meat & bread, two men also, and in the afternoon 5 men came   I played on the melodeon for them. They were pleased & wanted Hannibal to dance. Got some cows shoed. Made fruit cakes, washed &c

30. Put's birth day   Got into the Black Hills, which look beautiful to the traveler   Plenty of cedar & pine trees. Stony way. Got a drink out of a spring which came gushing out from under the hill. Camped on the Platte late after traveling 27 miles over mountains more delightful than any we have seen before.

31. My Birth day, aged 19. See some spots in the hill side occasionally which are as red as brick, sometimes rocky & red   Beautiful scenery, *splendiferous*   Commenced writing a kind of journal for Betsy. Camped near nice springs near an Indian trading establishment for the night & again lay down our wearied limbs to rest.

June 1   Nothing of any importance took place that I remembered of. Very windy & dusty. Bought some fresh antelope of a trader. At noon had a heavy hail storm — while eating in the open air, then rain. In 2 hours the ground was as dry as ever.

2nd   Have not got out of sight of Laramie Peak yet. Could see at sun rise plenty of snow on the top of it. Spent the forenoon in shoeing cows near a trading establishment Some Indians came in our camp & one asked me if I was going to have a pappoose. Ha! ha! ha! Much lightning & heavy thunder & large hail! tremendous time getting supper. Wet beds. 'Tis sublime, sublime.

3rd   Passed some strange looking hills like pyramids. Bad road among them. fine weather after the shower. Think we have got through the Black Hills. Had some mush & milk for supper & a fuss also about milk & vomiting up supper   over the left

4   Sunday. What a sight we have seen today; we met 402 Indians, or more. I am certain of this many for I counted them besides ponies & dogs, & plenty of children about 2 to a man & 3 ponies to a person & 5 dogs half wolf. They had their tent poles fastened on to the ponies on each side, & the provisions &c packed on his back, & on those poles. Dogs were loaded also. We met them on the hills   Very bad roads & we could see them for 3 miles. Were about 2 & ½ hours in passing them. They were Souix [Sioux], had weapons but were very friendly. Were either moving back into the Buffalo country or going to war with the Pawnees — we could not find out which. Their ponies were decorated with leather coverings & beads worked on them, with many strings cut of leather attached to the edge. Feathers on the horses heads, sometimes a bell on the neck, & a red string or something fastened to the tail, near the cropper. This sight was astonishing, equal to 50 caravans or circuses.

5. Still see nearly the same thing, nothing strange. Saw a

dead horse which had got frightened & his rope & had fallen
& broken his neck. I now by the request of the boys &
mother take the charge of cooking into my own hands, which
is my part. They are fond of clean victuals.

6. Got to Uta Ferry about 2 o'clock   Indians visited us
again. Bought a raw-hide for shoes for the cows   Drove
cows in the afternoon. encamped late.

7   Tried to get an early start to reach the watering place
before day as we get no water in less than 26 miles from the
Platte. Had a hail storm & rain at noon. Passed Rock
Avenue & alkali swamps, Mineral lake which looks black if
disturbed. Encamped within a mile of water which is
impregnated with sulphur. Very weary, late, no wood,
plenty of sage brush & grease wood which is but a shrub.

8   Delightful day. passed some graves & climbed Prospect
Hill; got tired before I reached the top & hung on to Isaac's
coat tail   Camped at noon near a wide stream clear as
crystal. Put washed my head. Reached the Sweet Water at
night near Independance Rock. Oh, yes, saw a lake of Alkali
all crusted over like a frozen pond with Saleratus some which
we gathered.

9   Rode David At the rock of granite (?) with Wes &
Put   all around it were names without number but none
which I could recognise as being acquainted. About noon we
came up to the Devil's Gate & it is a Devilish Gate in earnest
& Rode Nell down to it & saw the river come rushing
through. the rock on each side is 400 feet high & you could
throw a stone across at the top. Camped near a blacksmith
shop quite an establishment   hewed logs & shingled with
mud   Hailed & rained all the afternoon

10   *a very unpleasant occurence, girls rode with wet under
clothes all the forenoon,* camped at noon near a mountain of

rocks which stands out   very distinctly. we see nothing but
rocky mountains on either side and snow on the tops of some

11   Very sandy road up hill & down   saw some Snake
Indians trading. Traveled near 30 miles   pushed on over
sandy roads & horses gave out & it was dark before we
reached water, all tired & hungry. [In margin: The snow
capped mountains. Fremont Peak] Been raining hard. The
ground all wet. *Sublime.*

12. Recruited all the forenoon. Lightened our loads
considerably. threw away the side saddle & men's saddle &
blankets, some other clothing & traps, dinner box &c.
walked mainly all the afternoon. Encamped on the Sweet
Water a most splendid & delightful camp

13. What awful rocky hills we have to pass over. so many
flowers that fill the atmosphere with a very pleasant odor.
camped at noon near a icy cold spring   the boys had very
unpleasant feelings concerning Ed who had been
complaining about the walking

14. We are on the Rocky Mountains & expect to go through
the South Pass today   camped at noon off of the road a
piece near the Sweet water, where there was some traders
encamped or living. Rained some. Is very cold. Air is very
rare & rather difficult to breathe. cannot hardly discern that
we are in the south pass or near it. We have been ascending
gradually for some few days past & now will soon see the
waters of the Pacific running in the opposite direction. Pass
through about 2 oclock   saw it at some distance   a flag
erected at the summit. Found a blacksmiths shop   got a
cow shod. Encamped near Pacific Springs   ground
surrounding *very miry.* Bad watching, very cold

15   Rainy all day, nearly, extremely cold. Tremendous
time getting dinner. No stream near but rain, which came

down plentifully. Traveled about 19 miles & camped without water or wood. Got some water out of the road. Cold cold cold

16   White frost. Sun shines. still see snow covered mountains. Baked at night till 11 o'clock & had some conversation with will, he being reminiscent.

17   Saw a new grave. P. Jewet or Levitt from London Mo. Traveled 17 miles without water   Encamped on the big Sandy.

18   Ferried Green river at $5.00 pr wagon & 50 cts a head for horses. Swam the stock; swift current; quite an establishment here; court room, groceries, pies & cakes. Beer. dwelling houses, black smiths shop &c. Last year 11 men were drowned in trying to drive stock across on horseback; 7 at one time. Camped a mile or two down the river, & took dinner, then followed down 4 or 5 miles farther & stoped for the night   First rate feed

19   15 miles without water. See many Californians packing home on mules & ponies

20   Many sand or clay bluffs, one in the shape of a church bell. Crossed Ham's Fork, which is a very pretty stream.

21   Traveled about 18 miles without wood or water; very warm. Encamped on Black Fork; good camp; got dinner & spent the rest of the day in washing & baking pies & bread

22. Passed Fort Bridger. Stony road; camped at noon on a small stream. The ground surrounding is totally covered with Grass-hoppers. Could not set for them hopping into the dishes. Stayed all night near near a soda spring on one side & a hill on the other   covered with cedar   Had a concert, & company came in

23. Trav'led over hills & down gulches. Saw an antelope.

Reached Bear River at night. Bought at a station a dollar's worth of potatoes (about a peck)

24. This mountain air is very difficult to breathe; can not get enough scarcely into the lungs. Very warm & sultry. A woman near by camped started lying in a bed sick with mountain fever. Crossed the bridge free of charge the keeper knowing that we would ford it if we could not pass free & make a road for many others to see & follow. Rained again good

25. Crossed a mountain 2 miles up & 2 down. Many Utah Indians visited our camp at noon. Real imposers on emigrants, beggers Swapped an old white shirt for a pocket looking glass. We now follow along down Echo Creek Small caves in the Rocky mountains on either side of our road. Stucky is taken sick with the mountain fever We nearly all feel a little under the weather Mountain springs Sunday

26. Travelling on. Our sick is better Can see 12 different kinds of flowers within ½ a mile Some trading stations. Mother is taken sick. Oh Dear me! what if we all get sick! Reached Weber river Ferry.

27. She is no better; got some medicine of a company, a box of Lobelia; gave her 3 doses Did not start on till noon when she was some better after being washed with salaratus water, which eases the pain in the back. Many are having the mountain fever here in the Bear river mountains She took 5 pills at night.

28 Rolling on again. Awful roads in this canyon. Mother is better. On the recovery. Many new flowers & very fragrant The mule teams are ahead of us carrying merchandise to S. L. City & they bother us very much traveling so slow 6 mules on a wagon & stubborn at

that   We were at last obliged to stop for the night being blocked in by the mules. No feed at all. Tied the horses to trees & slept on the side hill

29   Descended the long hill which we have had such a time in ascending. Very dangerous. Came within 14 miles of G. S. L. City & encamped for the day. Washed & baked & wrote to Betsy part of a letter.

30   Entered the Great City; beautiful houses of Adobes; gardens well watered by a mountain stream made to flow along each side of every street, making water very convenient for irrigation, house water. The city is about 4 miles square and has about 25000 inhabitants. The buildings are neat but economically built

[This written by Wesley Tonner]
The Temple is quite a work. They are about building the foundation for a new Temple. I think it will encompass half an acre. They are also about constructing a wall around the city of clay — 12 ft high and 6 ft through at the base. We had a brief interview with Gov Young and Suite. (See letter enclosed.)

[Mary Burrell continues:]
The valley is improved north & south of the city. He is a pleasant man

July 1st   Spent the first part of the day running through town. Was treated by Wesley to soda water & ice cream & cakes, quite a rarity here in this wilderness. Towards evening started out, passed a spring so hot it would boil an egg. Encamped on the mountain edge. Ed's wagon ran down into the gulch

2 Sunday. Travelled through thick settlements   Grain looked well. Wheat in bloom. Corn looked well. Grass hard

to find, it being fenced up. Happened to good camp about 2 o'clock & stopped to recruit, when Frank & Mrs Hannibal had an explosion the result of which was dissolution (See note at back of book written by Wesley Tonner)

3   Remained in the same place throughout the day [The following in parentheses crossed out: (but it did not seem at all like the 4th & 5th of July to us)]. Wes had his shirt torn off by the boys. Very warm. Hannibals bought a yoke of oxen for $140, and Ed bought 2 yokes for $125 per yoke.

[The following is written inside the back cover:]
July 3rd   encamped 20 miles from the city. Mary sitting in the wagon Seeing her mother doing the same   Ike [Isaac?] Standing at the wagon foolin. Stucky laying in the tent singing   Put & Frank gone for good water. Ed gone to buy oxen. Louisa doing I dont know what. Myself sitting on the edge of the wagon box until it hurts me and what am I doing? Writing this nonsense —

4   Rolled on with the Bulls hearing the shouts of the drivers & the continued crack of the Buck skin when applied to the sides of said Bulls which had but little effect in spite of the physical energy which was displayed by said drivers   Traveled through brush & over hills but small in comparison to those which we had passed before. Wes lost the pistol in chasing after Franks mare, & after dinner Isaac & he went back to hunt it. Returned about 4 o'clock with the lost pistol, unexpectedly. I washed meantime. Stayed all night there. In the eve two Indians came. Put sold them his old coat for 50 cts. He put it on & called himself an Emigrant   Shot off his pistol much to our surprise, but knowing it had not taken effect we had considerable fun with him. [In margin: Bought a yoke of oxen.] Very windy in the night.

5   Passed over Weber River toll bridge and Ogdensburg.
Bought eggs   Forded Ogden River (there was a toll ferry).

6   Passed some Hot Springs, some like copperas,[7] at least
in color; tasted salt.   Bought some more cheese of very old
woman & children are after us to trade butter & cheese &
eggs for groceries or old clothes.

7. Hannibal bought another yoke of oxen $125, Nooned
where the mosquitoes were abundant very very numerous.
Reached 2nd Bear River ferry. Had the sick head ache

8.   Crossed the Ferry at $4.00 pr wagon   Were obliged to
go 8 miles out of the road to cross a small stream which has
brackish water. Nooned near the crossing. Filled the tin can
with the water & were obliged to use it for tea, as we could
find no other water.

9   Started before sun rise or breakfast & went about 4 miles.
Found water & had breakfast & now are 3 miles from where
we camped night before last on account of the bad crossing of
that small stream of brackish water. Traveled about 17 miles
& encamped near some brackish springs. Nearly all sick for
want of good water. Very warm & dusty

10. Went 14 or 15 miles & reached a mountain stream.
Nooned & went 8 miles further to a good cool stream

11. Many Indians came & were very troublesome, begging,
& ready to steal if a chance was offered. Got away without
any damage being done. Took water from the sink of Deep
Creek, & nooned among the sage   We Encamped at Pilots
Springs in a desert place.

12. Through a grove of cedar   Crossed several streams
coming from the snow mountains   Good cool water.
Threatened rain at noon Thundered, sprinkled a little.

---

[7] Copperas is not a copper compound, as one might expect, but an iron salt, ferrous
sulfate. It is green in color.

Encamped on a nice stream of soft water, very clear &
washed after dark.

13   Expected to reach the junction of the roads but did not.
Nooned in a wild wheat field. The grain was very high; up to
the horses heads. Many swarms of grass hoppers which eat
grass and grain out of the heads.

14   Passed the junction in the forenoon   Ironed. No
water except a small puddle to wash hands in. From the time
we struck the junction till we encamped we saw 7 dead cattle.

15   Saw 8 or 9 more dead cattle. Awful roads, hilly, 5 miles
descent, the last hill being very steep & dangerous   Emigrants need to let wagons down by ropes wound round the
alder trees at the top of the hill. A mountain stream runs
below as cold as ice water. In 2 miles we struck Goose Creek
& nooned   Rolled on 4 miles perhps & Hannibals wagon
wheel broke off at the axel in crossing a small run. Mended it
with a cedar stick.

16   Goose creek valley is the place for thieves it seems. We
were told this morning that 100 head of cattle were stolen 5
miles ahead of us last night & in the attempt 3 men were
shot, 2 badly wounded emigrants, & a few miles back 4
horses were driven off before the guards face & eyes. Night
before last 7 were stolen   Still we escape. Foster came up
with us with a shout! hurrah! have had an addition of a *son*.[8]
Lay by 3 days only. Wightman & wife have left them. Dined
with us. The Hannibals wagon in order to start. Traveled
about 5 miles & encamped with many others. Nothing was
heard of the Indians as was anticipated   Those cattle are
found & they are now in search of the stolen horses

17   Had another pudding made of wild currants. Traveled
about 30 miles   Almost a desert: nothing but Sage hills,

---

[8] Fred Foster was the baby. Lucy Foster Sexton, *The Foster Family, California
Pioneers* (Santa Barbara, 1925), p. 180.

very strong. Encamped in Thousand Spring Valley in a field of wild grain. Poor feed, 'tis so coarse & dry. No Inds

18   Went on a short distance when two men leading horses came running back with the intelligence that about 20 Indians had chased him back & he was oblige to fly or have his horses taken from him. He roused 15 or 20 armed men & went forward ready for them but when they arrived at the spot the Indians came running to make peace saying that the horses had got frightened at them, when they came to ask for something to eat; said they were good Indians. Shuishones — wanted to shake hands. Previous to the last meeting they had one Indian on a Pony up on the hill to take items & report to the rest who were awaiting to hear the report; but the report no doubt was that there was a vary large train close at hand & were making preparations to give them powder & bullets without delay; & thus they were baffled in their expectations. 'Tis expected they will attack some small party that may come along and as I write 60 Indians are camped back 2 or 3 miles   So we know not but we may [blot] attacked this night   There are 19 or 20 men here tonight to defend [blot] going to guard at a time

19. No harm done. No Indians appeared as was feared. Saw 7 on the road. Springs gushing out of the road-side under a rock. First rate camp at night. Still another arrangement on the cooking. Mother bakes while I cook in week about with Louisa.

20. Hore frost. Started early & went through the canyon safely — very rough roads. A warm spring comes bubbling up from under a rock as large as a wash tub   Got started thinking Indians were among the stock, but they were squaws. Encamped on the head waters of Humbolt

21   Good roads, fine feed, very dusty. Foster & [blot] shot several ducks & divided with us; fish plenty in the stream.

Saw Mr Pervis of Joliet; sent [blot] address to Plainsfield [blot] him. Camped in a perfect meadow [blot] intended to have a concert but it turned into a supper of Ducks.

22. Ive got my old customers to deal with again. as usual could not get dinner. Finished the first knitted sock for Wm [Hannibal] which I commenced the 19th   Fosters men shot 2 geese & gave us one   Had a jaw with Stucky for calling me a liar, which did not set very well on my rennet[9]

23. Passed some of Zumwalts train; camped with loose cattle. Came to the forks of road; one led over the mountains. the other through the canyon crossing the Humbolt 6 or 7 times, very deep. Went the latter route which is 20 miles shorter   Blocked up the wagon boxes, avoided the worst crossing & camped.

24. Had our goose for breakfast   Traveled on. Crossed the river 3 times in the forenoon. Mrs. Hannibal got left because she would not get into the wagon quick enough   Ed had to bring her on horse back. Very warm nooning. Did not cross again. Encamped near the mountain early. Plenty of wild currents. Had a concert in the evening.

25   Went over the mountain a stretch of 20 miles with out feed or water. Mountain very high but not very steep; very warm & fatiguing to man & beast   Saw a "flying cloud"[10] along with 3 or 4 young men in Co. Very good looking but badly dressed. Reached Gravelly Ford & encamped. Mrs. Foster has the sick head ache

26   Ed went to the upper ford & left a notice on a board for

---

[9] Rennet, which is obtained from a calves' stomach, is used to separate the curd from the whey in the making of cheese. Evidently what she means here that her stomach was upset.

[10] In Mary Burrell's day the clipper ship was the equivalent of today's space shuttle. The *Flying Cloud* was a ship built by master shipbuilder Donald Mckay. It was launched in 1851 and sailed around the Horn from New York to San Francisco in 89 days. She is evidently referring here to an extra-fast covered wagon.

Cub[11] that he had crossed to the South side of Humbolt the 26th. Left about ½ past 10 o'clock & traveled about 15 miles or less & stopped for the night. Bought 4 nice Salmon trout of some nearly naked Indians for a loaf of bread & some crackers. We ate the whole 4 for our supper. Splendid   One Indian stole Joes fish hook & has followed on after him threatning to shoot if not delivered. He gave it up & ran for life.

27. I am going to cook the rest of the way through if my health permits. Ascended some very high hills. Some had been volcanoes & there were lumps of lava as large as my head tumbling down the mountain side which was much steeper than the roof of a house. Rained some last night. No water   at noon Encamped near a Tule swamp where there were heaps upon heaps of mosquitoes, horrible to tell. A spring was at the left of the road; the water was sweet, quite sweet, — we feared it was poisonous as it made some of the boys feel strange

28. Left this miserable place & traveled about 12 miles & when we came to the river where we camped for the night the boys took a bath, while we washed & boiled ham   good feed —

29. started in the midst of a large train of emigration. Nooned without water except what we packed. Traveled about 20 miles when we passed a good spring to the left of the road at the foot of a high mountain. Passed on about two miles further and encamped beside a slough.

30   Went on without any good water. Passed through a dry canyon a few [blot] of which were very rocky   Traveled about 20 miles & came to the river once more & camped

---

[11] "Cub" was the nickname of Cuthbert Burrell, her father's brother, who had preceded them to California and was settled in Green Valley, Sonoma County. He is listed in the 1860 Federal Census as a farmer, 58 years old, born in England. They expected him to come out to meet them.

having about 3 pints of service berries picked for a Dumpling which went well. They are very tart.

31. Was so slow in starting that many trains got ahead of us & we took their dust all day. Touched the river at noon. but could not alight for the slough which runs along each side of the River   many mosquitoes —

[August] 1. Very sandy, hard for teams, warm, many dead cattle, as often as 2 in one miles distance. We are troubled with to many slow trains ahead & behind & we are obliged to travel among them & be afflicted with their dust   Got more service berries & had a concert in the evening. The boys mowed grass for a bed

2. Nooned near a slough, just no place at all to noon; no grass whatever to be got by the cattle. Crossed them over a mud hole & nearly mired them in going over & coming back. Went a little farther & encamped near the river & made a willow bridge for the stock to cross over to get grass & cut grass for the horses which are tied to the wagon for fear of getting sloughed   Sold a table spoon full of acid to a trader for $2 for his mules. Got lots of service berries on the bank

3   Rolled on through the deep sand from 4 to 5 inches deep. traveled about 4 miles & stopped to rest for the long stretch tommorrow. — 18 or 20 miles without grass or water. Had some fiddling & dancing, washing, baking, knitting, reading old compositions of Ws' [Wesleys'], scholars & more than all, more than all. [The following words are crossed out: "stuck my nose in where I had no business"]

4. Left the river   traveled 9 miles then came to a fresh stream, filled our kegs   traveled 3 miles & encamped on the river. Animals very tired.

5. Found that two of Hannibals oxen was missing. After hunting for them nearly all the forenoon concluded they were stolen. Traveled about 8 miles & encamped on the river

where 6 horses got stuck in the river. Sold old Susan for $15, went 7 miles & encamped. I am Humbolted pretty badly these 2 or 3 days past.

6. Sunday. Travled short distance & nooned after which we travled on till night and had to stop without grass within about 5 miles of the meadows

7 Started early. Soon arrived at the meadows. Nooned. Bad water. See many bull-rushes growing in the water. Travled about 9 miles & encamped in a large plain of alkali. Good grass but poor water. Enough to kill every thing. Waded in & cut grass to carry on to the desert. Foster lost his [unreadable] steer. We all feel under the weather.

8th   Left this stinking place, & reached the head Lake about noon where the boys again waded up to their waists to get grass. Foster lost another steer. We then started on about sun down   filled our kegs with pretty good water. Rolled on the desert leaving the Lake. About 9 o'clock reached some stores all lighted up which looked like a circus or city-like. Were halted by old Holmes, who persuaded us to encamp until his wife's train should come up so that we could travel together. Said Cub was not there nor would be. Well, he directed us to a slough & it being after dark could not see what kind of a place it was, how many dead cattle & horses. Here Foster lost a fine ox which he brought from Plainfield or Kanesville   This slough is an outlet to the Lake 10 miles apart. Our two companys were rather under the weather but we did not take any notice of it.

9   A trader came along & gave us some directions how to treat the one horse which had become swollen about the neck & head. Applied turpentine & camphor outwardly while he poured laudanum down his throat. We soon saw that others were swelling fast. In 10 minutes 16 horses were swollen, all

except Hannibals two & the two which we got of Halstead. We applied turpentine to all which removed it immediately but put the horses into torment. We soon sent for the trader & he hastened to our relief. Removed the horses & camp also to a running stream, an outlet of the Lake. Put the horses into it & all hands poured water upon their heads & necks then made a kind of paddle, a piece of board filled with tacks and slap this into the swellings. Well, Well we worked till noon & we started on the desert again, but the two iron greys died. The evening was fine   arrived at the slough about 9 o'clock. Here we watered and fed our stock and to our pleasurement found that the horses were better. Traveled on briskly until daylight, when we stopped again and fed ourselves work cattle & horses. during the night we left the road on the desert.

10th. Started on and soon struck the sand. 12 miles of Sandy road. got half way through and stopped again and fed and watered. got to Carson river and watered. Here are a number of trading posts that have assumed the name of "*rag town*".[12] No grass here. Traveled up the river about 3 miles to willow town. Here we encamped for the night at a Smith-Shop purposing to have wagons repaired. During this day we lost one fine ox. I would also insert here that we struck the river about half past 2 o'clock —

11th   Remained here having the wagons repaired until near evening, when we rolled out and traveled about three miles   encamped on good grass. Stock doing well —

12th   Collected the stock and to our astonishment found that our best horse ("Bill") has again taken the swelling in his breast   We used every means in our power to save him.

---

[12] "Rag towns" cropped up all along the trail, the incipient towns. Some of them grew up to maturity, others became ghost towns.

Spent the whole day, but alas! he died about evening.
During this day we lost a good cow also

13th   Traveled about 16 miles across desert and encamped
on good grass   during the night another cow died

14   Traveled 8 miles across a desert   nooned on good
grass. moved on and encamped near night on the opposite
side of the river near a company of Pyute Indians. grass
good —

15th   Traveled considerable distance (meantime crossed
the river) encamped for the night. good grass   during the
night two cattle died, one of our's & one of Foster's. Would
feel pretty well myself if I had not eaten so many beans. They
make me feel so w----y

16   Started in pretty good season crossed a 10 mile desert &
after passing along the river 1 mile camped in good grass   2
Californians stayed with us. Had a concert

17. Found that during the night 2 of Fosters cows had died
& one of the horses had taken the swelling. 7 miles brought
us to clear creek, passing what is called Gold Canyon or the
first diggings. In the afternoon came to some ranches. Fine
country for farming   Fences made of pine trees & sawed
boards, log houses — pretty comfortable   We now are in
Carson's Valley.

18. During the night the boys attended a dance. Black horse
died last night & Foster & us parted. Came up with him at
noon & was surprised to see Cummings[13] & Mather [?] who
had come to meet Foster. Numerous springs in the valley.

19. Traveled about 8 miles and encamped near the mouth of
the Canyon at a very large spring of clear cold water. Several

---

[13] This was William Cummings, the husband of Mariett Foster Cummings, whose
diary appears in this series, Volume IV (California Trail, 1852) pp. 117-168, especially
pp. 117-119.

houses near. One butcher shop   bought 40 lbs of veal. The boys [unreadable] at raking and binding. Rested ready for the Cannon & Pistol in the morning. Carsons Valley is about 50 miles in length N. & S. & about 20 in width. There are several beautiful farms which are well watered by Carson's River, & its numerous tributaries running from the snow mountains. These small streams are very convenient for farmers who have milk cows by causing the cold water to run through their milk houses, keeping the mik or butter very cool & nice. There are mountains on either side & are covered with heavy Pine which is being sawed   will amply supply the inhabitants of the valley for years. A saw mill is now partly complete which will be of great service to the inhabitants. There is a grist mill also in progress & I will here insert that a small saw mill is now in operation at the mouth of the Canyon. Emigrants here can purchase fresh provisions & all kinds of vegetables, as well as fresh animals. Undoubtedly Gold mines exist in these aged mountains & will yet be discovered though not yet very extensively worked. At the base of these mountains there is a fine grass where numerous herds of cattle graze.

[August] 20. Sunday. Spent the day in traveling through worst of Canyons, distance through 5 miles. Were nearly all day in going that short distance. Encamped in Hope Valley with Foster. Rained in the night. Put taken sick by eating berries.

21. Raining still. Started early & soon came to Red Lake (or a small lake) at the foot of the first range of mountain summits of the Sierra Nevada mountains   here we were delayed by teams ahead of us being stuck, having 16 yoke of oxen on. Still raining & very cold. On ascending it is very dangerous as wagons continues run back when they get as far up as Slippery Rock, which is 13 or 14 feet in length & very

difficult for cattle to keep from falling. Descent is not as bad. 'Twas nearly dark before we reached a camping place in Red Lake Valley which is surrounded by mountains, some capped with snow. Grass very short.

22   Gathered up & one cow was missing   Climbed up the second ridge which was steep & lengthy but not as rough as the first. Very cold. Passed just at the foot of a large snow bank which was melting some. In ascending we found 48 different kinds of flowers, some very pretty. Encamped a short distance west of the summit on very risky ground, rocks upon rocks. Drove the stock on the hill side; very cold. very windy. very damp and very uncomfortable. &c

23   Still rattling over rocks, up & down hills, some very steep. very thick timber. Pine & Balsom. No feed scarcely. Encamped at Tragedy Springs, among a drunken gang. Saw the effects of Liquor to our hearts content. Frosty.

24   Left Tradgedy Spring   traveled to two miles beyond Sleek Springs road   very hilly but not so rough as formaly   Drove the cattle one mile to poor grass

25   Traveled to Camp Creek. nooned. killed a rattlesnake   traveled about 4 miles when we came to a cut-off leading to Diamong Springs. We took this road and shortly encamped. feed close to road. roads very dusty   These mountains are well timbered. air quite cool. nights exceedingly so.

26   Left Alder creek. good road till noon, when we reached *Sly Park* being the first Ranch we saw in Cal. here we nooned. In the after noon we traveled several miles and encamped on Whiskey Flat diggins

27   Traveled (Sunday) to Diamond Sprs. Nooned. after noon traveled Mud Sprs and encamped on [?] grass

28   Traveled through mining country until noon when we

came in sight of Sac. Valley. Nooned near the old Mormon
Station. In the evening encamped in the valley —

29   In the afternoon passed some pretty good farming
country   arrived in Sac. City in the Evening

30. Stopt at noon. ferried the Sac. River   traveled about 12
miles and encamped on Pooter [Putah] creek. Bad water

31   Traveled through farming country. encamped in Ulati
valley.[14] tolerable grass.

Sept. 1st   Started in good season   passed through Suisun
valley. over a ridge to Green Valley.[15] Here we stopped at C.
Burrell —[16] thus ending a journey which for care, fatigue,
tediousness, perplexities and dangers of various kinds can
not be excelled.

LETTER OF WESLEY TONNER
FROM SAN JOSE TO ILLINOIS

September 10, 1854

Dear Friends

   I at length have the pleasure of informing you of our safe
arrival in this far-off Country. Without stopping here to tell
you anything about this country I will refer you back to
where I last wrote you which was at S. L. City   We
remained there about one day and would have been pleased
to remain longer, but our time would not permit. This is a
beautiful little city placed at the foot of the Wasatch
mountains. For water facilities it exceeds perhaps any thing
in the world — being watered by streams of fresh water

---

[14] Ulatis Creek in Solano County is named for the Ululato Indians who once lived in
the neighborhood. Erwin G. Gudde, *California Place Names* (Berkeley, 1969).

[15] This was their first California destination. The beautiful Green Valley was named,
not for the lusciousness of its growth, but because a Spanish official got sick there and
vomited "green." *Ibid.*, p. 128.

[16] *See* footnote 11, above.

flowing from the mountain and made to run along each side
of every street. The buildings are neat but economically
built. The City has about 8000 inhabitants besides a great
number that live out in the farming portion of the country.
The Lake lies about 30 miles n. w. of the city   We passed it
in leaving at the city. I have never yet told you that we had a
melodian and violin with us. With the aid of these
instruments we had many concerts, and made many an
evening which would have been dull and lonesome pass off as
but a moment. And I tell you there would be no small noise
when us *Cowdrivers* would join in the Chorus Boys carry me
long — Lily dale, Young folks at home, Old Folks at Egg
Hill &c. Sometimes we would have visiters from other
camps young boys for instance who had left dear Bro's &
Sisters at home — and when we were engaged in singing and
playing these mourneful melodies — the tears could be seen
starting from the eyes of these little prodigals if you will allow
me the word. Our Melodian got considerably abused and we
concluded to sell it to the Mormons. Some of the Brethren
told us that Gov. Young would be likely to buy it. So we
soon all but the old lady jumped into the wagon and "took a
ride" to the Gov's. Without much regard paid to ettiquete
we soon entered the office and made known the object of our
visit. The Gov said he was well supplied with music. (So I
thought from he has fifty wives.) However some one called
for a song and one of our feminines played, and the Cowdrivers sung until we had sang all we knew and more too. We
then sold the melodian at a good profit. I will here leave the
Mormon subject until I see you when I can tell you much
more than I have and with more ease. This is Sunday and I
must stop writing and get ready to go to meeting. Meeting is
over   I have returned home   Home did I say? Yes,
although among strangers I am treated as kindly as if I had

brothers Sisters & Parents here. but it is not the same. —

Now follow me if you please (in mind) over a worthless country until you arrive at Goose Creek abut 180 miles from the City   This is a perfect *"Hell hole"* for stealing cattle, fighting the emigrants &c. During this season not less than 150 horses have been stolen on this stream in a distance of only 20 miles, as this is the distance we travel on it. As an instance of matters at this place, I will relate to you the preceedings of one night while we were there. Previous to this you must be aware that the Road to Cal is now lined with Trading Posts, kept by Frenchmen mostly, who I believe are to a man worse for stealing than the Indians. A man on a mule attempted to drive our horses out of camp. But I happened to be standing guard on said night & as soon as I saw the chap & stopped him in his wild cause by making towards him with a Revolver cocked and in my hand, He pretended to be on the hunt of some Packers and asked a question to that effect which I answered immediately and he passed on. I wish I had shot the rascal & I would have done it had he not spoken when he did — About one hour after this, just before the moon arose to put a stop to his fun, this rascal returned — passed our camp at some distance & at the camp below us where they were not guarding drove out four horses and escaped with them doubtless in the same way he wanted to steal ours. The same night the Indians undertook to steal from a camp 5 miles above us, which resulted in a fight in which two of the emigrants got wounded one shot in the neck the other in the arm. I believe they both got well

Pass over another space of country and you will find it about the 9th of August at the Sink of the Humboldt. This sink is now nothing more than a lake about 10 miles squ filling the valley from the base of one mountain to the base of

the other. The sink has broken out lately, forming an outlet
or slough which makes the real desert about 10 miles shorter
than formerly This though is a grave yard for cattle. The
night before we started on the desert, and next morning all
horses were sick with what is called an incurable disease.
Two died and the rest we cured for the time being, but a few
days after three more died with a return of the disease. Out of
49 horn cattle we got 35 of them through and that by
frequently trading off lame ones for others. Carson valley is
pleasant. Crossing the Sierra Nevada mountains is too hard a
task to put down on paper. On the 29th of Aug. we entered
Sac[ramento] City in the evening — Remained all day and
left next day at noon. Crossed the Sac. River and traveled
west until we reached Green Valley. Situate in the Eastern
Border of the Coast Range Mountains about 11 miles N. E.
of Benicia. Here we stopped with our cattle. Our joy at the
thoughts that are ever no more to drive cattle through alkali
dust, guard them amidst the bites of venomous insects,
through storm and through rain &c, was inexpressible   I
forgot to tell you that we bought 3 Yoke of oxen before we
left S. L. settlements and put them to one wagon, thereby
giving our poor jaded horses a chance to recruit some [In
margin: "And I am now as good an oxdriver as can be scared
up"] On the 4th [of September] some of us started for San
Jose by public conveyance. It costs about 12 or 15 cts. per
mile to travel in this country. $1.00 per meal   While riding
in the stage in coming to this place I paid 50 cts for a pie.
And it was no great scratch pie neither. Boarding is from 8
to $10 per week. Wheat is worth from 1½ to 2 c per pound.
Wages for common labor from 2 to $5 per day and 40 to $50
per month, and very hard it is to get employ at all. I intend
working at the carpenter business for about $4.00 per day
and board myself. Since I have been here I have been

stopping with a Brotherinlaw to the man I came with
They are bully folks. very clever indeed. He is in his dis-
position very much like Bro Bill. They are just as clever to
the other boys.

Before leaving Kanesville or Council Bluff city we got
into a bitter scrape with the Indians. Perhaps you heard of it,
and perhaps not. I would have told you about this before
this, but I was afraid it would make mother feel more uneasy
about me while traveling through an Indian country and not
chance for writing often

You are aware that we were encamped while there on a
little stream a few miles south of the City. There was one
other camp on this stream about ¾ of mile above us. On
Sunday the last day of April (I believe it was) 11 Indians
attacked said camp without any cause and banished them
away from the camp shooting at some of the emigrants
causing them to fly to our camp for rescue. We boys each of
us mounted a horse with what arms we had & proceeded to
the Seat of War. I had the day before bought a Colts
Revolver & soon found a good chance to use it. When got
near the camp we found the Indian in possession and one
Indian laying groaning that had been wounded in the scuffle
before the emigrants fled. There were but three of us to do
any thing and we found that our Pistols could not compete
with the Rifles of the Indians. Meantime we sent a
messenger to town for reinforcements. We tried to get the
indians on the run by keeping a proper distance and firing
with pistols into camp. They soon began to run each one his
own way. We kept sight of them as well as we could for we
did not dare go too close lest he would pick us off our horses
with his rifle. You will perceive that we had lost sight of
them all by this time except one. Another fellow and myself
kept watch on this fellow until the force would come from

town. We cast our eyes at the prairie & saw coming mounted on horse one of the Indians we had started and was coming too full flight with rifle in hand. We thought it our safest plan to wheel which we did, and made for camp. Indians after us. When we got near the camp we met a reinforcement from town. — and the Indian now wheeled running towards the Indian we had been watching. His horse could out strip ours, but followed as close as we could and when we again got sight of them they were both on that horse. We urged our horses and when we got within about 300 yds. they stopped their horse and both fired into our crowd which now numbered about 20 horseman. Now was our time when we knew their guns were both empty. And then commenced a chase which was worth seeing. the fellows then had the best horse, foremost. We ran across that Missouri bottom I should think about two miles. When we came up pretty close to them. My horse was the fastest except a mule which led our van. As soon as a fellow thought he was close enough he would shoot. Soon the formost Indian fell dead from his horse pulling with him the other one. This one had draw a Butcher knife and empty gun to fight with, and he done well for he came near getting into timber and escaping in spite of us. [Following scratched out: "from the fact that we have now"] nearly all our guns empty. While trying to drop the villain with my revolver he ran up and gave me a dig in the leg with his knife, before I could wheel the horse. We killed these two and the one that was wounded, afterwards died. So we heard none of our crowd were hurt any except myself and that but slight. There was some talk of having us arrested — a man told me so the next day in Kanesville. I told him they might crack away. However they thought best to leave it alone I guess. I do not think there was any wrong about it. I fought for my rights, and tried to kill them lest they might attack our camp   we knew not when.

We understood afterwords that the Indian Chief said we had served them right, that they had no business to cross the Missouri and molest the emigrants. We also heard that there was a reward out for those that had a hand in killing the Indians, & that orders were sent to Laramie to stop us there. But we traveled on unmolested and not afraid. If any body had tried to take us after we were on the Plains they would have got reward with our Pistols for here we had the law in our own hands. I have received but one letter here instead of about six 6 as I expected. When you write direct to San Jose City, Cal.

Yours as ever   Wesley Tonner.
The letter I received was from Tom.

"Northren Route to Calafornia"

⅔ Elizabeth Myrick

INTRODUCTION

On the 29th of October, 1849, two young people, Horace Augustine Myrick and Elizabeth Tilton Perkins, were married by the Rev. John Lewis, a Congregational minister, in Lima, Grant County, Wisconsin. They lived in neighboring Platteville. Over the next few years they made moves characteristic of mobile Americans on the advancing frontier that brought them ultimately into the northwest corner of California in the redwood country of Humboldt County near the small town of Rohnerville, not far from Humboldt Bay in the Eel River valley.

Elizabeth Myrick was the recorder of a diary that told of the long overland journey to California in 1854.

It was very soon after their marriage that Horace made a long preliminary journey to California as a participant in the gold rush. He got there just in time for the word to come that a strike had been made in the Trinity mountains, so that's where he went. He took ship from San Francisco to Humboldt Bay and was living in Weaverville when the 1850 United States census taker interviewed him and recorded him as 35-years-old, born in New Hampshire; his profession, a miner.

Another 1850 census taker wrote down the name of Elizabeth Myrick in Grant County, Wisconsin, saying she was 24-years-old, born in Indiana.

Shortly after the census taker's visit, on September 10, 1850, Elizabeth gave birth in Platteville to a baby girl and named her Harriet Olive Myrick.

Horace returned from California a year or two later with the news of fine farming country in the beautiful redwood empire of coastal northern California. He had observed it on his journeys to and from Weaverville in Trinity County. He told neighbors and friends about all of this and by 1854 had interested several families in going overland with covered wagons to the Pacific shore.

There were John Porter and Caroline A. Langdon, William H. and Julia A. Simmons, Elisha L. and Nancy Davis, and the Grant Myers family, all of whom became pioneer settlers along the banks of the Eel River in Humboldt County. There were other individuals and families who went along to become settlers in other parts of California.

Another baby girl was born to the Myricks in the newly settled land. This was Altheda Myrick, first white child to be born in the Eel River valley. Her date of birth was August 11, 1855. According to the 1860 census records there was another child born to Elizabeth Myrick in 1857, a little girl named Lucy. Nothing seems to be known of her.

The Myricks farmed the rich Eel River valley for many years. Their's was a general farm with livestock and crops. Some huge redwood trees had to be cut down, and the stumps remained for years. They took their crops to Humboldt Bay for shipment to San Francisco and beyond.

Family records tell of the death of Elizabeth Tilton Myrick in Rohnerville on February 17, 1892, and of Horace Augustine Myrick on September 10, 1895.

Elizabeth Myrick's diary is plain-spoken, written by a plain-spoken woman. There are no flights of fancy. She saw what she saw and wrote it down with no flourishes. She did note in that year of the Kansas-Nebraska act that the germs of settlement were being established along the route through present Nebraska and Wyoming in 1854. She used the term "trading post" for such a settlement, or sometimes "grocery," even once "dogery." These posts were often run by Frenchmen, either from Canada or Louisiana, and there were Indian wives and children about.

The diary itself is a small book, 3¾ by 6¾ inches in size. On the first page she has written, "Elizabeth T Myrick   Blank Book

Purchased Council Bluffs City   May the 10 1854." On the next
page are written the words, "Northren Route to Calafornia."

She kept her diary faithfully through July 29 with the words,
"camped on goose creek." The actual locale was about where the
boundaries of the three modern states of Idaho, Nevada, and
Utah meet in what is now called the Sawtooth National Forest.

Why did Elizabeth Myrick stop writing her journal? We don't
know. She had not run out of blank pages in her book. These were
later filled with records kept in Rohnerville telling of her income
from washing clothes for such as Henry Rohner, the Swiss
immigrant for whom the town was named. She sold many dozens
of eggs and pounds of butter. And she wrote down her purchases
from Rohner's store such as "1 thimble 1 tooth brush 1 slate."

It was a telephone call from Wendell C. Gulliksen of Salem,
Oregon, that alerted us to the existence of Elizabeth Myrick's
diary. He is a descendant of the lady. Later we got to know his
brother, Jorgen Gulliksen of Fortuna, Humboldt County,
California, and he added to our knowledge. A photocopy of the
original 1854 diary was sent to us by a nephew, David Gulliksen,
of Stockton, California. It is kept safely in a bank box there. The
family also made available to us their family papers collected over
many years for which we are grateful. They have enthusiastically
given us permission to publish the diary.

ROSTER OF THE MYRICK WAGON TRAIN OF 1854:

Mr. and Mrs. Blundells and their little boy. This is the spelling as it
    appears in the Parrish letter. It is variously spelled in Elizabeth
    Myrick's diary. Parrish says they were in Tehama, just south of
    present Red Bluff, in the Sacramento Valley.

Mrs. Cummings gave birth to "a fine son this morning." Thus wrote
    Elizabeth on June 7. This was Mrs. Jonathan Cummings. They pre-
    empted a homestead on the Eel River some miles upstream from the
    others in the party. The town of Cummings in Mendocino County is

named for the family. According to Wendell Gullikson, there is only one house left. Erwin G. Gudde, *California Place Names* (Berkeley, 1969), p. 82. The Eel River flows through both Mendocino and Humboldt counties. It is the longest flowing river out of the west side of the California Coast Range.

Elisha and Nancy Davis, 31 and 30-years-old respectively, settled on a farm near that of the Myricks in the Eel River valley. Both families were visited by the census-taker on the same day, July 7, 1860. Elisha's brother, Eli, a young man in his 20's lived with them.

Mr., Dr., and Mother Davidson (variously spelled) are mentioned by Elizabeth many times. Parrish in his letter tells of Vance and Doc Davidson. He says Vance was mining on the Feather River. We know nothing more about them.

"Heartsaugh" was living in the rich mining town of George Town in El Dorado County, according to William Parrish. Elizabeth had mentioned a "Mr. Hartsough" on June 17. He had been elected captain of the wagon train. For an apt commentary on George Town see Erwin G. Gudde, *California Gold Camps* (Berkeley, 1975), p. 129. According to the Gulliksens the name is now spelled "Hartsook." There is a resort some ten miles south of Garberville with that name. The 1860 census of Mendocino County lists an Isaac Hartsook, a 41-year-old English farmer, living in Mendocino township with two sons, George, age 20, and Isaac, Jr., age 18.

Newton Hough is mentioned by Elizabeth in her diary on July 12. A Charly Hoff is named in the Parrish letter. Nothing more is known about them.

John Porter and Caroline (Simmons) Langdon, were important members of the wagon train. They were New Yorkers by birth. Their Rohnerville farm was named "Langdons' Ranch." They were neighbors of the Myrick, Simmons, and Davis families. They were all visited on the same day by the census-taker, July 7, 1860. Elizabeth Myrick in her diary tells of the birth of a baby boy on May 30 to Caroline Langdon on the plains of Nebraska. He was given the name, Thurston Platte Langdon. Shirley Langdon Wilcox of Arlington, Virginia, a descendant of the Langdons, has been most helpful in supplying information about them and other family relationships. She also kindly let us have the use of William C. Parrish's letter of December 17, 1854. It had been written to the Langdons and is among the family papers. Caroline Langdon was a sister of William Simmons.

"Mr. Myers" is mentioned by Elizabeth in her June 28 entry. This was probably Grant Myers, who went into ranching some 20 miles south of Rohnerville. There is a town there named for him, Myers Flat, Humboldt County. Erwin G. Gudde, *California Place Names* (Berkeley, 1969), p. 216.

Henry Parr is so-far unidentified.

William C. Parrish, the writer of the letter which here follows the diary, was living in Sutterville, Amador County, when he penned his missive on December 17, 1854. We know nothing more about him except that he was a busy miner. For information about Sutterville see Erwin G. Gudde, *California Gold Camps* (Berkeley, 1975), pp. 341-42.

William H. and Julia Ann Simmons are so listed in the 1860 census. They settled on the banks of the Eel River as neighbors of the Langdons, Davises, and the Myricks. Caroline Langdon was William H. Simmons' sister. When they crossed over the trail, they had a six-year-old son, Lofton F. Simmons, born in Michigan. They were both New Yorkers by birth.

THE DIARY

May 10 [1854]   Rose early this morning and washed some clothes in the afternoon   went to council Bluff City bought a few articles   Saw an elk.

11   Started on our journey, got to Council Bluff   Stayed there half the day   Seen 2 beggar indians. There was a good deal of money given them by the emigrants   went from there to the Missouri River an camped for the night

12   Crossed the river in a steam ferry boat   went a quarter of a mile an camped   oweing to a hard storm of wind and rain the same visited us to day   there is a company of 48 persons from Savannah (Ill.) (men, wemen & children) they have joined our company making in all 64 persons

13   Raining this morning   a very cold windy day

crossed 2 creeks   the men had to dig the banks to make it passable

14 Sun   Started early   we are now on the banks of Elk horn river waiting to be ferried across, have to pay 2 dollars for each waggon across   the cattle swim across the river seen a grave where the indians had buried their dead. they bury their dead on top of the ground all in a heap thrown up onto a mound. Met 6 indians.

15 Mon   got to Platt river in the forenoon   now we [unreadable] the Platte river valley and will be for 5 hundred miles   had a hard storm of wind and rain   seen 4 graves to day

[May] 16   Tus   Cold wind this morning   traveled six miles. camped   it is too rainy an windy to travel   we are on the big Platte river where some poeple say it storms every day or two   a company with a drove of cattle overtook us this evening

17   Wen   Very cold & windy   another drove of cattle overtook us to day   Seen one grave   camped on the river

18   thur   clear cold wind this morning   one cow missing the cow found an [unreadable] to the camp tonight   we are camped on the looking glass

19   Fri   Clear & windy this morning   met an army of indian fighters going to fight the Pawnee indians   They were dressed in full indian uniforms with their guns bows an arrows an lances an bayonets & shields   camped on a small creek

[May] 20   Sat   clear an Pleasant   passed a train where the indians had stolen 13 horses the night before   eleven men were out in search of them but could not find them but found where the indians had sheared off the main [mane] of their horses   camped on large fork of big Platte   there is 5 trains in company camped in sight

21   Sun   crossed loup fork   it is a very difficult ford   it is full of quick sand on the bottom of the river   camped on the west side of loup fork   rained to night

22   Mon   Clear and pleasant   in camp all day on loup fork   some of men are fixing   Mr. Davidson mending buggy   some are hunting some are fishing   some are cooking   some are washing   The wemen are washing cooking and airing their clothes   Some are patching an mending their clothes   I have been sewing the waggon sheets for the boys and the buggy

23   tus   fair an pleasant   traveled all day   seen nothing of importance   camped on prarie creek

[May] 24   Wedn   Fair and warm   in the after noon traveled all day on the wrong road   camped again on the prarie creek   Seen white wolves

25   thur   Clear warm an pleasant   one of Mr. Brundles sons was thrown from a mule he was riding an badly hurt   passed the station wrote one letter an put it in post office kept by Dr. Clark[1] the United States Indian Agent   passed the station an post office. Crossed wood creek on a toll bridge at 50¢ per waggon   traveled 8 or ten miles & camped on the prarie where there is no water for the cattle we carried some to cook with   Mr. Davisson left our company this evening   one train overtook us that came from ST Francisville Clark Co Mo   Rained in the night

---

[1] This was probably George W. Clarke, who was appointed on August 14, 1854, to be Indian agent to the Pottawatomies farther south in present Kansas. Louise Barry, *The Beginning of the West: Annals of the Kansas Gateway to the American West, 1540-1854* (Topeka, 1972), pp. 1191 and 1201. This remarkable book is fundamental to the study of the eastern take-off points for the western trails. Mary Burrell also made comment in her diary entry for May 13 about "Dr Clarke." That was twelve days before Elizabeth Myrick's mention of the man. Mary places the encounter on Wood River.

26 Fri Raining this morning cloudy at noon Mr Davison has caught up with us again. Seen several companys ahead on their way to California. Raining this evening. Camped to night on the big Platte river.

27 Sat Seen other trains Pleasant day camped on a creek plenty of wood & water

28 Sun Forenoon Showery with some wind we stayed in camp to day 5 or 6 trains some with droves of cattle passed us this morning on buffalo creek Mr Davison is about to leave us again he is dissatisfied with the company because they dont do just as he says after noon Mr Davison has consented to stay with the company

[May] 29 Mon Rained the forenoon the after noon clear and pleasant camped on big Platte plenty of water and grass Seen several trains on the other side of Platte passed 2 droves of cattle one man was accidently shot through the waist & side though not mortally wounded after night a very hard storm of wind & rain

30 Tus clear warm & pleasant muddy roads in the morning Seen pararie dogs to day gathered a variety of beautiful wild flowers see a great deal of prickly pair camped on Platte Mrs Langdon had a fine son.[2]

31 Wed clear & windy this morning In camp all day Mr Langdon and Mrs Simmons washed I baked some bread

June 1 Thurs foggy in the morning fair an warm at noon cloudy and windy & like for rain this evening Passed by a large Spring to day camped on a Slough not far from big Platte passed through a Swampy country to day

[2] The newborn was Thurston Platte Langdon. He was given the middle name, "Platte," in honor of the river. The parents were John Porter and Caroline (Simmons) Langdon. Information has been supplied us by Shirley Langdon Wilcox, of Arlington, Virginia, great-great-grand-daughter of the Langdons. See roster above.

2   Fri   Clear pleasant   the wind blows considerable this evening   camped on a small creek near big Platte   we bid farewell to the timber this morning   we will have to burn buffalo chips and brush when we can get it for 200 miles   rained in the night

3   Sat   raining & windy this morning   Showery & hard wind all day   traveld through the sandy bluffs   passed by a camp noon that was called post office   some of the company left letters there   camped by a Spring near Platte

4   Sun   Clear windy & pleasant to   traveld through Sand mud & alkali water & camped on rattle snake creek about noon   half the day lost   2 indians belonging to the pottawattamie tribe stayed with us to night

[June] 5   Mon   Clear & cold very windy   traveled through swamps & sand bluffs   over took Mr Davison that is taking a drove of sheep through   Mr. Brundles little boy fell out of the wagon to day but not much hurt. Camped on Platte this evening   the boys gathered buffalo chips   the plains abound in the most beautiful wild flowers I ever seen   cold enough for shawls   your garden flowers in the States would envy them for their beauty   The Turkish crown is a species of the Prickly Pear only it is of a more beautiful form and has a pink & yellow flower on it   camped on Platte

6   Tus   Very cold wind to day   Seen a large train on the other side of platte   a drove passed us to day   we passed a dogery[3] where they had whiskey candy nuts an other articles to sell   Camped on green river   plenty of grass an water but no wood   have to burn buffalo chips   cold enough to sleep under blankets & 2 heavy quilts   woolen clothes are comfortable.

---

[3] A doggery was a saloon of a cheap or disreputable nature, or sometimes a grocery store with the same characteristics.

7   Wed   clear & pleasant. Mrs Cummins has a fine son
this morning   We started on our journey in 2 hours after it
was born   noon   Mrs Cumins is getting along well. Passed
an indian camp

8   Thur   cold & cloudy windy this morning   Some of
the boys are out hunting Buffalo & Antelope   traveled over
high bluffs to day and seen snow at a long distance on the
mountains   passed 4 graves to day   One the man died the
5 of this month   his name was Kimble   the last one the
man died last night at half past 11 oclock   his name was
Graham   he left a wife & one child to mourn their
loss   noon   very cold and windy   Mr Simmons went to
get some wood   brought a lot of cedar   2 more graves
seen   Camped on Platte   2 indians visited us to night an
sold mokisons to the boys   passed 7 graves to day

[June] 9 Fri   Cloudy and cool this morning   passed 2
wigwams where there is lots of squaws & children   passed 2
more wigwams seen an old indian one hundred & six years
old   Noon   In sight of what is called the chimney
rock   passed 3 graves this morning   traveled over some
rough country this evening an camped on Platte   a troup of
indians passed us since we stoped   cold night   the water
froze the eighth of an inch of ice

10   Sat   Passed a camp where the men had been fighting
one shot the other it is thought mortally wounded
Noon   walked out through lots of prickley pear (Cactus in
smaller quantities) an camped on or near Platte

11   Sun   traveled over a hard gravel road   passed by a
traders camp   They were white men   they had squaws for
wifes   camped on a small creek   the boys are singing this
evening   Some of the oxen are lame

12   Mon   very warm   noon   still very warm   no grass

for the cattle   some timber in sight on Platte   more of the oxen lame   clear very warm

[June] 13   Tues   Passed traders camp   noon Camped on platte   I washed this after noon   We are in 4 miles of Fort Larimie & hard storm of rain to night

14   Wedn   cloudy & calm but pleasant this morning very windy & showery   in camp all day   2 miles from Fort Larimie

15   Thurs   Clear & pleasant   started early this morning passed by Fort Larimie on the oposite side of Platte   come to the black hills to day   passed 2 or 3 white indian stations. noon   like for rain   passd one grave   2 graves more camped in the black hills

16   Fri   Fair & Pleasant   passed Dr Davidson company this morn   His sister died this morning with the colera She was sick but 24 hours   pased 5 graves besides hers hatty [Harriet] fell out the waggon this evening traveled over very rough hilly road to day camped near a creek

17   Sat   clear & cool with wind this morning   pased one grave   Still among the black hills   several trains in sight noon   Took dinner on Platte   camped on the road 1 mile & half from Platte   Mr Langdon gave up his office of captun ship. Mr Hartsough elected captain

[June] 18   Sun   clear & pleasant this morning   noon very warm   come through some very high rugged hills Took dinner on Platte camped on Platte   Windy & like for rain this evening

19   Mon   Cloudy & windy & cool. Traveled over high hills and a very rough road this fore noon   noon   Stoped on Platte for dinner   a hard hail storm met us there an give

the men & horses & cattle a good pelting   cold wind this
evening   camped on Platte   plenty of grass & wood

20   Tues   Clear & cold wind   good traveling   noon
took dinner on camaleon hill   see the horned long tailed
toads   Camped on Platte near a grocery kept by white men

21   Wed   Clear & pleasant   traveled over very rough
roads   noon   pleasant   took dinner in Platte river valley
in a grove   Mr Davises drove passed by us   we passed a
black Smith Shop   3 or 4 miles further passed 2 groceries
one white woman was living with a man out of civilization
camped on Platte

[June] 22   Thurs   Clear & warm   passed another traders
shop   trail led over rough hills   Seen ice on the hill on the
opposite side of Platte   noon   took dinner on Platte   an
indian passed by us on horse back & leading one horse
Camped on Platte

23   Fri   Clear & warm   passed a grocery   left Platte
this morning   traveled all day with out crossing any water.
no grass for the cattle   Seen lots of Alkalis on the
ground   come to the willow Springs in the evening   there
overtook several trains & droves of cattle   met 2 or 3
companies from Calafornia   they packed on mules
camped on a branch

24   Sat   Clear   Started this morning before breakfast
traveled 2 miles then took breakfast & found grass for the
cattle   noon   come to a good Spring of living water &
found plenty of grass for the cattle   a great deal of alkali on
the ground   met a company returning from Oregon to the
States   Passed a lone house   a family lives there an keeps
Store   camped on Sweet water.

25   Sun   Clear & warm & very windy   the company
stays in camp all day   we are on the rocky mountains close

by independants rock   it has hundreds of names written on
it by the emigrants   I went over the independents rock with
a company of ladies and gentlemen. it is a great national
curiosity

[June] 26 Mon   Clear & warm & windy morning
pased the Devils Gate in the mountains   passed a store
camped in the mountains on Sweet water   good feed for
the cattle

27   Tues   Clear & rather cool & windy morning   Harriet is not well   passed 1 grave   Henry Parr lost his pocket
book an has gone back a haf days Journey to hunt for it

28   Wed   warm & very windy. Dr Davisons boy fell out
of the waggon & is badly crushed to pieces though not
mortally   noon   Cloudy   after dinner we had a very hard
shower of rain & wind   very cold hard wind all afternoon
cold rocky mountain fashion   camped on Sweet water
Mr Myers was taken suddenly sick with the Colera mor-
bus an was sick all night   Six Snake indians visited us to
night

29   Thurs   Clear & cool wind   Mr Myers is better this
morning. it is very windy all day   camped on the mountain
by a little Spring   grass & water rather scarce   in sight of
the snow caped mountains though one hundred miles off

[June] 30   Fri   Hard wind all day & quite cool   camped
on Sweet water. Some what showery this afternoon

July 1   Sat   Clear & warm for the weather in the
mountains   hard wind   Mrs Brundle is very sick all
day   we Stayed in camp all day   Mr Myers brought some
snow water off the mountains where there is a snow drift

2   Sun   Clear in the morning   at noon there come a hard
storm of wind & rain an some hail   we are over the Rocky
Mountains   camped on a small creek

3   Mon   Clear an warm this morning   I in company with
several ladies gathered some specimens of icing glass in rocks
at the foot of the mountains   One days journey west of the
Rocky mountains the Savannah company left us   they took
the road to Salt Lake City   we took the northern route. we
camped on Sandy creek in company with Dr Davison train

4   Tues   Clear warm & windy   Crossed big Sandy an
struck the desert   its productions are sage brush prickly
pear a little starved gras & a few stunted flowers over the
hills   Camped in the desert by a huge Sulphur spring
some emigrants here from Calaforney   they say there is
some indians with them. Several trains are camped here
this evening

[July] 5 Wed   Clear & warm the fore noon   in the after
noon there was a hard Storm of wind with but a few drops of
rain   we are camped all day in the middle of the desert in
consequence of there being no water for 30 miles more of the
desert. 15 Snake indians visited us to day   our company
started this evening at six oclock & traveled till mid night
then stoped untill day light

6   Thu   Clear warm an windy   traveled ten miles over
rocks an hills to Green River just through the desert. no feed
for the cattle. There is a ferry of 14 little flat Boats kept just
large enough for one waggon a piece   the owners charge 8
dollars per waggon   Our train thought that was too much to
pay for so little so they went down the river 3 or 4 miles an
crossed over to an Island an staid all night   found plenty of
grass for the cattel horses & sheep   Also plenty of first rate
wood called the Balm of Gillead[4]

7   Fri   Clear & warm   3 trains here together on the
island   men are fixing the waggon beds for ferry boats to

---

[4] Balm of Gilead is an old term for the black cottonwood tree.

carry the provisions an dry goods over the main channel of
the river   the men are taking goods a cross the river   in
camp all day   the men did not get through carrying the
freight over the river. Staid on the island another night [In
margin:] I setting watching the thousands of grasshopper
that inhabit this island

8   Sat   Clear & warm   Got all over the river against
noon   it took the ballance of the after noon to [de]ploy &
reload the waggons   Camped on Green river

[July] 9   Sun   Clear an pleasant   traveled over the Green
River hills or mountains   noon   took dinner on Fount in
nell[5] an found plenty of good grass for the cattle   traveled
on & at night camped on Fount Du Nell   Heard that the
Savannah company was not far behind us on the road
Found good gras   no wood but willows   cool nights

10   Mon   Clear & warm   traveled over the mountains
noon   gathered some gum off the Fir trees a grove in the
valley   camped ten miles from no where in the mountains.
plenty of snow close by. good water an some stinted
grass   this afternoon passed the conjunction of the 2 roads
that divided east of the desert   passed some traders an
indians huts

11   Tues   Clear & warm on bear river mountains. the
worst roads and the tallest hills to climb we have seen   lots
of Firr groves   had plenty of snow to eat   it looked
singular to see snow on the mountains an flowers an grass in
full bloom an growing Close by it   Mrs Davisons is sick
with the mountain fever   Camped on hams fork

---

[5] Fontanelle Creek, Wyoming, is a tributary of the Green River. The present name is
a mis-spelling of Fontenelle. Lucien Fontenelle was a well-known Frenchman out of
New Orleans, who was active for many years in the fur trade. There is a fine biography
of him by Alan C. Trottman in LeRoy R. Hafen, *The Mountain Men and the Fur Trade
of the Far West*, V, pp. 81-99.

12   Wed   Clear an warm   traveled over more mountains
some very steep ones   Caught up with the savannah
company   camped on Bear river

[July] 13   Thur   Clear & warm   traveled on bear river
till the after noon then crossed on a bridge   Mr. Newton
Hough joined our company to day   camped on little branch
in the mountains of bear river   cold frosty nights

14   Fri   Clear & warm. traveled over high mountains
Noon   took dinner in Bear river valley   the missouri train
caught up with us this morning   other trains in sight
good roads this after noon camped on a small creek in Bear
river valley   began a pair of mits

15   Sat   Clear and warm   very dusty road   finished the
mits at noon   can see trains as far ahead of us as we can see
and as far behind us as we can see   Camped on bear river

16   Sun   Traveled six miles and come to the soda springs
an camped for the day   The Soda Springs keeps constant
boiling   some of them are upon mounds   Sunday evening
I with a company of ladies an gentlemen walked 2 miles to
visit the Steamboat Spring   it is a natural curiosity   it boils
furiously all the time   we then went to another large soda
spring about 20 yards off from that   there is a good beer
spring all ways effording [affording?]   never failing pure
clear beer   They are all on bear river

[July] 17   Mon   In camp all day   mother Davidson is
too sick to travel   Mr. Parish was out on the mountains
an found a lake 1 mile wide an long, 10 an 15 feet
deep   around it there is petrified vegetation   they are
curious looking things

18   Tues   Clear   left the warm soda springs   traveled
over mountain   Camped on a branch of the head waters of
the Columbia river

19   Wed   Clear warm the fore noon   traveled only 8

miles to day over the mountains   camped on the Braport
[?]   the after noon there come up a shower of rain hail an
dust

20   Thur   Clear & warm   traveled 22 miles an camped
on a branch in the mountains   Good road to day

[July] 21   Fri   Clear warm

22   Sat   Clear & warm

23   Sun

27   Thur   Clear an warm   passed the Castle rocks [City
of Rocks] the fore noon   noon   come to the conjunction of
the Salt river on northern roads traveled 6 miles further an
camped in the mountains   raining this evening

[July] 28   Fri   Clear an warm   camped on goose creek

29   Sat   Clear warm   traveled half the day an camped on
goose creek.

[The diary ends here right near the point where the present
states of Idaho, Nevada, and Utah make contact.]

LETTER OF WILLIAM C. PARRISH

This letter is from William C. Parrish, of the same overland party
as Elizabeth Myrick, to John Porter and Caroline (Simmons)
Langdon, of Humboldt County, California. It is now the
property of Shirley Langdon Wilcox, of Arlington, Virginia, who
has provided us with a photocopy of the manuscript original and
given us permission to publish it. The "Bey" he writes of is
Humboldt Bay.

                              Sutter Ville   Dec. 17, 1854
Mr. Langdon and family
    I embrace this opportunity of writing you a few lines.
After so long a time. I had no Idea that it wold be three
months before I would write to you but time passes very fast

in this country. And I have been very busy. And I thought
that I would not write untill I found a place where I would
stop for a time. And I have found a place where I shall stay
for some time   I think I have spent some time traveling and
Prospecting. And I find that it Costs some thing to run a
round in this Country   I have had the best of health since I
left you   I am on Sutter Creek about three miles above
Volcano in Amadore County about 50 miles south of
Hangtown. I And [unreadable] Augustin are to gether
Sampson is on Feather River near where Vance Davidson
Stoped   Augustin has Just returned from there And he
heard from All of the folks that came across in our train   he
heard from Doc. Davidson's folks [unreadable] they got in
safe   We have heard from all but you and Henry Simmons
and the folks that were to the Bey. And we want to hear from
you   Our Cattle we left at Butte Creek. We have a good
mining Claim on this creek   we are in New Diggins
plenty of water with out buying it   if our claim pays as well
as it has prospected It will pay 4 hands 5 dollars per day for 2
years   Wages here are from 40 to 75 dollars per month
Stock is low. Provisions tolerable Cheap. The wet season has
not set in yet   the weather has been very pleasant this
fall   Charly Hoff [Hough] is near Diamond springs
Heartsaugh [Hartsough] is at Georgetown   Blundells are
at Tahama. The most of the miners are doing nothing for
want of water. We are in a new part of the mines and I think
that we will make Grub this winter   there are some good
Claims here and some that have never been tutched yet. I
have not seen any place yet where I wanted to stay and live
out my days at. Although I like the Country better than I
expected to.

I want you to write and tell me just how times and things
are in your part of the Country. I expect to spend five or six

years in this Country   I may take a notion to come to the Bey before I leave the State. I could not get a School to suit me   I like mining very well. Let us know what kind of a school you have what wages are prices of stock &c. Tell us about all the folks that went to the bay with you where they [are] what they are doing and so on   Give my respects to all acquaintences that you see   Tell them I want them to write

Direct your to Volcano Amadore Co. Cal. I remain yours respectfully.

Wm.C. Parrish

INDEX